The Life & Times Of A Lawman

*To Nell
An old friend
with love and best wishes
Edvina Hanushuk*

7/13/12

The Life & Times Of A Lawman

A Biography

by

Edwina Hauversburk

FirstPublish
A Division of the Brekel Group, Inc.
control your own destiny

Success is to be measured not so much by the position that one has reached in life as by the obstacles that one has overcome while trying to succeed.
  Booker T. Washington
  (1856-1915) Educator

Copyright © 2001 by Edwina Hauversburk.
All rights reserved. Printed in the United States of America.
No part of this publication may be reproduced, stored in
a retrieval system, or transmitted, in any form or by any
means, electronic, mechanical, photocopying, recording,
or otherwise, without the prior written permission of the author.

ISBN
1-929925-82-4

Library of Congress Cataloging in Publication Data
2001094497

Edwina Hauversburk
The Life & Times Of A Lawman

10 9 8 7 6 5 4 3 2 1

FIRSTPUBLISH
A Division of Brekel Group, Inc.
300 Sunport Ln.
Orlando, FL 32809
407-240-1414
www.firstpublish.com

Introduction

Dave Barry, Pulitzer Prize winner and syndicated columnist for the Miami Times, once said, "When they close that lid for the last time, it's better for someone to say 'Why wasn't he famous?' than to say 'Why *was* he famous?'.

That's pretty serious stuff coming from a man who makes his living writing comedy, and for sure it's one of those comments that won't stand debating. But it seems to me that fame can be pretty fickle when you get right down to it. Sometimes a person can become notorious from pretty silly reasons and not because they did something so noteworthy. It all depends on whether some observer was impressed enough to record it. Very simple, really.

Take Mrs. O'Leary, for example. Would she have been so well known if her cow hadn't burned down Chicago? Or Typhoid Mary, if she had been properly treated instead of running around infecting people? Of course both those cases became well known because the news media jumped on them. But what about the ones that were ignored? No journals kept, records made, or notes taken. Would the world have known about the Long Rangers heroic deeds if Tonto hadn't sent up smoke signals? Oops, I don't think that one fits, but you get the idea I'm sure.

I began to think about all that one day while strolling through an old cemetery in Dillard, Ga. Old cemeteries have always fascinated me. I was studying the eroding moss-covered tombstones, reading the epitaphs, and wondering about the people who were buried there. What kind of people were they? Was society better because they existed? Or were they cheating, wife-beating, lazy low-lifes? Did they die of natural causes or were they stomped by an irate mule, shot by a jealous husband, lynched for robbing the local bank, or poisoned on some homemade hooch? Was she a teacher, the local prostitute, or a discontented housewife who deserted her husband and twelve kids to vamoose with a traveling salesman? There's no way of knowing. Most likely they were all just ordinary run-of-the-mill folk, but no one will ever know for sure because nobody wrote down the details of their lives, and a bit of history was lost forever. How sad.

It seems to me that people come in varieties, like pickles or ice cream flavors. Some are just born to greatness, their names recognizable even centuries after they walked this earth, like those who were elected to high office or who discovered the cure for some catastrophic illness. Many became famous for their wealth and philanthropic endeavors, others for their literary, artistic, and scientific talents, and some for their daring feats or explorations. The list is endless. But wait! Let's not forget those who attained their spot in history because of their lust for power, or greed, or cruelty to man. That bunch probably didn't want to be remembered for their wicked ways but they will be. Forever and ever. *Because somebody wrote it all down.*

On other end of the scale are those who seem born to mediocrity and they really don't give a happy toot. They just drift placidly through life, accomplishing little of note, then die, leaving nothing to remember them by except a few words on a tombstone. That bunch is content to live in their own little microcosm, their existence akin to that of a dozing bullfrog on a lily pad, never making waves or even so much as a ripple on the tranquil surface of life's pond. Indeed, their only link to immortality, besides their tombstone, is the begetting of offspring.

Well, the truth is, a person can become quite famous, at least on a local level, for begetting. There was Henry Crawford Tucker, our ancestor down in Colquitt County, Georgia, who managed to sire 32 children, all single births, before his horse did him in when he (not the horse) was in his eighties. And he would have probably continued to begot if that horse hadn't broken his neck. I'm not making this up. His log house still stands, is recorded in the national historic registry, and his history can be found in the genealogy section of the Colquitt County library. Which shows nothing, actually, except how well informed I am on the virility of my ancestors and how good they were at begetting.

However, somewhere between the two aforementioned groups, the well knowns and the unknowns, is a third group of people who should be written up in the history books but won't be. Those are the folks who stand out from the crowd and should be remembered for their achievements. Unfortunately, like so many before them, they will live and die and eventually be forgotten because no one bothered writing down the details of their lives.

After giving the matter a lot of thought, I decided to do my bit to correct that travesty of justice by writing a book, a biography. My motivation in undertaking this project is to give a very special man the recognition that I think he deserves. Much of his biography as recorded here will be in his own words, for one of his many attributes is the ability to spin a yarn. A goodly portion will be descriptive to give a true picture of the era in which he lives (and has lived). Other parts will be presented from the first person point of view since I shared closely his first eighteen years and remember first-hand many incidents. It stands to reason that my memories will be the most accurate since I am older . . . by eighteen months actually.

I obtained a lot of information from older relatives, some of whom are now deceased. I have relied too on the memories of close relatives and friends, and thank them for their input. Between all of us this biography should be an accurate portrayal of one man's life, his fearless feats, daring-do's, close brushes with death, his crazy sense of humor, and his struggles to achieve the goals he set for himself. My hope is that his story will be worthy of its own place in the history books, at least the family history books, and that someday someone will find his biography to be of such interest that they will pass it along. If they happen to be descendants, then I hope they will feel a great deal of pride in knowing that this unique man happens to be a part of their family tree . . . as I do.

1 | CHAPTER

He has always had a flair for the dramatic, my brother Quentin. Nothing he does is ever simple. The unexpected is his modus operandi, and trouble is something he attracts like an old, mangy, hound dog attracts fleas. It didn't suddenly begin at some particular point during his lifetime, either. He jumped right in at the very beginning, like he just couldn't wait to generate a little excitement.

First, he put in his appearance a couple months early, on one of the coldest days of the year, right in the middle of the Great Depression . . . March 2, 1932. Then, he managed to get himself born into a family so financially strapped they almost missed having that proverbial pot to tinkle in. But Quentin has always liked a challenge, and I suppose his dallying with the difficult started at the beginning, too. Or maybe it was just in his genes, for it was something he never outgrew, that's for sure.

Anyway...times hadn't always been so hard for the Whittle family. Sometime in the distant past our ancestors had been quite wealthy, owning large tracts of land in Pike County, Alabama, and Colquitt County, Georgia, where they dabbled in politics, and were active in civic affairs . . . people of substance, you might say. Some cousin even traced them back to the gentry in England. By the 1900's, however, all the blue-blood had pretty well petered out and the wealth along with it, leaving mostly a bunch of sharecroppers and blue-collar workers...good salt-of-the-earth kind of folks with a few lowlifes thrown in, like most families. Circumstances were destined to improve over the years, but for the Whittle clan, and a lot of other folks, times were tougher than hog's hair during the depression.

At the time of Quentin's birth, Daddy was sharecropping in South Georgia. What that meant was, he worked his buns off farming for someone else who had more land and money. In return he and the family were allowed to live in a tenant shack on the property and receive a small portion of the harvest. It wasn't the best of situations but one that Mother and Daddy were thankful for, all the same. With an unemployment rate of 25% in the U.S., many people didn't have that much.

Quentin's premature birth could have been due to a couple things; lack of prenatal care and Mother's lifestyle, in part anyway. Her days were long, lasting from before light until after dark. Although she worked as hard as any man, many of her chores were different. She did fascinating stuff...like cleaning pork entrails at hog-killing time to make casings for sausage. Then, of course, there was the weekly laundry. Since there was no electricity or plumbing, clothes had to be washed by hand, on a rub board, with homemade lye soap, and then boiled in a cast-iron wash pot. I think Mother's soap did most of the cleaning because that stuff was strong enough to dissolve paint. And, of course, water for the laundry had to be drawn from the well, one bucketful at the time.

In her leisure time, Mother milked four Jersey cows twice daily, churned butter, and made cheese. Between times, she sewed, quilted, tended chickens, cooked, cleaned, and doctored anybody with any complaints. Actually, nobody complained much no matter how sick they were because her home remedy was often worse than the complaint. There were exceptions, of course, but Mother's treatment for constipation wasn't one of them. It couldn't be tolerated by many, even the strongest among us.

Thinking back, I know Mother and Daddy's life style must have been exhausting. And even though they were still a young couple, I sometimes wonder how they had enough energy left to make any children. I guess there are some things a person's never too tired for.

Anyway, they were successful three times before Quentin's birth. Winston, and Myra were born in 1924 and 1925 respectively. Then I came along in 1930 and Quentin in 1932. There were 13 months between Winston and Myra, and 18 months between Quentin and me. I think Mother had a few miscarriages in between, some of them probably due to the aforementioned workload she carried, or maybe to the fact that she was Rh negative and Daddy was Rh positive. Not much was known about Rh incompatibility back then, especially not South Georgia tenant farmers.

With so much against us, I guess we children were lucky to get born at all. Mother wasn't a large, robust woman, either. She was only five-foot-two inches tall and weighed about 98 pounds, soaking wet and *un*pregnant, as the saying goes.

The house we were living in when Quentin was born was in such pitiful shape that even the termites didn't want to live there. It's still standing, I hear. Mother used to say that when it rained she had to wear a hat and coat in the kitchen to keep from getting wet. And she could count the stars through the roof at night. We only lived there about a year and she said she wasn't a bit disappointed to leave.

The main part of the house consisted of two rooms, side by side, which served as bedrooms and living room. Tacked on to the back was a one-room lean-to that served as the eat-in kitchen. And on one end of the front porch was a small room where Daddy stored his corn. There wasn't much furniture, just a couple bedsteads, Mother's sewing machine, dressers, trunks, and chairs. No closets. Nails were driven into the walls to hang clothes on. You might say we had the basics and that was all. Daddy made the dining room table out of scrap lumber and none of the chairs matched. Our furnishings were "southern primitive"...I think that's the term the antique store owners use today before they slap a big price tag on them. I'm told that people actually put out good money for that stuff. Amazing.

Our furnishings may have been primitive, but our house was clean. Mother made sure of that. Every Saturday, after doing the laundry, she scrubbed the floors using a corn-shuck mop and her lye soap. Besides having a clean house, Mother always made whatever hovel we lived in look like a real home. That's because she was so creative. She made all sorts of household stuff, like curtains and bedspreads, out of bleached flour sacks. Even underwear. I'm not making that up. We children were way up in school before we had under-drawers that didn't say "self-rising" across the seat. Mother baked *a lot* of biscuits.

Now that the family circumstances have been described, let's get back to the birthing.

The night was bitter cold, as I mentioned earlier, and the wind was whistling around the old sharecropper's shack, flapping the rusted tin roof and fanning the flour-sack curtains at the windows. When Mother started having labor pains, Daddy hitched up the mule and went to fetch Dr. Slocum over in Doerun, a small rural town a few miles away. After examining Mother and deciding the time wasn't right, he made himself comfortable in a rocker near the crumbling fireplace and dozed. He was used to waiting.

Grandmother Whittle was there, too, bustling around, throwing lighter-knots on the fire, and being generally useful. Grandmother always bustled. That's the only way to describe her movements because she never wasted any. To her, there just weren't enough hours in the day to do all that needed doing, so she went at everything full tilt. Just watching her could be exhausting. But, it was a foregone conclusion that if there was a crisis in the family Grandmother would be there.

She was a little less than five feet tall, plump, wore rimless glasses, and was usually dressed in a long-sleeved print dress covered by a starched and ironed white apron. That was her usual attire unless she was going visiting or company was coming ... then she took off the apron. She was very fastidious and very much a lady. Grandmother Whittle never raised her voice and she certainly never swore, heaven forbid. As far as I know, she never had any vices at all. Unless you want to count the hot toddy she had at bedtime sometimes. A hot toddy was a shot of whiskey mixed with warm sweetened water. Not many people knew about Grandmother's toddies, for she was very discreet. It wasn't an *every* night ritual, for heaven's sake, just in case you're getting the wrong impression.

On the day of Quentin's birth, Grandmother woke up Myra and Winky, fed them breakfast and hustled them off to catch the school bus. They were barefooted as usual, though there was frost on the ground. Their lunch of corn bread, fried side meat, and maybe a baked sweet potato, if they were lucky, was carried in a lard bucket.

When they left that morning they knew something was up, but they didn't know what. Such things as sex and childbirth weren't discussed much back then...rarely by adults and never,

ever, with the young ones. If children were smart enough, they figured out the facts of life by watching the farm animals. If not, they sometimes grew up thinking new babies were found in the turnip patch.

Since it wasn't customary for the husband to be present during the birthing, Daddy was pacing around outside, trying to keep warm and worrying, of course...something he had a lot of experience at. Dying in childbirth wasn't uncommon and Mother hadn't seen the doctor since her last delivery. Medical care was like anything else. If they couldn't pay for it, they did without it. It was a matter of pride. And if Mother couldn't treat it with her home remedies, it didn't get treated. Most of the time anyway.

Finally, Quentin quit fooling around and put in his appearance about midmorning. According to Grandmother's measurements, he only weighed 2 pounds, was twelve inches long, and his thigh was the same size as Daddy's thumb. He was definitely the runt of the litter.

Dr. Slocum handed him to Grandmother and said, "He's too small and premature to live. Just wrap him in a blanket and leave him over in the corner. Cecil can bury him later."

Now *that's* a dramatic beginning.

Dr. Slocum wasn't an unkind, callous man, and Grandmother understood what he meant. She didn't fault him for it; to her mind he was just being realistic. She also knew the odds against Quentin surviving, but that didn't matter a whit to her. Grandmother could be as tenacious as an old bulldog when she set her mind to it, and she decided right then and there that she wasn't going to let Quentin die without giving him a chance.

After Dr. Slocum had been paid . . . probably with eggs, butter, syrup, and whatever else was available, except cash, which wasn't...he left and Grandmother got busy. She cleaned Quentin with oil, wrapped him in flannel, and put him in a makeshift crib made from a dresser drawer. Then she packed hot bricks around him to keep him warm. For days, every few minutes, she fed him breast milk with an eyedropper, a few drops at the time, and kept rotating the bricks as they cooled. No one knew when she slept, or if she did.

Surprisingly, to everyone but Grandmother, Quentin kept on living. Myra said his crying sounded like a newborn kitten. She also said he looked like a rat, and was ugly as sin. Her memories of that day, coming home from school and seeing him for the first time, are quite vivid.

He was named Quentin Owen, and Grandmother dutifully recorded his name in the family bible. The Owen was a family name from the Carter side. I don't know where Mother got the Quentin unless it was from the Roosevelts, which is puzzling because Daddy never had any use for the Roosevelts. Although I think they did have a son named Quentin.

So, Quentin survived. Given the primitive circumstances of his birth, the odds against his survival were astronomical. It wouldn't have happened, I feel sure, if not for Grandmother's fierce determination and God's intervention. And since he survived in spite of the odds against it, I guess he was just meant to be. But there is one thing for sure . . . even though there have been innumerable times in Quentin's life when he has had a close brush with death . . . none have been closer than at the beginning.

2 | CHAPTER

Grandmother may have given Quentin the first nudge, but he quickly developed a will to live all on his own. Seems like once he got the hang of it, he just grabbed life with both hands and hung on. Despite his shaky beginning, he wasn't a bit sicklier than the rest of us, and we were a pretty healthy lot. Except for the usual head colds and childhood illnesses, he never had anything serious and didn't see a doctor from the day he was born until he was in his teens. He probably wouldn't have seen one then, either, but a rabid dog bit him, and since there wasn't a home remedy for rabies, he had to have the series of shots.

Furthermore, he didn't have a dental cavity until he was in his thirties, nor a broken bone until just a few years ago. Now, that's really amazing considering how he's always putting himself at risk and managing to get in all kinds of dangerous situations. Quentin's whole life is full of stuff like that, as you will see. I've been trying to figure out why that is so and have decided that, since he was premature, he must have been born before God could get around to instilling a sense of fear in him. Or maybe he just decided early on that God had appointed him his own special guardian angel so he didn't have to worry about it.

I seem to be getting ahead of myself again. Lets get back to the beginning.

A few days after his birth, Quentin became strong enough to nurse on his own, and from then on he thrived and developed rapidly. It wasn't long before he graduated from the dresser draw and claimed his corner of the bed. After rolling off a few times, he eventually mastered the art of staying on top instead of under.

At first he was nicknamed "Pee Wee" because of his tiny size, but he outgrew that name pretty fast and it was soon shortened to "Pete", a nickname still used by many relatives and close friends. Daddy coined it but I don't recall Mother ever calling him anything but "Quentin." And he never called her anything but "Mother", as did the rest of us. Of course, when he was preschool age, his pronunciation was "Mudder", which brings to mind an incident that occurred while mother's youngest sister Lill was living with us. She was in her teens at the time, the same age as Myra, and she always seemed more like a sister than an aunt.

According to Lill, she was helping Mother with the weekly laundry, using the old rub board and boiling clothes in the cast-iron pot in the back yard, while Quentin and I played under a nearby tree. We were doing skin-the-cat off the lower limbs when, suddenly, Quentin began screaming bloody murder and hobbling cross-legged to the house with a death grip on his crotch.

From all the commotion, I guess Mother figured he was dying for sure. Now, Mother was always kind of emotional, not exactly what you would call cool-headed in an emergency, and she started wringing her hands and crying, "Oh, mercy! What's the matter, honey, what's wrong with you?"

He sniffled a couple times, looked up and her and calmly said, "Mudder, I think I cracked me nuts."

Well...Lill thought it was funny at the time.

I digress...let me get back to the story again and get things in order.

Quentin's size and name wasn't all that changed. It wasn't long before he developed into a sturdy, handsome little fellow with blond hair and deep blue eyes. Now, that was truly a blessing and a relief to the whole family, because it would have been a crying shame if he had gone through life as ugly as he started out.

He had a cowlick on the crown of his head that looked like a rooster tail and refused to be tamed no matter what he did to it. Though-out his growing up years, Quentin must have used gallons of Vitalis on it without success. Ruined the top of Mother's maple chest-of-drawers, he did, slinging that stuff all over it. In time, a military barber took care of his rooster tail for him. That was later, of course.

One of the things that I always thought contributed to his good looks was his cute, well-shaped little nose. Now, it's for sure he didn't get that nose from the Loyd side of the family (that's Daddy's maternal side of the family tree) because a big nose is a distinct trait. I wasn't so lucky and Quentin used to tease me unmercifully about it. His favorite digs were, "Hey, is that your nose or are you eating a banana?" and "Is that your nose or are you smoking a cigar? Tee hee!!"

He was the only person who could get away with insults like that without hurting my feelings and ending up with all kinds of bodily injuries. But... I knew he would never deliberately hurt me, and he knew that I knew. By the same token, and even though he has forcefully denied it over the years, I don't think he was all that devastated when I chased him all over the yard with my tweezers and pulled out his only two chest hairs. He was about fourteen at the time and, to my thinking, unduly vain about his chest hair. I had my revenge, and he made no more derogatory remarks about the size of my nose.

As I mentioned earlier, Mother never had a child after Quentin, although she did have several miscarriages. We found out many years later that Mother and Daddy had Rh incompatibility; she was Rh negative and Daddy was Rh positive. If the baby is Rh positive, the mother builds up antibodies in her blood, which tries to destroy the baby. It's a condition called erythroblastosis. With each pregnancy or miscarriage of an Rh-positive fetus, more antibodies are built up. Usually by the third pregnancy, the baby didn't stand much of a chance. That means that if Quentin had been positive instead of negative, he would have been stillborn or died shortly after birth. Replacement transfusions on newborns, a procedure developed and used for many years, was unheard of back then, and Rhogam, the shot used today to counteract the build-up of antibodies, wasn't developed until years after that.

Before continuing, there is one thing I must make clear. Even though Quentin was the baby of the family, the runt of the litter, and premature to boot, he wasn't spoiled rotten, as one would have expected. That was probably because nobody had to the time. Putting food on the table was an on-going struggle and everybody in the family had to work, including the children, according to their capabilities. Myra and Winky chopped and picked cotton, hoed peanuts, split firewood, and generally did the work of adults. By the time Quentin and I had reached the ripe old age of three, we could gather kindling, feed the chickens, gather eggs, and run errands for Mother. Mostly we tried to stay out of everybody's way so they wouldn't find things for us to do. That didn't usually work, nor did hiding in the cotton patch.

Now I think I know where the old saying "going to bed with the chickens" originated. By late afternoon we were all exhausted and nobody complained about going to bed as soon as it got dark and the evening chores were done. There wasn't much time for playing. Working was an accepted part of our life. From the time we were knee babies we were taught that to be called "lazy" was the highest form of insult. It ranked right up there with unflattering remarks about one's ancestry, and anybody so labeled was lower than a snake's belly. That work ethic, so carefully instilled in us by our parents, has served us well over the years. We Whittles may have been called many things, and probably were, but never "lazy", at least as far as I know, and we all take great pride in that.

I can remember one time Mother telling Daddy about some local man that she held in high regard. She went on and on about what a fine upstanding fellow he was, the pillar-of-the-church type, a regular paragon of virtue. Then Daddy came back with, "Yeah, but Mae, that sonofabitch is lazy as hell!" That ended that discussion.

Let's back up just a minute. I don't want to give the wrong impression here. We may have had to work hard as we were growing up, and we may have missed out on a lot of material things, but there was one thing we had plenty of and that was love. By today's standards we probably would have been considered "socially and economically deprived", but we didn't know we were. You see...there wasn't a government social worker around to tell us we were. As a result, we grew up as happy as dead pigs in the sunshine, secure in the love of our parents and each other, and knew without a doubt that each of us was just as important as the other in our little family niche.

That feeling of security may be why Quentin was such a happy, contented little fellow...at least most of the time. There were a few exceptions, of course, like the time when he was about 18 months old and decided he wasn't getting his fair share of attention. He got down on his all-fours and started beating his head on the floor and crying pitifully. Periodically he would stop to catch his breath and look around to see if anybody was paying any attention. Didn't take him long to realize it wasn't working. Daddy strolled casually past, glanced down, and said, "What's the matter with Pee Wee? Is he having an Esmeralda fit?"

Now, no one ever knew where *that* term originated—-probably with Daddy—-but it was used thereafter to describe the temper tantrums of the children, grandchildren, great-grandchildren, and more than a few of the adults in the family.

Quentin's Esmeralda fits didn't last long, though. It was obvious that his ploy wasn't working, and so he eventually quit.

As it turned out, entertaining Quentin while Mother was busy, which was most of the time, became one of my chores. If she had to help with the fieldwork, like picking cotton or hoeing peanuts, she would put Quentin in a cardboard box padded with a quilt, and place the box under a nearby tree. I had to amuse him, but it wasn't a hard job. At least I don't recall that it was. It could be that my memory is a bit sketchy since I was only three or so at the time. But any bad habits he later developed, like biting, spitting, scratching, and eye poking...I absolutely refuse to take credit for!

CHAPTER 3

We moved about once a year, or anytime Daddy thought he could improve the family financial situation. He wasn't successful but it wasn't due to lack of effort on his part. I guess he inherited Grandmother's determination, along with her sense of family responsibility, because he just kept plodding doggedly along. He didn't have a whole lot of choice, with so many people depending on him. During those depression years, there were almost always relatives living with us, either Daddy's brothers or some of Mother's folks. That was because families helped one another back then, with no questions asked and no payback expected. There wasn't any complaining about it either. It was just done, that's all.

Even with all those extra mouths to feed, we weren't nearly as bad off as some people. Up until 1935 we had Jersey milk cows that provided more dairy products than we could possibly use. The excess, if not traded on the rolling-store* for other things, was fed to the hogs to fatten them. Then, as soon as the weather got cold enough, came hog-killing time. That gave us hams, side meat, sausage, cracklings, and lard for biscuits and making lye soap. Since Mother always had chickens and a vegetable garden wherever we lived, we didn't go hungry, but there was a lot of times when it was kissing close.

(* A rolling-store was a truck equipped with all kinds of stuff like groceries, piece goods, sewing notions, canning supplies, wash tubs, and the like, that traveled around the country doing door-to-door business)

When a hailstorm wiped out Daddy's bumper watermelon crop, he began thinking about giving up farming altogether and leaving Georgia completely. The idea took root about the time I was born in 1930, but it took him four years to act on it. He wasn't what you would call an impetuous man. The thing that really decided him, I think, besides losing his crops to hail, was finding Mother stuck under the bed afterwards. I didn't make this up.

During the hailstorm, Daddy took cover, probably under the wagon since there's not much in an open field to hide under. Then, as soon as the weather cleared enough, he high-tailed it home to check on the family. Mother was nine months pregnant with me at the time and about as big around as she was high. Well, when those huge hailstones—about the size of a baseball according to Mother—began coming through the roof, the only safe place she could find for her and the children was under the bed. Myra and Winky got out o.k. but Mother stuck, and there she stayed until Daddy got home. He had to lift the bed off her. She was not a happy person.

Circumstances didn't improve much after that, and with each year of failure Daddy's urge to leave Georgia became stronger. In 1934 he finally decided to bite the bullet and go for it.

Grandpa Carter, Mother's father, lived in Tampa and was acquainted with a cattle rancher by the name of Whitehead who owned a huge spread in Pasco County, Florida. Although the details aren't too clear, Grandpa apparently interceded on Daddy's behalf. Mr. Whitehead and Daddy started corresponding with the outcome being that Daddy was hired to work the cattle.

Now, Daddy didn't know diddley-squat about being a cowboy, but he was desperate enough to try anything, so he set about making arrangements to move the family lock, stock, and barrel to Florida. That was a monumental task in itself, not because we had all that many possessions, but because that was a long ways to travel back then. No interstates, just narrow, twisting two-lane roads. It took a lot of planning.

About three miles away, there was a small country store located in the fork of the road that ran between Moultrie and Doerun. The settlement around the store was called Jackson at that time but was later changed to Sigsbee. The storeowner, Clyde Smith, often took Daddy's excess produce, i.e. butter, eggs, etc., in exchange for staple goods such as coffee, flour, and sugar. They had become well acquainted and Clyde agreed to provide two trucks and two drivers for the big move that was expected to last from before dawn until after dark.

We set out before daylight on November 1st, 1934 with all our household goods on one truck and the farm animals on the other. Myra and Winky rode atop the furniture while Quentin and I rode in the cab with Mother and Daddy. I imagine we probably resembled the Jhoads in *The Grapes of Wrath*. Mother had packed a lunch for us to eat along the way, and we stopped in Brooksville, Florida about dusk-dark for our evening meal. Myra said we had Vienna sausage and crackers, which Daddy purchased from a small country store by the roadside. Maybe that's when Quentin developed his liking for Vienna sausage. He has consumed many during his lifetime and still takes them on his fishing trips.

By the time we got there, we were all cold and totally exhausted. There was no moon and the night was blacker than a crow's hiney when we finally rattled down a long lane and pulled up in front of the tenant house where we were to live. It was located about as far back in the boonies as you could get, or it seemed like it anyway. There was a big forest within stone-throwing distance in front of the house, and every now and then panthers would scream and scare us kids nearly to death. After listening to that catter-wallering a few nights, we got used to it.

Our nearest neighbor was almost a mile away, and Daddy had to haul our drinking water since there was no well on the place. The house itself wasn't all that bad, pretty good actually, compared to what we had just moved out of. It didn't have plumbing, but then we didn't expect any. The rooms were larger, there was a screened-in porch, and the yard had lots of shade from huge oak trees. The house may have just *seemed* roomier because by that time Daddy's brothers, who had been living with us in Georgia, had moved on to greener pastures.

Sometimes you gain a little and lose a little. Poor Mother's laundry arrangements had gotten even worse, as unbelievable as that may seem. Once a week she would dump the dirty clothes in the sled, a long wooden structure with runners on the bottom. She plopped Quentin and me on top of the clothes and hitched the mule to the sled. Then, wearing a pair of Daddy's overalls, she climbed up on a stump, and straddled the mule.

Somehow she always managed to get the mule going. I don't remember her cussing, though, like Daddy always did. He said that cussing was the only language a mule understood and he was real good at communicating with mules. Anyway, we proceeded to the pond about a quarter-mile behind the house. While Mother washed clothes in the pond, Quentin and I played along the bank and dabbled in the water, trying to catch minnows and tadpoles. Mother always kept one eye on the laundry and one on us. That's because she had an ungodly fear of water all her life and was totally convinced one of us would drown if the water was more than two inches deep. Another reason for her concern was the huge alligator that lived in the pond. He never tried to bother us but would just lay offshore and watch us with eyes that looked big as saucers. He probably thought we were too skinny to make much of a meal anyhow.

Mostly, we were pretty obedient little kids, but Quentin's curiosity sometimes got him in trouble. Like the following winter when Daddy burned off the stubble from the fields. The pasture ran up fairly close to the house and Quentin was totally fascinated by that fire. He might have turned into pyromaniac except for what happened. Mother told him to stay away from the fire, but he kept getting closer and closer and ended up burning the soles of his feet pretty bad. Going to the doctor wasn't an option. Mother's home remedy, whatever it was, must have done a pretty good job because he never had any scars. That was probably because we kids didn't have shoes, and the soles of our feet were as tough as any shoe leather.

We didn't have any toys either, except for the tire swing Daddy put up in one of the big oaks trees. Then, Quentin found a little red truck that had been abandoned by previous tenants. It was all scratched up, had no rear wheels, and wasn't much, but it was beautiful to Quentin and he treasured it more than life. He played with that little truck every day, pushing it around on the ground among the chicken droppings, making all kinds of truck noises, and then parking it under the back steps every night.

We did get a couple new toys later that year...a rarity, and the memory is so sharp I couldn't forget it if I tried.

It was in 1935, and while we were still living at the Whitehead place, that Grandpa Carter died. That meant we had to go to Tampa to the funeral. We children had never been to a large city before, and we were so bug-eyed over the sights and sounds that we were literally speechless. There were a lot of relatives there, most of them strangers to us, so I'm sure they must have thought we were a little retarded. Maybe even more than a little. Quentin's behavior didn't do much to change their opinions either.

Mother's youngest brother, Kelso, known to outsiders as "Jack", took Quentin and me to a large department store and bought us each a toy. I got a little harmonica which disappeared shortly thereafter...I can't imagine why... and Quentin got a tiny truck. He immediately pulled off one of the wheels and poked it up his nose. Kelso sat him up on the kitchen table and worked for hours trying to get it out. No saint ever had more patience. Quentin didn't cry much, considering the digging and prodding that was going on and the hysteria of some of the women. If the truth be known, he probably enjoyed all the attention. But anything can get tiring after awhile, so he sniffed out instead of in and the wheel fell out on the floor. I don't remember if his truck disappeared like my harmonica or not. After all the trouble it caused...it probably did.

Somebody once said it's better to have bad luck than no luck at all. I think they're full of beans. People who come out with stuff like that probably never had any of the bad kind. Daddy had more than his share.

He was given a steer, as part of his pay, which he fattened, butchered, and took to the cold storage plant in Dade City, a few miles away, for safe keeping. The plant burned down one night shortly thereafter. We could see the western sky all lit up, and we could smell smoke but didn't find out what it was until the next day. No insurance, of course. Daddy was able to save a little of the meat that was so charred it was almost inedible. We weren't used to having much meat so that burnt meat was right tasty to us.

Sometimes Daddy would kill a squirrel or rabbit and Mother would make a stew. And sometimes he would catch a soft shell turtle in the pond and she would flour and fry the turtle like it was chicken and serve it up with a platter of buttermilk biscuits. That was good eating. Mother had a knack for making nothing taste good, but then she had a lot of experience at it.

In the fall of 1935, Daddy was forced to face the fact that cowboying just wasn't his forte. He was doing pretty good at it until the day he was rounding up cows and his horse stepped in a hole. They were going full tilt when the horse stopped but Daddy didn't. He landed on his head, pretty hard at that, broke his nose and almost broke his neck. He was laid up for days. Even Mother's home remedies didn't help much. It was about then that he decided to pull up stakes again.

Daddy's oldest brother, Hubert, and his family lived in Dundee, a small town in Polk County, in the central part of the state and right in the middle of citrus country. They had been over to visit a few times. We thought they were wealthy because they owned a car and dressed nice. Looking back I realize they really weren't all that well fixed, just fixed a lot better than we were. On one of their visits, Uncle Hubert advised Daddy to go over to Dundee and apply for a job at the packinghouse there. He figured Daddy stood a chance of getting on even though jobs were still scarce. After studying about it for a while, Daddy decided it was worth a try, so he set about moving us again.

The first thing he did was sell the livestock and buy a rusted-out rattletrap truck, that being all he could afford. The fact that it even cranked was a miracle. Daddy's plan was to drive over to Dundee, apply for a job, and find us a place to live. That all hinged on his getting the job, of course. He decided to take Winky with him, and they started out early one morning, taking a load of syrup to swap for any necessities they might need along the way, since they had little cash. The trip they expected to make in three or four hours ended up lasting all day. They set a record for flat tires, and by the time they reached Uncle Hubert's in late afternoon, the inner tubes' patches had patches. That's what they always said, anyway.

Daddy did get a job at the packinghouse, preparing fruit for shipping, and it paid six dollars weekly. That was for six days a week, twelve hours a day, and he was glad to get it. The unemployment rate in the U.S. was still running about twenty-five per cent. Hoboes were a frequent sight all over the country, knocking on back doors, asking for work or something to eat. They were mostly good, decent men, down on their luck, and traveling around trying to find work to support their families. No matter how desperate they were, they didn't steal. The crime rate was very low. Times have surely changed.

The only affordable house Daddy and Winky could find was located about two miles out of town or, as Mother put it, on the back side of nowhere. It wasn't much but didn't leak and it had all kinds of outbuildings, too. That was because it was an abandoned chicken farm. Thinking back, there is one thing I distinctly remember about that place... the constant odor of chicken poop. It wasn't so overwhelming in dry weather, but gosh did it stink when the rains came! We eventually got used to it and having all that chicken poop did have an up side; Mother had an inexhaustible source of fertilizer for her garden.

I don't remember how the actual move was made from Pasco County to Dundee. Uncle Hubert may have loaned Daddy the money for truck tires. If so, it had to have been a loan because Daddy didn't take handouts. Anyway, we did get settled in and Daddy started working and drawing his weekly salary of $6.00. Even an idiot can figure out that a family of seven...Mother's Uncle Davis was living with us at the time...couldn't live very high on the hog with that kind of income. Actually I don't think we ever got much above the hooves. But, once again, Mother had chickens and a garden so we managed. Sometimes, on a Sunday afternoon, Daddy would take us all fishing at one of the many lakes in the area. They were clear, cold, fresh water lakes and the fish out of them were delicious.

Those outings were good for all of us, especially Mother. She didn't have much of a social life. Come to think of it, I don't think she had one at all...unless you count the visits from Uncle Hubert's family, which were infrequent. She played a lot of make-believe games with us kids, and showed us how to make things out of wet clay and leave them to dry in the sun to dry. She would sit with us beside an anthill and watch the ants working, or call our attention to a beautiful sunrise or sunset. Besides instilling in each of us a love of nature, she also taught us to appreciate music. Mother had a beautiful voice and sang a lot back in those days. Guess it helped keep her from going bonkers. Someone once said that you can't feel depressed when you're singing. That's mostly true, too.

The old truck finally quit running, but before it did Daddy and Mother took us to a traveling circus that came to town. It was just a small operation but looked like a fairyland to us. I don't know how Daddy got the tickets. Another time he took Quentin and me to town and bought us an ice cream cone, our first. It was vanilla. Nothing ever tasted as good before or since.

To me, anyway. Quentin swears he doesn't remember that ice cream but he does remember another first... his first banana.

After the truck quit, Daddy had to walk the two miles to and from work everyday. When his shoes wore out, he folded cardboard and put inside over the holes. Usually, on Saturday afternoon, after he got paid, he would stop by the store in town and bring home a sack of groceries, usually no-nonsense-stuff like sugar, flour, and coffee. Quentin and I would sit on the front steps and watch for him. That particular day he pulled a bunch of bananas out of the sack and gave one to each of us. We didn't know what they were and he to show us how to peel them.

As Quentin said, "I sat on the front step, eatin' my banana. That was the best thing I had ever tasted in my life. It was so good I just kept right on eatin' till I finished off the inside of the peeling, too. Wasn't much left to that banana when I finished with it. After that we usually got a banana in our Christmas sack. None of 'em ever tasted as good as that first one, though."

4 | CHAPTER

Having so few possessions did have one advantage...it made moving a whole lot easier. In the summer of 1936, after a year at the chicken farm, we moved once again, this time to downtown Dundee. I turned six that August and was ready to start first grade, then Quentin would be starting a couple years later. Mother and Daddy didn't think we could walk that four-mile round-trip to school every day. There were no school buses running out there. Of course, Myra and Winky had been hiking to school all along, in all kinds of weather, too.

The old frame house we moved into in town was referred to as a "shot-gun house." That meant that all the rooms were arranged one behind the other so that if a gun was fired through the front door the bullet would come out the back door without hitting anything. It was small, too, but it did have plumbing, our first experience at such a luxury. Well, that may be stretching it a bit. Actually, what we had was a half bath...just a tiny room off the back porch that contained a permanently stained sink and a smelly commode. Even after it was cleaned, it still looked and smelled the same. Not as bad as a privy, though, and it did work. And, since our house was only two blocks from downtown and just three blocks from the elementary school, we thought we had "arrived" at last. Prosperity was just over the hill. We might even get to carry sliced bread in our lunch instead of biscuits...someday.

I don't want to mislead you here. Don't get the idea that Dundee was a *really big* city. Maybe I had better describe it in a little more detail before continuing.

The business area consisted primarily of two grocery stores, one drug store, one hardware store, a shoe repair shop, two churches, two filling stations, a post office, and the school. One block north was the police and fire station, and one block west was the train station and community center. One block west of the fire station was the citrus packinghouse and canning plant.

During the land boom in the early part of the century, a German fellow by the name of Kletzen, bought up land and laid out the town. I'm sure he must have had great expectations for the area, maybe hoping to attract rich Yankees who would winter over like they were doing along the lower east coast. Dundee should have blossomed, but as far as I know it never has. I don't know if Mr. Kletzen's money ran out or he just died of disappointment. At any rate, he wasn't around when we moved there, and Dundee just kinda drifted along, not growing and not shrinking, just stagnating mostly.

The town was laid out in equal sized blocks. They were twice as long as they were wide, with four running east/west and six north/south. All the streets were paved and there were sidewalks around every block, with curbs and sewer drains. The main thoroughfare was lined with huge eucalyptus trees when we lived there, but they got diseased later and had to be cut down. Main street was, and is, arranged like a T with a one road going to Lake Wales, one to Haines City, and the other to Winter Haven. There was a traffic light at the intersection, the only one, and I think its still there. Dundee *is* on the map and a lot of people I run into nowadays have even heard of it. But, I never could figure out why Mr. Kletzen decided to name his town Dundee in the first place. If memory serves, Dundee is a city in Scotland and Mr. Kletzen was a full-blooded German. Another of life's mysteries.

Dundee wasn't what you would call a pretty town back then. It could have been, but there was too much poverty and the living conditions of most of the residents reflected it. The town sat in a beautiful location though, surrounded by rolling hills of orange groves and pristine lakes. To us country folks, Dundee was a regular thriving metropolis. And we children loved it.

In time, we found out there were a couple other benefits to "city" living besides the advantages I have already mentioned. For one, Mother could start going back to church again. Her faith was a very important part of her life and she loved to take part in church activities, especially singing in the choir. So she made us all go, little heathens that we were, except Daddy. He wasn't much on church going except to gospel sings, which he loved, and to funerals, which he hated and only went when he was forced to. It wasn't that Daddy was atheistic, or even agnostic, but because he had little liking for the trappings of organized religion.

The second benefit was the social advantages, which mostly revolved around the church and school. For the first time, Quentin and I began to cultivate friendships out side the family. Up until that time we had no one to play with besides each other. This may have been responsible for another first...our first fight. Actually, it was a totally one-sided affair with Quentin the attacker, and I the attackee.

Quentin swears he doesn't remember why he did it and neither do I, but I certainly remember every other black and blue detail. As I remind him often, his cruel attack upon my bodily person at such a tender age has left me with declining memory loss. He still refuses to take the responsibility for this no matter how much guilt I try to dump on him. Instead, he claims I was too hardheaded to have been hurt that much.

It happened late one afternoon as I was just sitting on the back door steps, washing my grubby feet in a wash pan and minding my own business. Quentin sneaked up behind me and hit me with a brickbat. That hurt like crazy and I started screaming my head off. I thought for sure I was dying, considering the size of the bloody goose egg that popped up on my head. It didn't knock me out though.

What Quentin didn't know was that Daddy was standing in the kitchen, looking out the screen door, and saw what he did. Daddy was already taking off his belt when he came out the back door, something Quentin noticed right away. Daddy only stopped long enough to see if I was okay and in no danger of dying. It must have been during those few seconds that Quentin decided he really didn't want a licking, so he took off around the corner of the house. That was his second mistake. He ran as fast as his short little legs would go but Daddy was gaining fast. They hadn't made a complete circle of the house before Quentin realized he couldn't out-run Daddy. He dropped to his knees and scampered under the house, which sat about eighteen inches off the ground. It was too low for Daddy to crawl under, or maybe he just decided he didn't need to. Quentin felt safe.... for a while anyway.

He squatted there among the spiders, rats, and God only knows what else, until the sun set and his little hidey-hole became pitch dark. Staying under there didn't seem like such a good idea anymore. There were rustling noises. He began to imagine all kinds of boogers just waiting to pounce on him. The more scared he became, the less frightening Daddy's belt seemed. After awhile he even convinced himself that Daddy had forgotten all about him. Daddy hadn't. When Quentin slowly inched his way out from under the house, there stood Daddy, leaning against the house, patiently waiting, and the belt still in his hand.

I got over my injury pretty fast but Quentin had trouble sitting for awhile. He learned a couple things from that experience, though. One was to be sure Daddy wasn't around before he beaned me with a brick bat, and the second was to *never, ever* run from Daddy under *any* circumstances.

Altogether we lived in and around Dundee for eight years. During that time, we moved about four times, yearly at first. The reasons for some of the moves are long forgotten, but I know for sure that not paying the rent wasn't one of them. Daddy was a stickler for paying his bills; they always had first priority when he got paid. Then, if anything was left over, we ate. He may have spent most of his life broke but he always had a triple A credit rating, something he took great pride in.

Getting back to the moving. A year later, in 1937, Mother and Daddy decided to move again, this time to a frame house a couple blocks away and only one block from school. The house was roomier, which was good since Grandma Carter and LaBelle, Mother's sixteen-year-old sister, were living with us part of that year. Later, after they left, some of Daddy's folks moved in for a while. We definitely needed the space.

This place sat almost on the sidewalk and had an open porch across the front. It also had a faucet on the back porch but no other plumbing. In other words, no indoor john. And we were all so used to having one by that time, too. We were back to an outhouse and only a one-holer at that. What a letdown. But Mother didn't object too much to the move, mainly because we children no longer had to cross Main Street to get to school.

Main Street was extra wide, about four car widths plus room for angle parking on each side. Its size didn't really matter to Mother. She was totally convinced one of us children was going to get smashed flat crossing that street twice daily. It was a raceway, as far as she was concerned, and a heavily traveled one at that. Why, those cars tore along there going at least forty miles an hour, and often too...about one an hour at least. To her, anything more would have constituted gridlock. As you may have guessed, Mother tended to worry a lot.

Quentin was too young to remember much about living in the Harden house, as we called it; that's because the little old lady who lived next door owned it and her last name was Harden. But he does remember *two* things: the car tire he rolled up and down the street for entertainment, which was fun, and the little red-headed boy who beat him up every day, which wasn't.

The boy was a first grader, the son of the local barber, and he had to pass our house to get to school. His favorite way of finishing off the school day was to beat the living daylights out of Quentin. Besides being a year older, he was taller than Quentin and heavier, too, and I used to wonder why Quentin didn't just hide from the little bully. But every afternoon like clockwork, about the time school let out, Quentin would go out and sit on the front steps and patiently wait for his daily whipping. I suppose standing up to that kid day after day fulfilled Quentin's little five-year-old sense of honor, or something like that.

There was another incident that happened while we were living there. Quentin says he doesn't remember it but I do. That's because I *am* older, as I keep reminding him, and that gives me an advantage.

After starting school we children were permitted one pair of shoes a year. They were invariably plain, brown, lace-up shoes that can only be described as utilitarian. Ugly they may have been but to us they were beautiful...even when the heels ran over, the tongue came loose and we had to curl our toes when they became too small. Our Saturday night ritual, besides an all-over bath, always included polishing our shoes. To make them last as long as possible, we were only permitted to wear them to school, in extremely cold weather, and to church on Sundays.

Since we went barefooted the rest of the time, we regularly got ground-itch, a common occurrence back then, especially in the south. In itself it wasn't so bad, but it's what it led to that was a real bummer.

Every summer, as sure as the world turned, we were subjected to that horror of horrors...*the hookworm treatment*. We did everything we could think of to get out of it. When Mrs. Summers, the public health nurse, began showing up around town, Quentin and I tried to make ourselves as scarce as possible. We hid behind bushes, ducked behind Mother's skirts, and tried our best to become invisible, but nothing worked. That woman had an eagle eye that seemed to improve with age. She could spot a gnat on a tree at one hundred paces, and she could always spot us anywhere. When she did, out came those dreaded words: "Miz Whittle, those children look wormy."

While we cowered there, mortified and hoping nobody had over-heard, she would begin digging around in that cavernous medical bag she always carried. She seemed to have an endless supply of those little packets of clear gelatin capsules, and she could rattle off the instructions for their use without thinking hard, or even taking a breath.

"Leave off their supper and breakfast. Give two of these in the morning, to be swallowed whole, mind you, and follow in two hours with a good dose of Epsom salts." Those capsules contained the bitterest, foulest tasting substance known to mankind so its no wonder the hookworms couldn't survive. That's also why the capsules had to be taken intact. I could handle them o.k., but Quentin was only five and he hadn't learned to swallow pills whole. Which turned out to be a major problem.

Mother tried everything she could think of but nothing worked. She would force his mouth open, throw the capsules to the back of his throat, pour in some water, and then hold his nose. Might have worked with most kids, but not with Quentin. He spit out the capsules with such force they stuck to the kitchen wall. Having the patience of a saint, Mother just retrieved them and tried again...and again.... and again.

By mid-morning she was reaching the end of her rope. She had pleaded, begged, and then threatened with no success. She and Quentin were both exhausted and in tears, but those darn capsules, a bit misshapen and sticky, were still intact.

In the meantime, I had taken mine, swallowed the Epsom salts without throwing up, and was busy beating a path back and forth to the privy. Between times I stood at the kitchen window, feeling sorry for Quentin, and just looking out. That's how I managed to spot Aunt Ora marching down the street in our direction. I whirled around, my eyes as big as saucers, and yelled, "Aunt Ora's coming!!" Without even blinking, Quentin grabbed those capsules from Mother's hand, threw them in his mouth and started chewing like crazy. The expression on his face never changed, and Mother just stood there looking totally stunned.

To understand Quentin's reaction, you would have to know Aunt Ora.

She was a big, raw-boned, rather plain woman who towered over her husband, our Uncle Hubert. If opposites attract, as they say, then it was certainly true with Aunt Ora and Uncle Hubert. He was a sweet, pleasant-natured man who always treated us as if we were very special. Aunt Ora, on the other hand, was over-bearing, critical, and just loved to boss us around. With a few well-chosen words, she could make us feel about as significant as a pissant. She intimidated Mother, and we children were terrified of her. She dominated her family and did a pretty fair job of dominating ours, except for Daddy and he just ignored her.

They lived a block away, across main street going west, with their two youngest children: Doris, who was grown and worked at the packing house, and Trammell who was in high school in Haines City. Those two were always nice to us, like they were glad to be related. The oldest daughter, Romelle, had gotten married about the time we moved to Dundee and seemed to be a regular chip off her mother's block. In ways, but not in looks. She was very pretty.

Their house was much nicer than ours, had an indoor john, and nice furniture. I mentioned their car earlier. The reason they got along so well during the depression was because Uncle Hubert drew a steady salary all those years. I don't think it was a huge sum but it was regular, him being the police chief and all. Actually, he was the entire Dundee police force. His major duties were locking up the town drunks, Mr. Douberly and Mr. Pierce, every Saturday night, and keeping the grass cut between the sidewalks and streets. There was no crime in Dundee to speak of. Nobody locked their doors. Most people didn't even have a door key and weren't overly concerned about getting one.

Getting back to Aunt Ora. About once a month she would come marching down the street like a drill sergeant, doing her Christian duty, checking on the poor relations. She had one of those "its a distasteful job but somebody has to do it" attitudes. We children tried to make ourselves as scarce as possible but Mother always invited her in, conducted herself like the lady she was, and just suffered Aunt Ora's visits. Other than that, there wasn't much socializing between the two families until many years later.

5 | CHAPTER

If you're getting a little tired of all the moving...well, let me assure you it's more fun reading about it than doing it. Yes, in the spring of 1938 we moved once again, this time back across Main St. one block to a corner house. Nobody can remember the reason for that move either but it was probably just out of habit. We were pretty well conditioned by that time, kinda like Pavlov's dogs. As it turned out, though, that move had a different outcome. We actually ended up living in the "Reagan House" (named after the previous tenants) for *five whole years*...a record of stability for the Whittle family.

Quentin turned six that spring and started to school in the fall. Since we were living back across town, we children once again had to cross Main Street to get there. Mother wasn't a bit happy about that and a few other things, too, which I will get to shortly.

According to Quentin, crossing that wide street twice a day had a lasting impression on him. That's because, when he was in the fourth grade, he was chosen to be the crossing guard at the intersection near our house. There were a lot of kids living on our side of Main Street, and the school authorities felt a crossing guard was needed there. Why they chose Quentin is still a mystery. Anyway, they issued him a special white belt that crossed one shoulder and buckled around his waist, a sign that said, "STOP", and a whistle. Even now he admits he liked that feeling of authority and the control he had over people, something that could have influenced his choice of careers later in life. At the time, though, he turned into a regular little Napoleon.

I remember distinctly how he used to make the rest of us children wait on the curb when there wasn't a car in sight. Then, when a car finally did appear, he would strut out into the street, blow his little whistle, heist his little sign, and make the car stop so we could cross. I'm sure the drivers gritted their teeth a lot, but I guess they didn't complain to the school because Quentin served out his time.

The Reagan House was small but in better repair than anything we had lived in before. The walls were plastered, there was a screened-in front porch, and yep...a real indoor bathroom off the kitchen. Mother was so proud of that porcelain tub, but Quentin and I weren't all that excited about it. We weren't into bathing unless made to. Up until that time, Mother would make us bathe in the rinse-water tubs after she finished the laundry. That wasn't so bad, except when we didn't get clean enough to suit her and she scrubbed us with her lye soap.

There was no hot water during the summer months unless it was heated on the kerosene cook stove in the kitchen, so cold baths were the thing. But when the weather turned cold enough for heat, there was a wood heater in the dining room that had a water tank attached. At least we had warm baths for part of the year.

Sometimes, after supper, when it was freezing outside and Daddy got that old wood heater fired up, Mother would gather us around it and we would sing together. She always sang alto, Winky tenor, and the rest of us soprano, all except Daddy. He never joined in but seemed to enjoy it anyhow. I figure that's where we all developed a love for music. Except for Mother, none of us were blessed with any musical talent, but we could carry a tune and we did love to sing. We still do.

Our yard was small but nice. It was shaded by a variety of fruit trees: oranges, tangerines, grapefruit, a cattley guava, and an avocado. There was a paved walk to the front door, one to the back door, and there were sidewalks around two sides of the house, since we lived on the corner. On the back of the lot was a small garage, which abutted the alley.

We kids were happy living in the Reagan House but there were a couple things Mother detested about it. For one, when we moved in, Mother discovered the place was infested with bed bugs. She waged war for weeks trying to get rid of them. She doused all the wall crevices with kerosene—-her main treatment for a lot of things—-and soaked the bedsprings weekly. It's a miracle she didn't burn the house down, but as she frequently said, "Only trashy people have bed bugs and we aren't trash."

The second thing she hated was the size of the place. Every room was tiny and just a couple people would have felt crowded. As it were, there were six of us plus various and assorted relatives who often came to stay for weeks at the time. I can't recall anyone ever complaining about the extras. If Quentin and I had whined about spending most of our childhood sleeping on floor pallets instead of a bed, we would have been shamed unmercifully. Actually, I don't think the thought ever crossed our minds. Providing for family was done gladly. There was no such thing as welfare, federally subsidized housing, or food stamps back then.

I must be honest here. There was one thing I did hate and didn't feel a bit generous about, and that was when *certain* relatives came to visit. (I'm not gonna name them because they may read this someday and I wouldn't want to make them feel bad after all this time.) Anyway, they always seemed to arrive just as we were sitting down to Sunday dinner, that being the best meal of the week and usually the only one with meat. Since, traditionally, the children always ate *after* the grownups, we were lucky to get a chicken neck and biscuit. It was misery, smelling all that good food, and watching it disappear before our very eyes.

During the time we lived in the Reagan House, Daddy managed to eke out a living by picking and packing fruit in season and doing odd carpentry jobs. He had a talent for woodworking, not much experience at it, but a real feeling for it. Grandpa Carter had taught him a lot the basics when they both worked at the shipyards in Tampa back in the mid-twenties. To give the impression of experience, he ordered some tools from Sears Roebuck and left them outside to age in the dew for several days. He was all prepared...and when construction began on a new elementary school in 1937, Daddy was hired on. He had regular employment there for several months with weekly paychecks. That was nice.

Quentin got *his* first experience in the labor market when he was about eight or nine years old. Every spring the big citrus companies would hire young boys to plant orange seedlings, do grafting, and that sort of thing. Quentin got himself a job and was transported by truck each Saturday morning to the groves. For working from daylight until dark, he made one dollar.

He remembers it like this: "That was awful hard work. The sun baked down on my head, my hands got raw, and my bare feet got blistered in that hot sand."

Eventually, he had saved up enough to buy himself a secondhand bicycle from a man who was traveling through town with a truckload of bicycles. It was kind of stripped down, no fancy chrome or anything, and it could have been stolen. Probably was. But to Quentin it was the prettiest bicycle ever made. He rode it back and forth to school. Once in a while he would give me a tow on the crossbar, and sometimes he would even let me ride it by myself.

If there was anything left over after paying the bills, Daddy would give us each a nickel allowance. Making that nickel last a whole week was a challenge. Even with all-day suckers at one cent each, silver bells at five for a penny, and by chewing the same piece of bubble gum for several days, that nickel just didn't make it.

Quentin learned early on how to supplement his income, so to speak. He began scavenging down at the town dump for empty soda bottles. They paid two cents each for those at the grocery store. Stomping around in the town garbage did have a down side, however. Quentin was forever cutting his feet on broken glass or stepping on rusty nails. Mother made him soak his feet in a basin of kerosene, her cure-all. Guess she figured if it killed bedbugs, it ought to kill germs. Must have worked, though, because he never got tetanus or had bad infections of any kind that I can remember. But he did come close to getting himself killed a couple times while we lived there.

The first time happened like this:

There was a family named Williams who lived catty-cornered across the street from us. They had two little girls, Ann and Margaret. Ann was a year and a half older than me and was a year ahead of me in school, but she became my bosom buddy anyway. Margaret was Quentin's age, in the same grade, and became his most frequent playmate. Nobody called her "Margaret" though. Everyone called her "Sister" until she was nearly grown.

Between the Williams front porch and the sidewalk was a huge camphor berry tree. It must have been ancient because its roots spread out from the tree base in every direction and stuck up like some old woman's arthritic fingers. We spent many happy hours climbing that tree. In fact, it was a favorite with the neighborhood kids and there was most always one or more perched among the limbs. Quentin especially liked to climb it and pretend to be his favorite all-time hero...Tarzan the Ape Man. He had a Tarzan yell that was the envy of all the kids. When he was in top form he could be heard all over town, and he sounded like a hound with his tail caught in the door.

One hot summer afternoon Ann and I were involved in our own pursuits...hiding in the bushes down near the lake behind their house watching the boy scout troop go skinny-dipping...while Quentin and Sister were playing in the front yard. Quentin climbed the old camphor berry tree and began scampering around among the limbs, pretending to be Tarzan. Sister seemed more interested in her doll than him so to get her attention he yelled, "Hey, Sister, watch this. I'm Tarzan!" With that he gave his mighty Tarzan yell and jumped from one limb to the next. Well, that was his intention but he didn't quite make it. His trip down was faster than the one up and he landed with a loud plunk right between two of those big roots. He just lay there, not breathing or moving and was white as a sheet. That scared the pea-turkey out of Sister and she started screaming at the top of her lungs. Ann and I heard all the racket, ran up the hill to the house, took one look at Quentin and we started howling, too. I thought for sure he was stone-cold-dead.

Mrs. Williams came running out of the house. Well, actually, it was more like waddling real fast because she was short, fat, and kinda butt-heavy like a duck. She could really move though when she had to, and she had a real cool head in an emergency. She grabbed Quentin under the arms, drug him up on the porch, propped him in a chair, and threw a glass of ice water in his face. I guess she never considered that he might have some broken bones, just figured that if he didn't start breathing it wouldn't much matter how many broken bones he had anyway. Getting him to breath seemed more important at the time and it worked, too. He gasped and started turning a nice shade of pink.

In the meantime, Mother had heard all the commotion and came running across the street, totally convinced her biggest nightmare had come to pass...one of her offspring had finally been killed. Unlike Mrs. Williams, Mother wasn't much help in an emergency...she was more into hysterics.

As soon as Mrs. Williams got Mother calmed down, and I'm not sure how she did this unless it was her ice-water-in-the-face remedy, Mother began rocking Quentin back and forth and trying to convince herself he was indeed still living. Then, she reached in her apron pocket, handed me a dime, and sent me to the store to buy Quentin a pound of little green grapes. He loved those almost as much as candy and we didn't get them very often. At a dime a pound they were considered a luxury, much to expensive.

I never figured out why Mother did that unless it was symbolic, like a sacrifice of thanksgiving, or something as deeply meaningful. At the time though, my impulse was to jump out of that old tree myself so I could get some grapes. I really did consider it but decided they wouldn't be worth the pain. Besides, I honestly didn't think Mother would survive another go-round.

The second time Quentin nearly killed himself was when he set the man's orange grove on fire. That was right after he got the bicycle.

It happened on a Saturday, a beautiful spring morning, sunny and a little breezy. Mother was working at the canning plant, Daddy at a construction job, and Winky was delivering groceries for Smith's Grocery Store. That left Myra to keep an eye on Quentin and me. She was about sixteen and a very conscientious baby sitter, or whatever you want to call it for two kids our age. Anyway...she kept me so busy helping her clean house I didn't have time to get into trouble. I can't say that for Quentin.

He and Ronnie Rutherford, one of his neighborhood buddies, were riding their bicycles up and down the streets and through the alleys when they got the notion to build a hideout. That's what got them into trouble...big time.

They began collecting discarded lumber and any other junk they could think of a use for, and transporting it all down to Lake Minzie on their bicycles. The lake was located across the street and at the bottom of the hill in front of our house. It was round-shaped and deep...bottomless according to the old-timers.

That may have been a tale, made up just to scare us kids and keep us from playing around it, which we were forbidden to do anyway. The lake was surrounded by orange groves, and, closer to the shoreline, tall, dry reeds. We were having a drought at the time.

Shortly afterward the town fire alarm went off. In Dundee the sound of a siren was rare so it always generated a lot of excitement. As soon as the fire truck appeared half the town chased it to its destination, either on foot or by car if they had one. Part of them were volunteer firemen but the rest were just satisfying their curiosity.

The siren got closer and, not wanting to miss anything, Myra and I ran out the front door just about the time the fire truck came flying around the corner, heading off down the dirt road toward the lake. That's when we noticed the big, black, smoke-clouds coming from that direction. And it was about that time that Myra realized Quentin wasn't anywhere around. She started calling him and running towards the lake, taking a short cut through the orange grove. I was close behind and running like mad trying to keep up.

When we got to the lake the first thing we spotted were Quentin and Ronnie's bicycles, lying near the reeds that were burning like crazy. By that time, and with the wind blowing the way it was, the fire had already crept up and spread into the grove. The firemen were pumping water from the lake and doing their darndest to put it out, but they didn't seem to be making much headway.

Myra quickly reached the conclusion that the fire had forced the boys into the lake. Since it dropped off at the edge and neither of them could swim, she figured they had both drowned. She was awfully upset, and since she was, I was. Both of us started bawling. She decided not to tell anyone the boys were missing, at least until she could get word to Ronnie's parents and then tell Mother and Daddy herself. She knew how fast a rumor could travel in Dundee. It would make a greased bullet look slow.

We pulled their bicycles up the hill to the road and then rode fast to the Rutherford house, a block away. The first thing we saw was Quentin and Ronnie playing ball in the front yard, looking as innocent as newborn babes. Or trying to. They might have gotten away with it, too, if they hadn't been covered with soot, their hair and eye lashes singed, and stinking like smoke.

As soon as Myra sized up the situation, she broke a switch off a nearby bush, grabbed Quentin by one arm and began dragging him home, right down the middle of the street. I rode his bicycle along the sidewalk and tried to get mad at him, too, but I couldn't. With every step, she switched his legs and chewed him out, all at the same time.

The conversation, if you want to call it that, went something like this:

Myra: "Have you gone crazy? What were you thinking of?"

Quentin: "I'm sorry, Myra. I didn't mean to set the reeds on fire."

Myra: "You KNOW you're not supposed to play near the lake! And you KNOW you're not supposed to play with matches! Where didja get them anyway?"

Quentin: "Ronnie snucked 'em out of his house...and we used that ole cardboard roll Mother's rug came on for a stove pipe in our hide-out...and it caught on fire...and we couldn't put it out...I'm sorry!"

Myra: "It's too late for 'sorry'! Daddy doesn't have the money to pay for that man's grove. What do you think Daddy's going to do to you when he finds out? Huh?"

I think it dawned on Myra at that exact moment what Daddy *really would* do to Quentin. And being the tenderhearted person she was, she couldn't bear the idea. By the time we got home, Myra was doing more thinking than hitting. Quentin, realizing right off the bat that she was softening up some, tried to look his most pitiful.

By the time Mother and Daddy got home from work, a couple hours later, Quentin had gone through a transformation, you might say. They were either too tired or too distracted to notice that their baby child looked mighty weird. Myra had done her best in the short time she had. She had stripped him down, washed his smoky clothes, made him take a bath (that in itself should have made them suspicious), and then trimmed his singed hair, eyebrows, and eyelashes with Mother's sewing scissors. We were on pins and needles for the rest of the afternoon, just waiting for Mother and Daddy to notice something out of the ordinary, but they didn't.

Actually they didn't know about what happened until years later. At the time, though, the only comments made were over supper that night. Mother and Daddy talked about what a terrible thing it was, that poor man's grove burning and all, and they wondered how the fire got started. Quentin tried to look as small as possible and not call attention to himself, while giving Myra apprehensive looks from under his eye lashes...what he had left anyway.

For several weeks afterward, Quentin was a regular little angel. He was at Myra's mercy and knew it. All she had to do was smile at him sweetly, tell him to do something, and he would jump to it like he had been hit with a cattle prod. Eventually, things settled down and the fire was pretty near forgotten. Until I started writing this book, that is, and remembering about it and lots of other neat things in Quentin's life. He'll swear I made this all up.

But before I leave the subject entirely, there is one other thing I must mention. Besides improving Quentin's behavior, the fire also served another purpose: It created a lot of excitement for the local folks and gave them something to think about besides how they were gonna pay their grocery bill. As I mentioned earlier, not much happened in Dundee except an occasional domestic squabble or dogfight. Well...there *was* that time when the local barber fell out of his fishing boat on Lake Marie and nearly drowned because his cork leg kept floating. Now that was really exciting.

6 | CHAPTER

Some of these tales may not be in proper sequence. I've forgotten the exact time frame of some of them, but I haven't forgotten what happened. A few of the memories aren't too pleasant to recall but most of them were happy, for us kids anyway.

There was the time, not too many months after we moved into the Reagan House, that Daddy had to go to the hospital. It was in '38 or '39, I think, before we had a car. Daddy had been picking fruit for the packinghouse and rammed a spur from an orange branch into the palm of his hand. It had already starting turning red by the time he got home that afternoon and wasn't long before he had a full-blown case of blood poisoning. He was running a fever of 104 when Doris, Uncle Hubert's middle daughter, came by for a visit and saw the shape he was in. She took him over to the county hospital in Bartow right away and had him admitted. If he hadn't been so sick he probably would have objected to taking charity because that was the kind of hospital it was. Knowing Daddy, he probably would have just sat there and died. If being stubborn was a virtue, he was truly gifted.

As it happened, he was in the hospital two weeks and wondering all that time if they were going to take his arm off. There were no wonder drugs back then but the treatment they used proved to be effective. I can still remember that they used hot Epsom salts compresses constantly. Doris took us over to see him a couple times and I watched the nurse doing the treatment. Why that should have interested a kid my age I don't know, but it must have impressed me enough to make nursing a career after I became an adult.

Daddy's hand eventually healed but it took several weeks and he was out of work all that time. We had no income except charity goods. That was tough for Mother and Daddy to accept but it was a necessity. Temporary, thank goodness.

They say that even black clouds have silver linings, and seems like that's true. Even in the midst of our misery, we had happy moments. Take that Christmas, for example.

On Christmas Eve Santa came to visit in a big truck and left us the best toys we ever had.

Quentin got a big blue tricycle and I got my first doll. The toys were recycled second-hand stuff and Uncle Hubert was dressed like Santa Claus. We didn't know that at the time but it wouldn't have made any difference anyway. In retrospect, I know Mother and Daddy must have been embarrassed, knowing how proud they were. But I guess they loved us too much to refuse those gifts, especially after seeing our excitement.

Quentin could hardly wait for daylight so he could ride up and down the sidewalk, showing off his tricycle. Sometimes he would let me stand on the back and hold onto his shoulders while we flew down the hill. That was a lot of fun but going uphill was the pits. That's because he made me push it back up...with him on it.

Quentin didn't get to enjoy that tricycle for very long, though. Rudolph Feagle, who lived next door, sneaked it for a ride and bent the front wheel. Daddy tried to straighten it but it never would roll right after that. Quentin wouldn't play with Rudolph after that or have anything to do with him. I don't think Rudolph cared much. He wasn't a mean kid, just lacking in smarts. Actually I'm being real kind here . . . saying he was dumb as a toad would be more honest.

In 1939 the situation in Europe was heating up and most people figured the U.S. was about to be involved in a war. Hitler was invading all the surrounding countries and appeared to be making plans to conquer the whole world. Things were beginning to change around our part of the country, too. Many of the military bases were enlarging and there was a growing demand for civilian highly skilled carpenters. Daddy began finding work on a regular basis, but the jobs were scattered all over Florida. Sometimes he would be gone for weeks at a time. Since he rode with men from the area, who had cars, he could only come home when they did, like on weekends and holidays. Daddy didn't like being away from home, but he did like the salary he was making. And, unlike many of the men he worked with, Daddy didn't drink it up, gamble it away, or spend it on wild women. Daddy always brought home every cent he ever made above work expenses.

Finally, when he was working in Tampa at the base there, he saved up enough to make a down payment on a car. He came breezing up one weekend in a 1930 Model-A Ford. It was just a black, stripped-down, two-door sedan but we were as proud of that car as if it were a gold Cadillac. It costs $150 and the payments were $10 a month. After that, we sometimes got to tool over to Winter Haven or Haines City on a Saturday afternoon and see a movie. Quentin and I could get in for a dime and spend the entire afternoon watching a double feature, cartoons, news, and a serial, like Fu Manchu.

After WW II officially broke out in December of 1941—- that's when Japan bombed Pearl Harbor—- Daddy was never without a job. He worked long hours and put in a lot of overtime. It must have been around then that he began hankering for a place of his own, preferably a farm. He never took to city living, not that Dundee was any city, but he didn't like living so close to other people that he couldn't spit out the window without hitting the neighbors. His dream was to farm for himself on his own place. No more share cropping. So he opened his first bank account and began to put away a few bucks out of every paycheck.

When Daddy's next job took him to Buckingham Gunnery School in Fort Myers, he decided it would be cheaper to take us all with him than try to drive home every weekend. Gas was rationed then anyway, and you couldn't get tires. So, he rented a really nice, completely furnished, three-bedroom house a block from Fort Myers Beach, and that's where we lived for the entire summer. Quentin and I thought we had died and gone to heaven.

We had new bathing suits and we spent every day at the beach, gathering shells, playing in the surf, and building sand castles It surprised all of us when Mother gave us that much freedom, especially around the water. She was a lot more relaxed that whole summer, even mentioned getting some shorts to wear because it was so hot, but Daddy wouldn't let her.

He didn't think it was fitting for a woman her age. She was about 39 that summer and had a knockout figure. But she obeyed. That's just the way things were, and a heck of a long time it was before women's lib, too.

This story is supposed to be about Quentin so I guess I had better get back to our hero.

Two exciting things happened to him that summer, one bad and one good. He almost lost his toe while playing along the edge of the surf. That was the bad. Quentin swears a crab tried to bite it off and I have always contended he stepped on a sharp shell. At any rate, it was split pretty bad and probably needed sutures but nobody mentioned going to the doctor. Mother whipped out the old home remedies and got busy. He ended up with a bad scar but managed to keep his toe.

The good thing happened on the pier one night. After supper all the families would congregate to enjoy whatever breeze they could get off the gulf, do a little fishing, and talk about the latest war news. The main subject that night was about the German submarines that were operating off the gulf coast. That was scary to the rest of us kids, but Quentin wasn't paying attention: he was too busy fishing. He rigged up a cane pole, about six feet long, put some bait on it and was fishing along with the adults. They, of course, had all kinds of fancy, expensive, salt water fishing gear. They didn't catch anything but Quentin caught a ten-pound snook. Nobody could figure out how he landed that big fish on his teeny little pole. I don't think he knew either, but it surely had to be one of the biggest thrills of his life.

When we moved back to Dundee in time to start school in September, a lot had changed over the summer, or so it seemed, and it was all exciting. For one thing, there were more military convoys passing on Main Street. When we heard them coming, Quentin and I would run down, sit on the curb, and wave at the soldiers as they passed. Sometimes there were trucks with German prisoners of war, too. We expected them to have horns or something but they looked pretty much like the American soldiers to us. Like most children we had no idea what war was all about, just what we saw in the newsreels at the movies.

Everybody around Dundee got all fired up and full of patriotism. We kids spent every afternoon after school collecting scrap iron and aluminum for the war effort. Then we piled it up on a vacant lot and waited for a truck to come by periodically and pick it up. Instead of Cowboy and Indian games, we started playing war games, using sticks for machine guns and mowing down the Japs and Germans.

In December, Winky joined the Coast Guard and was sent up north to boot camp. We put a star in our window to show we had a boy in service. Many of the houses in Dundee had one and sometimes two. Mother spent two days in bed when he left. Just grieving I guess. We didn't have much of a Christmas that year, but Myra tried to make it the best she could. She used some of the money she made working at McCrory's Dime Store in Winter Haven during that Christmas vacation, and bought a tree. She put it up, and decorated it with lights. Made us some chocolate fudge, too. It was really good and we didn't care that we had to eat it with a spoon.

Quentin turned eleven in March 1943 and we spent from June to October in Walnut Hill, Florida, about ten miles from the Alabama line. Daddy had a job at the Naval Air Station in Pensacola, about thirty miles away. He commuted every day in the old Ford.

We didn't actually move there, just camped as Daddy liked to call it. (I think he just said that to appease Mother.) Since we didn't own a house key, he just nailed up the doors to the Reagan House and left all our belongings except our clothes. At first we moved in with Daddy's sister, Aunt Imogene, and her family. She and Uncle Marland, and their big bunch of kids, lived in a big old farmhouse and had lots of acreage that Uncle Marland and his boys farmed. It was right on the main highway through Walnut Hill and had been in the Sharpless family for several generations.

After a couple weeks, Mother and Daddy decided to get a place of their own. Even a big house can get crowded when two families live in it, and as Daddy always said…one roof is not big enough for two women, for very long anyway. They rented an old tenant house just down the road from Aunt Imogene's and, with her help, threw together the basics for housekeeping. We were once again drawing our water from a well and using a two-holer out back. That seemed to be our destiny.

Mother wasn't a happy camper, you might say, but Daddy kept telling her it was only a temporary measure until he could find a farm to buy. He liked that area, we all did, and we hoped he would find something to his liking. What free time he had he spent looking, but farms-for-sale didn't seem to be very plentiful around that area.

Those summer months were sweltering hot, the days long, and Quentin and I spent most of them working in the fields, picking cotton or gathering stuff for Mother and Aunt Imogene to can. Everybody was encouraged to preserve all the food they could to help the war effort. I guess Mother and Imogene took that real seriously because they surely broke some sort of record that summer. They canned over four hundred cans of black-eyed peas, not counting the other stuff, and we got to help do it. That was not one of the most fun things we did there. The cans had to be sealed and then processed in a pressure cooker. Our right arms nearly got over-developed from running the sealer.

Occasionally, there was time for playing, though, and sometimes the two of us got invited to peanut boilings with the local farm kids, or Daddy would take us swimming at a spring-fed creek not far away. The water was icy cold but we loved it. That was about our only way of cooling off because that summer was a scorcher and we didn't have a refrigerator or icebox. That meant, of course, that we had no iced water, no iced tea, no iced nothing.

Once in a blue moon, Mother would treat us to an ice cream cone at Shell's store, and about as often, Daddy would bring a block of ice from Atmore, Alabama, the closest town of any size, about ten miles northwest. He would wrap it in burlap and put it in a tub. We sure did hate to see that ice melt.

Quentin quickly made friends with the little boy who lived across the highway. His name was Howard Shell and his folks owned a combination country store/ filling station and lived in the back of it. Howard was Quentin's age, but he was a tad taller and much chubbier than Quentin. Looked better nourished, you might say. He had sandy-colored hair, a round pudgy face and smiled a lot. They got along fine and spent a lot of time exploring the woods behind the house and doing whatever boys that age do for fun.

Quentin couldn't seem to go for very long without something exciting happening to him. That summer was no different.

One afternoon, while he and Howard were playing in the woods, Howard was bitten on the leg by a ground rattler. When nobody heard all their yelling for help, Quentin did what he figured he had to do . . . he carried Howard piggyback all the way home. We're talking *up*hill, with a kid that out-weighed him by several pounds. Nobody could figure out how he did that. I guess he must have had an adrenalin rush or something, but Howard swore it was true so that satisfied any doubters. Mr. Shell put Howard in the car and broke all the speed records getting to the hospital in Atmore. Howard's leg turned black, and he was pretty sick for a while, but he got over it o.k. except for some scars.

Something else happened not long after that, something really scary that nearly caused Quentin to lose his cookies.

We seemed to be located directly under the flight path between the Pensacola and Mobile air bases. That's where they trained a lot of fighter pilots to send overseas. Seeing planes flying in formation overhead became so familiar we seldom paid attention. That was true for the droning of the plane engines too. The sounds were almost constant and we were so used to them, we just tuned them out. That's why, the day there was a sudden change, I knew immediately something was wrong.

I was drawing water from the well and looked up in time to see two of the planes falling. They were turning round and round and making a high-pitched whine. That was really scary because I couldn't tell where they were going to crash. I just froze in one place. They disappeared behind some trees not far away with a loud crash and smoke. I only saw one parachute open.

Quentin was working in the field with Aunt Imogene's boys, not too far from the crash site. He started running in that direction, along with everyone else, curious to see what happened. He should have stayed away. The parachute of one pilot caught on the tail of the plane when he bailed out and it didn't open. He made a good-sized hole in the ground and it wasn't a pretty sight. Quentin took one look, backed up against a tree, and nearly passed out. He had nightmares about that experience for a while but he eventually got over it. Being the tough little nut that he was, nothing seemed to faze him for long.

7 | Chapter

Daddy's nest egg had grown, not as much as he wanted, but still enough to make a down payment, and he was getting anxious. The long hours and heavy manual labor at work, in addition to being around people constantly, was beginning to tell on him. As the days passed, Daddy became even more determined to find a farm, anything he could sink a plow into, but he wasn't having any luck finding a place in that area.

In the meantime, Myra had a job at the airbase in Mobile and was living there, but she spent weekends with us as often as she could. Quentin and I enrolled in the Walnut Hill School that fall and rode the school bus, which picked us up in front of the house. It was a new experience but one we liked. Quentin was in the sixth grade and I was in the eighth and the school was huge compared to the Dundee School, but we adjusted rapidly. Making friends seemed to come easily, too, and we fit in like we had lived there all our lives. Moving was unthinkable, we loved it there and didn't want to go anywhere. But life's not always fair, as we found out in short order.

About the first of October, Daddy decided to drive over to Havana, Florida, in Gadsden County, about 18 miles northwest of Tallahassee, to see Grandmother Whittle. She and her mother, Great-grandmother Loyd, had settled there several years before. While he was there, Daddy and his brother Barney, who also lived in Havana, decided to pool their money and buy a place that was up for sale. It was located about three miles north of Havana, three miles south of the Georgia line and one-half mile off U.S. 27, the main north/south highway through that area.

None of us saw the place until it was a done deal, more's the pity. I do believe Mother would have finally rebelled...if she had been given an opportunity. As I mentioned before, Daddy made the big decisions and Mother accepted them without question, at least none that we kids were aware of.

The day Daddy, proud as a peacock, loaded us all in the car and took us out to see our new home, was unforgettable. After one look I think Mother was in shock, a condition that must have lasted several years. She had lived in some crummy places but that had to be the worst of the lot. "The Farm," as it was called forever after, consisted of one pathetic, ancient farmhouse, one barn in worse shape than the house, and thirty-four acres of land. The place didn't even boast a decent out-house, for heaven's sake. Now, there are some things that are *absolutely necessary*. That's why, in the olden days, privies were called "necessaries." The truth was...that house should have been condemned for human habitation, but hadn't been, unfortunately.

It was very depressing, is what it was, any woman's worst nightmare. I'm sure it would have been rejected as a scene for the movie *Tobacco Road*, and I'm *not* exaggerating here. Most of the windows were boarded up, or filled with cardboard. There was no insulation and no heat except for two fireplaces, one of which was leaning and looked ready to tumble over if anybody breathed on it. The house had never seen a paintbrush. There was a rotten one-room shack a few feet behind it that didn't have a roof, but did have a bunch of chickens scratching around it. I guess they roosted in it because there was about a foot of chicken do-do underneath it. Daddy said it had probably been a detached kitchen at one time, as was common in antebellum homes, but was being used at that time as a chicken house. That explained it nicely. There was a smoke house near the back, too, but I don't think it had been used in years, probably because it was listing to starboard.

The back of the house, the part that served as the kitchen/dining room, was sagging and was partially supported by tree stumps. The L-shaped front porch was rotted through in several places, which caused it to sag in the center. There was no landscaping...just a packed-clay and sand yard with a ditch, apparently from erosion, running directly in front of the porch steps. Oh yes, they sagged, too. Actually, what with all the sagging, that place looked totally exhausted.

There were no power or phone lines and no water supply. The shallow well, which was located about fifty feet from the mule lot, had caved in. Access to the farm was by a narrow two-rut road along the side of a small clay gully, and that was almost impassable in rainy weather.

Actually, the farm's only redeeming qualities seemed to be rich fertile soil, and a good price. I don't think Daddy ever considered the appearance of the place, or how unlivable it really was. Or maybe he did and didn't think it was all that important. He had never been used to a lot of comforts, just the necessities mostly. I always thought of Daddy as being a diamond in the rough. His needs were simple...a bed, a roof over his head, and a bite to eat would suit him nicely, thank you. To hell with how it looked. So, once he got a look at that rich soil and heard the price, Daddy was hooked, he was in hog heaven, and he wasn't going anywhere...and neither were we.

I guess Mother was too speechless to complain, and even though Myra and I didn't want to disappoint Daddy, we had a real hard time working up any enthusiasm. To be honest, we were impressed with the many pecan and oak trees on the places, and it did sit in a pretty spot. Quentin, on the other hand, was too busy exploring the place to show any interest one way or the other.

The people who were living there at the time...yes, people were actually living there...had a mangy-looking old dog running around the yard. And some distance from the house was a tiny structure, about four feet high and four feet wide, made with a wooden frame covered with burlap bags. Propped at one side was a white enamel sign with blue lettering that said "Murphy." Quentin, being the smart kid that he was, figured that was a dog house and Murphy the dog's name, so he began chasing the dog around the yard and yelling," Here Murphy! Come on, Murphy!" He got some strange looks from those folks. We found out why later on. That thrown-together contraption was their privy, and the sign was a discarded oven door from an old wood stove. It just happened to be lying there.

After that day, if anyone in the Whittle family was in a crowd and had to go to the restroom, he or she asked to be excused by saying, "I have to go see Mrs. Murphy." It became a private family joke. We still do it and nobody has an inkling of what we are talking about, except any Whittles who might be there. If we get quizzical looks, we just smile innocently, keep our mouths shut, and let people wonder.

We moved to our "country estate" on October 1, 1943. Winky was still in service. Myra transferred from the base in Mobile to Dale Mabry Field in Tallahassee but lived at home and commuted to work by car pool from Havana. Quentin and I enrolled in the Havana school and had to catch the bus at the highway, about a half-mile away. We walked it everyday in all kinds of weather, and hated every minute of it. We didn't care much for the school either. I'll get to that later. But the truth was, we were not happy about the situation in which we found ourselves; none of us except Daddy, that is.

He bought himself an old mule named Rhodie, who looked as old as the house and in about the same pitiful shape, and some second-hand equipment and set about farming. He built a sled to pull behind the mule, taught Quentin and me had to harness her, and then gave us the job of cleaning the yards. That included tearing down the chicken house and hauling it off, along with the accumulated chicken poop. This was every-day-after-school and weekend work, in addition to helping Daddy clear the fields. After that he had us hauling dirt to fill in the front yard ditch. It wasn't long before we had as many callouses as any field hand. Well, that's pretty much what we were for the next several years, anyhow. Quentin always said we were Daddy's slave labor.

Since Uncle Barney's house sat on one acre, our house on one acre, and there were six acres of woods, that left only twenty-six tillable acres. To give Daddy his due, he really thought he could make a living off it. Or, it may be he let his deep desire to farm his own land overcome his good common sense. In a short time, we were in a financial bind. Myra was paying all the grocery bills out of her salary, plus buying stuff to try to make the house livable. Winky began sending a Navy allotment that October, also, which Daddy used mostly for seed, fertilizer, and such as that. Eventually, Mother got a job at the tobacco-packing house, running a stemming machine, to pay the basic household expenses. We were living about as close financially as a family could when Winky got married in 1945 and the allotment stopped. Then, when Dale Mabry Field closed at the end of WW II, Myra moved to Charleston, S.C. to work in Aunt Clora and Uncle Buddy's meat market there. (Aunt Clora was Daddy's youngest sister.) She got married the following July, in 1946.

Daddy began doing some truck farming, running-type green beans mostly, with some corn and peanuts. Quentin and I did all the bean tying and a good deal of the picking. Every summer, as soon as school let out, we were working in the fields, all day, every day, except weekends. We had to hoe five acres of peanuts one summer and it got almighty hot out in that patch. By the time we finished we not only *looked* like most of the Gadsden county field-hands, we probably would have *sounded* like them, too, if Daddy had permitted us to cuss. Quentin had a way of getting around that. If he got really frustrated about something, he would say," I think I'm gonna cuss...CUSS!" That usually started us laughing and we'd forget about how miserable we were...for a little while anyway. But, there was one thing we found out real fast—-after a few hours in that hot sun, those peanuts began to look an awful lot like coffee weeds. We probably hoed up as many peanuts as weeds. We didn't do it on purpose, I swear, but I did wonder a lot of times if Daddy ever figured out why he didn't make much of a peanut crop. He didn't plant many peanuts after that and we weren't a bit disappointed.

As I mentioned earlier, our world had been turned upside down in a short period of time and we were not the happiest kids on the block, or the farm in our case. Starting to Havana School didn't improve matters. One thing we found out right off the bat was that kids who lived in the country didn't rank very high on the Havana social scale. That was real puzzling to us. In Dundee and in Walnut Hill, we Whittle kids were invited to all the parties, and involved in everything. Now we were pretty well ignored, and that was hard to adjust to. I guess you might say that where once we had been *big* fish in a *little* pond, we were now *little* fish in a *little* pond, and our egos received a major shock from it.

In most small towns, and Havana was no different, much of the social life revolved around the churches and school. Getting active in church might have helped matters a bit, but after we moved to Havana Mother quit going altogether. I don't know why. We never asked and she never said. It wasn't due to a lack off faith on her part though, I'm sure of that, but she didn't attend church for the next six years. She never attended PTA meetings either, as far as I can remember, and that pretty well finished off our social life, for a while anyway. As a result, and over a period of time, we changed from two big extroverts into two little introverts.

I guess Myra got tired of our moping around. In 1945 she bought two tickets on the Greyhound, packed our bags, and sent Quentin and me to Dundee for a few days visit. We stayed with Uncle Ora, who made us welcome, surprisingly, and Uncle Hubert. We visited around town and hung out with old friends, but it wasn't the same. There were new people there and a lot of changes. We had been gone too long, there was no house on the corner to go home to, and we missed the folks.

Eventually we made friends around the area where we lived. We went to pileaus, to peanut boilings, on possum hunts and hayrides, and stuff like that. It was all good country fun, but it didn't happen all that often. And sometimes, on a Saturday afternoon, we went to the movie in Havana while Mother and Daddy did their weekly grocery shopping. Otherwise our social life didn't amount to a hill of beans.

Once in a while, Quentin, Daddy, and Uncle Barney would take Uncle Barney's old military jeep and go fishing down on the Ochlocknee River. The jeep didn't have a heater and they nearly froze in the winter. One dark night as they turned down the Glade Road off Highway 27, on their way home, there was a car blocking the road. That was long before the road was paved. The car was just sitting there with the lights out. Uncle Barney, who was a mechanic, thought the car had broken down so he walked up to see if he could help. What he saw was a black couple in the back seat...making out, big time. Now, Uncle Barney figured there was a time and place for such things and blocking a county road in the middle of the night to have at it wasn't one of them. He put the jeep in four-wheel drive and pushed the car over in the ditch.

Quentin said, "All I could see was the whites of four eyes peekin' over the back door as we passed. That musta scared them to death, but they shouldn't of been where they were, doin' what they were doin'."

When I was picking Quentin's brain for this book, I asked him what kind of memories he had of our life on the farm and he said, "Mostly I think about skippin' school because I was so ashamed of what I had to wear." Then he laughed and said, " I don't imagine we smelled any too good either, since we only had a wash pan to bath in, on a daily basis anyway. And I can't remember ownin' any deodorant until I could earn the money to buy my own."

On Saturdays we would drag one of Mother's old wash tubs into the back bedroom, heat water on the wood stove, and take our weekly all-over bath and shampoo. Mother did manage to keep us supplied with soap and Halo shampoo. She was strict about cleanliness, so I guess we were presentable and didn't smell too bad.

One of Quentin's main chores during the winter months was to cut and split firewood for the stove and fireplace. No matter how cold the weather, he would strip down to the waist. Since he had begun to get taller about then but hadn't put on any extra weight, his ribs stuck out and looked a lot like Mother's washboard. He developed a kind of rhythm when he swung the axe, and he kept time by singing along at the top of his lungs. Any song would do, and if he didn't know the words, he just made them up as he went along. One of his favorites was "Joley Blonde". That one had all kinds of possibilities and if he thought I was listening, his lyrics became more and more ridiculous. Even during those miserable years, Quentin had a crazy sense of humor, and he could always make me laugh. He still does and he still can.

For several years we had no heat except the fireplace in Mother and Daddy's bedroom. Many times, if the night was cold enough, Mother's slop jar would freeze solid under her bed. That's the truth, so help me. I would never exaggerate about something of such importance. What's more, we would have to thaw it out before it could be emptied. That was usually my job.

Since Mother and Daddy always went to bed with the chickens—-that's about dusk dark, for city people—- and Quentin and I had homework to do, we had to sit at the dining room table to do it. And since there was no heat, we would have to get all bundled up in our heavy coats to keep from freezing. Even then our fingers would get so blue and stiff we could hardly write. Since we had no reference books, not even a dictionary, I guess we did pretty well in school, considering.

I'm going to back up a bit here and catch up something important I left out. After moving to the farm, Daddy did make improvements, over a period of time, until the house was livable. Not pretty, nor comfortable, just livable. And one of his first improvements was to build a nice out-house. During the war building materials were almost impossible to come by, but he managed to scrounge up enough for that necessity, thank goodness. Then when REA ran electric lines to the house, Daddy ran us a line to the privy. What we had was the Cadillac of all privies...a two-holer with electricity, no less. And as Daddy explained, the extra hole was for company, and you certainly needed a good light to see what you were doing, by golly.

Basically, Daddy was a very serious-minded man. That's because, to him, living was a serious business and much of the time he seemed to be carrying around the weight of the ages. A belly laugh to anyone else was just a chuckle to him. Yet, every once in a while, he would do something or say something that showed he did have a great sense of humor. It must have been buried so deep it only erupted occasionally...like it couldn't be contained but just so long. For instance, when he finished the privy and took us out to see his handiwork, he had posted a sign on the back wall that said, "You can tell by the shape of the seat, it was made for your ass and not for your feet." Quentin, Myra, and I doubled up laughing, but Mother made him paint over part of it.

There was something else that puzzled me at the time but nobody else seemed to think it was odd. Daddy built that privy right out in the open. I understood why he built it so *far* from the house, but there was nothing to camouflage it. Our place sat up on a hill, too, so the privy sat there in all its glory, a shining beacon for all to see. Everybody within a mile knew when we had to go. Many years later, after the house had plumbing and an indoor bathroom and the privy was no long needed, the family congregated in the back yard for a grand ceremony. Quentin, or one of the grandsons, nobody can remember exactly, cranked up the tractor, tied a chain around the privy and drug it down to the woods. Everyone cheered and clapped. I don't think there was anyone who enjoyed the occasion more than Quentin. That privy had caused him some real grief at one time and he hadn't forgotten it.

In the summer of 1947, Aunt Clora came down from Charleston, S.C. to visit Grandmother Whittle for a few days. Grandmother had been living alone in a small house in Hinson, about a mile from the farm, after Great-grandmother Loyd died in 1943. Aunt Clora drove down in the meat market truck and brought her son Jerry and his motor scooter. He was to spend the remainder of the summer with us. He was the same age as Quentin, fifteen at that time, and about the same size, too. But where Quentin was blond and blue-eyed, Jerry had dark brown hair and brown eyes. They were both good-looking boys and the two of them got along like two peas in a pod. They made that summer altogether unforgettable...in more ways than one...and most of them we could have done without.

8 | Chapter

Jerry was known throughout the family for his pranks and practical jokes. I think he tried them all that summer, plus some new ones. I wish I could say that Quentin didn't take any part in it, but alas, that would be untrue. He not only took part but was a very willing and enthusiastic accomplice. They tried to see how much trouble they could either cause or get into. Some of it wasn't so funny. Like the time they connected some wires to the scooter and gave an electrical shock to all the farm cats. And we had lots of those, too. That mean trick got Quentin and Jerry a good scolding and shaming from Mother, and made me the butt of some of their practical jokes, since I was the one who tattled.

I need to explain about our overabundance of cats here, before I continue.

After Grandmother moved to Hinson, she worried that Clementine, her cat, might get run over. Since Clementine was a good mouser, Mother and Daddy agreed to let her live in our barn to keep down the rat population, even though Mother didn't like cats. As soon as Clementine moved in, she began to have a lot of wild cat parties, entertaining suitors at all hours, and before long that we had about two dozen of her offspring running around. They didn't all come along at the same time, of course, but they did accumulate and nearly drove Mother nuts with their constant meowing. Sometimes when Mother was cooking, they would line up at the back screen door and get with it, all up and down the musical scale. When she couldn't stand it anymore, she would take the broom and charge out the back door, swinging the broom from left to right and yelling, "Scat, you aggravating cats!!" Cats flew in all directions. A few minutes later she would go out and take a head count, checking to be sure she hadn't hurt any of them.

After shocking all the cats, Jerry starting looking around for another prank to pull or someone to play a joke on. The next one wasn't so funny either, to Quentin anyway, since he was the butt of it.

Because of a long-standing problem with asthma and sinus infections, Jerry had lost his sense of smell. One day when Quentin was sitting in the privy, Jerry sneaked up and propped the door shut so he couldn't get out. Then he scooped up a bucket of water from the nearby hog trough and threw it through the ventilation hole in the back. It all landed on Quentin's head. Since that water was full of rotted food and had been standing for weeks, it stunk so bad a starving buzzard would have turned up his nose in disgust. Quentin started gagging and retching and beating on the door. It finally dawned on Jerry that Quentin wasn't putting on, and he quit laughing long enough to unbar the door.

In all fairness I do think Jerry regretted his impulse when he saw how upset Mother got. She wouldn't let Quentin in the house, made him strip in the yard, and then burned his clothes. He didn't have many either.

I guess one reason I became the butt of so many of their jokes was because I was so convenient. They kept saying all the things that happened to me were just coincidences. I told them I'd believe that when a hound had piglets. Most of the time it was pretty harmless stuff, for the most part anyway. But then...

They found an old abandoned nest of rotten duck eggs, waited until dark, then hid in the cornfield and pelted cars when they passed. They swore they didn't know I was in one of those cars. It was my first date, actually. I don't recall that the boy ever asked me out again. He set great store by that little coupe, his first car, and rotten duck eggs do tend to make a big mess. As for stinking, they rank right up there with three-day-old road kill.

Jerry and Quentin did have a lot of fun with his motor scooter that summer. It was a bright-red Cushman and had a passenger seat on the back. Jerry drove while Quentin sat behind with his arms around Jerry's waist. There were only two ways that

Jerry knew how to drive that scooter ...fast and faster. We didn't know about a lot of the stuff they did until years later, and that was probably in their best interest.

Every night they would go to bed in the back bedroom, as they were told to, all docile and obedient. That should have made us all suspicious, but it didn't. After they figured we were all asleep, they would climb out the bedroom window, push the scooter down the hill, crank it, and then tear around the countryside. Just before daylight they would climb back in the window with no one the wiser, at least for a while. Mother couldn't understand why they were so hard to get out of bed every morning.

One night, after they had covered about every road and pig trail in our end of the county, they decided to go farther afield. Their meandering took them to Lake Bradford, which is southwest of Tallahassee and about twenty-five miles from home. A lot of high school and college kids hung out at the pavilion there, dancing and playing the jukebox and pinball machines. It stayed open all night, and Jerry and Quentin arrived about two o'clock. They played the pinball machines until their money ran out, which didn't take long, and then started home, allowing themselves just enough time to make it before sun-up.

Things didn't go exactly as planned. First, they were stopped by a city policeman on south Monroe Street in Tallahassee and questioned. Or, as Quentin put it, "He gave us hell for bein' out so late but sent us on home anyway. Then the scooter wouldn't go up that long hill in front of the capitol, and we had to get off and push it up. Then when we got to the Ochlocknee River on 27, Jerry was goin' too fast around that curve there and I fell off. Didn't have on anything but my overalls. Scooted down the road on my arms and legs. Except for skinnin' up my knees and rippin' my clothes, I wasn't hurt. Guess it was a miracle I didn't break somethin', like my neck. We didn't get home until just before Daddy got up. That was a close call."

Another of their foolish stunts almost got them killed.

Across the field behind our house and not far from our property line, was a Negro jook. Everybody around those parts knew that the owner sold moonshine and ran Bolita. It seemed to be a booming business, and there was always lots of partying going on down there. Sometimes it could get really loud and annoying, especially around one or two in the morning when working folks were trying to sleep. Complaining to the sheriff's department was a waste of time because they came out weekly and got their pay-off not to raid the place.

One night when the noise level got especially high, Quentin and Jerry decided to have a little fun. They sneaked out through the window as usual, only this time they took Daddy's 22 rifle and a pocket full of bullets. They crouched down and followed the cornrows to the back of the field. Since there was a full moon that night, it was easy going. Not far from the jook, they squatted and began to shoot at the tin roof. It made a gosh-awful noise and the people inside began screaming and piling out of the doors and windows. Quentin and Jerry thought that was about the funniest thing they had ever seen and began rolling around on the ground laughing.

Quentin said, "It was funny at first. Then all of a sudden we started hearin' gunshots and bullets began whizzin' just over our heads. We fell to our bellies and began crawlin' like crazy, expectin' them to come after us any minute. I've never been so scared. Thought sure I'd have to clean out my pants when we finally got home."

Their next prank didn't turn out so good either.

They were lying in bed one night after everyone was asleep, trying to think of something exciting to do, something they hadn't already done before. They were broke which limited their options. Then Quentin happened to remember the fifteen cents in change Daddy had left on top of the icebox the day before. We didn't have a refrigerator so Daddy would go into town and buy a chunk of ice every couple days.

They pushed the scooter down the hill, cranked it and took off to Havana. In the center of town, on the corner, was Hubert Lassiter's service station. It had a roof that extended all the way out to the sidewalk and there were a couple pinball machines against the back wall. Those weren't locked up at night and anybody could use them at five cents a game. As usual, at that time of night, there was nobody about except Mr. Haskins, the night policeman. He made rounds occasionally but mostly slept in the police car all night.

Quentin and Jerry were having a high ole time playing the pinball machine with the money Quentin swiped. As Quentin said, "We were really good at pinball. We won so many free games we could 'uv played all night on that fifteen cents, but we didn't get the chance."

The town was quiet as a tomb, no traffic and no activity, so any sound carried. As Quentin later told me, "I heard a sound that wiped the smile off my face real fast and tied my stomach in a knot. There wadn't any traffic at all, so when I heard that car comin' I knew immediately it was Daddy. I recognized that old Model-A engine when he was still halfway to Hinson, and I knew I was in big trouble. He drove up to the station, called me over to the car, and calmly told me to get in. Jerry followed us on his scooter. Daddy didn't say a word all the way home except to ask me if I took the money off the icebox. I said, 'Yessir.' I knew better than to lie to 'im.

"When we got home he took me out to the barn, took down a leather strap he used to harness the mule, and began to beat hell out of me. It's not the pain of that beatin' that I remember most, but the fact that Daddy was cryin' as hard as I was. I had never seen him cry before, or afterward. I've never forgotten that. And I've never stole anything since then, either. He impressed me real good!"

Sometime ago I had a chance to ask Jerry about that summer. He said the thing he remembered most was Quentin's pet chicken. He said, " Pete had a bow-legged pet hen. He tied a string around that chicken's neck and she would follow Pete all over the yard."

I don't remember that myself but I don't question it. Sounds like something he would do.

Quentin and Jerry became fast friends that summer of 1947 and remained so over the years. They spent more time together and had a few more wild experiences later on. Seems like every time they got together they went a little nuts. I'll get to that later.

After finishing high school in 1948, I worked as a clerk and soda jerk at Powell's Drug Store in Havana to earn money to go into nurse's training. Sometimes Daddy would let me take the Model A to work, and sometimes he would let Quentin and me drive it to town to see a movie. Everybody knew when we were out and about.

If it wasn't the rattle of that old Model A, it was the looks of it that drew attention. Daddy had the back end cut off and made it into a flatbed truck to haul beans to market. Then,

Mother's brother Kelso came for a visit and painted some nifty mermaids on the sides. He was a good artist. The worst thing about it, though, was the lack of brakes. There were times when we almost had to drag our feet to get it to stop. That's the truth. We caused quite a bit of road kill, too, because of it...mostly chickens. There wasn't much traffic on the roads then, thank goodness. Sometimes the truck wouldn't go at all and we had to get somebody to give us a shove. We started calling her "Jerking Josephine", a name we thought was descriptive and appropriate. Actually, she seemed like part of the family by then anyway.

9 | CHAPTER

When I entered nurse's training in Jacksonville in 1949, Quentin was the last chick left in the nest. I think he missed me. All the chores we had previously shared, he now had to do all by himself. Well, there was one he didn't share anyhow because he figured out how to get out of it. That was milking Janie, the cow. We were supposed to take turns but every time it was Quentin's turn and he went to the pasture to get Janie, she would turn tail and run. That was a puzzlement since Janie was a sweet old cow, docile as a tame pup, and she certainly never gave me any trouble. But Quentin would come back to the house, an earnest expression plastered on his face, sounding so sincere, and say, "Edwina, I just don't understand why she won't come to me like she does to you. I guess you'll have to go get 'er." So I ended up doing most of the milking. Twice a day, too. Doesn't it say in the bible that a person's sins will eventually find them out? Or something like that? I guess it takes awhile though . . . in this case twenty years.

Lonnie Lassiter, the black man who owned the land adjoining ours and who was our neighbor for many years, told me the true tale in 1968. He said he would sit on his front steps in the late afternoon and laugh at Quentin. He said, "Mr. Quentin would call that ole cow and when she'd git close he'd rare back and throw a rock at 'er. 'Course she jes ran off agin." Uh huh.

When I told Quentin about this incident, and said, "Have you no shame?" he just laughed and said," Edwina, you were always so gullible." I reminded him at the time that with age comes wisdom and the loss of gullibility, or whatever. I don't think he believed me.

As the time for his graduation from high school drew near, Quentin began to worry that he might not get that diploma. He had to have at least a C-minus average to graduate and his average was too close for comfort. Don't get the notion he was dumb; Quentin just didn't apply himself most of the time. I like to think it's because I wasn't there to prod him along, but in all honesty there were other reasons. Havana School, though small, was very strict. The teachers believed in giving lots of homework, and there was no acceptable excuse for not doing it. Dying might have worked, but even then a doctor's certificate probably would have been required. I may be exaggerating just a tad there. But mostly I think Quentin just had other things on his mind besides schoolwork. Like girls.

Daddy finally got rid of the old Model A and bought a 1937 Ford sedan. It turned out to be a real lemon and didn't run half the time, but when it did Daddy let Quentin drive it occasionally. That was about the same time he began to notice girls. There were two or three he especially liked, and those were the ones he took "rabbit hunting." That's what he called it anyway. Personally I think there's a better name for it. At any rate, they were out in the woods...at night...to all hours. He never said if they caught any rabbits but I imagine his "rabbit hunting" did interfere with his homework. Also, at about the same time, something else was happening at school to make Quentin's life miserable and hinder his chances of graduating. It came about like this:

The schools back then were controlled by the county school board, which, in turn, was strongly influenced by the parents. In Havana the parents decided the students needed to be taught religion. So, a bible teacher, Ruth Moore, was hired, and her class on bible study was included in the curriculum. There wasn't much choice of electives at Havana High and that may be why Quentin ended up in bible class. His grade point average needed jacking up real bad and he figured a bible class would be a cinch, easy to pass, even though he hadn't been to church since leaving Dundee. He figured wrong.

To start with, Miss Moore, who was apparently a fine, Christian, spinster-lady, and who could quote endless bible passages without even stuttering, didn't know diddley about how to relate to teenage boys. She started right in on Quentin, pressuring him to join the Baptist Church. As he put it, "Miss Moore was bound and determined to make me see the light, give up my sinful ways, and join the church. The more determined she became, the more I resisted."

We Whittles are notoriously stubborn and hardheaded, as I mentioned earlier. I think it's in the genes. Anyway, over time, it became a battle of wills, and it appeared Miss Moore was going to give Quentin a failing grade.

"I began to dread goin' to school even more than I had before, if that's possible," Quentin said. "Besides Miss Moore stayin' on me constantly, there were two or three girls in that class who were religious nuts, and almost every day they prayed aloud in class for my sinful, immortal soul. That was mortifyin'. It looked like I was going to flunk that class, and I had to have that credit to graduate. I was gonna quit but Mrs. Jessie Truluck, my English teacher, found out about the spot I was in and talked me out of it. I finally decided the best way to get them off my back was to just join the church and be done with it, so I did. Things eased up after that."

(Interestingly, one of the girls who caused him so much grief moved to a big city a couple years later, became a regular party animal, drinking, carousing, and having a grand old time of it. I guess she must have backslid).

Quentin graduated from Havana High School in May 1950, with a C-minus average. His grade didn't matter all that much to him; just being out of school did. But then he was faced with a blank future and no earthly idea what to do with it. College wasn't an option, but there were two others possibilities he gave serious thought to. One was going down to Tampa and applying for work at the huge train depot and train yard there. Trains had always fascinated him so training to be an engineer sounded good. Or, two, he could join the service and let Uncle Sam teach him a trade. He decided, however, that he'd better get a job before making a decision, and save some start-up money. Any kind of job would do temporarily. As it was, buying a bus ticket to Tallahassee would have been a financial drain. Sometimes fate intervenes, and that's about what happened, you might say, in the form of Uncle Leo, one of Daddy's younger brothers. He came by the farm for one of his rare visits and changed Quentin's life in the process.

Uncle Leo was a restless sort of man, always on the move, never staying put for very long. As a journeyman electrician, he followed the work all the way from the Keys to Alaska, and seemed content in the doing.

He was stocky, muscular, and good-looking in a rugged sort of way. The most noticeable thing about his appearance was one ear that stuck out from the side of his head. It looked like somebody had taken a bite out of it, which is most likely what happened. For most of his adult life, Uncle Leo's idea of a good-time Saturday night was to get drunk as a skunk and see how many heads he could bash in. Sometimes he didn't fare any too well himself, hence the weird shaped ear, a constant reminder each time he looked in the mirror. Actually I think he was kind of proud of it.

Nobody ever knew what his motivation was but one day, out of the blue, he just hauled off and quit drinking, the hard way, cold turkey. He never touched another drink until the day he died, and nobody was happier than Grandmother Whittle. I don't guess anybody had more reasons for worrying than Grandmother, and Uncle Leo provided more than his share of them during his hell-raising days.

When he stopped in one place long enough, Uncle Leo would remember he had family. And when he was in the vicinity, he would pop in for a short visit with Mother and Daddy, always in a hurry, always unannounced, but always made welcome. One of those visits happened the day after Quentin finished high school. Uncle Leo was passing through, as usual, on his way to a job in south Florida.

Now, Uncle Leo loved to talk, mostly about himself, all the places he had been, all the money he had made, the sights he had seen, etc. He tended to brag a lot and was sometimes, I suspect, prone to exaggerations and delusions of grandeur. Basically, he was a generous-hearted man, though, and when he heard Quentin needed a good-paying job, he immediately set about getting him one. The fact that Quentin wasn't trained in anything, only knew fieldwork and farm chores, didn't matter, at least to Uncle Leo. Quentin needed a job so he would get him one, a good one, too, by god. Simple matter, really.

He contacted a few friends and had Quentin signed on as a wench truck operator with an electrical concern in Naples, Florida. His starting salary was $1.75 an hour, a mind-boggling amount to Quentin, who had no money, no car, and few clothes. Of course, he didn't know pea-turkey about operating a wench truck. That bothered him some. The fact that the job was based on a lie didn't set right either, but none of it bothered Uncle Leo. Not a whit. After giving it some thought, Quentin decided he would be stupid to turn down that kind of money. Besides, it would be his passport out of Havana. If Uncle Leo could live with the way he got the job, then so could he.

He packed his few belongings and the $7 he had saved from picking beans and took off to Naples with Uncle Leo. He had no idea how he would live, or *where* he would live until his first paycheck, if he even made a pay check. Whether he could make it through one day without getting fired was questionable. Then, on the way down to Naples he began to have doubts that they would even get there. Uncle Leo drove like he did everything else . . . like a bat out of Hades. They left Havana early Sunday morning, and then stopped overnight in St. Petersburg so Uncle Leo could meet with a union man and get Quentin a "third-year apprentice lineman union card." That's what it said . . . and that's because he had to be one to operate a wench truck. Seems like he was getting more hog-tied in lies with every breath Uncle Leo breathed, or so it seemed. It wasn't that Uncle Leo was basically a lying man. He just did what he felt he had to do in order to do what he wanted to do. Simple, when you think about it a few hours.

They finally arrived in Naples on Monday. As soon as they got there Uncle Leo began driving up one street and down another, looking for Quentin a place to stay. He finally found what he wanted about two blocks from the electrical company headquarters. It was a weathered frame house with a hand-painted sign in the window that said *Rooms For Rent*. Uncle Leo hustled Quentin up to the door, introduced himself, rented a sparsely furnished attic room for $7 a week, and then talked the landlady into giving Quentin credit until payday. Only Uncle Leo could have done that. He could charm the socks off anything in skirts, even ones old enough to be his grandma. He was married four times that I know of.

After giving Quentin directions to the electrical company where the trucks were parked, Uncle Leo told him how to locate the hidden key to the wench truck, patted him on the back, jumped into his car and took off. Quentin was left standing there feeling like he had been run over by a steamroller. His first time away from home, he didn't know a soul, and he only had $7 to eat on for a week. That must have been a lonely feeling. Frightening, too.

After unpacking his clothes, he walked the two blocks to Ernest Waters Construction Co., located the truck and found the key. So far, so good. After walking around the truck several times, looking it over from one end to the other, he started it up and found out he could actually drive the darn thing. He drove it back and forth until he began to feel more confident about handling it, and then he taught himself how to use the wench. By dark, he figured he could give a good imitation of somebody who knew what they were doing.

The next morning he met the foreman, W. A. Barnard, who introduced him to the four-man crew. That's when he found out he had other duties besides operating the wench truck. He was supposed to keep the time sheets, inventory the truck equipment, and keep up with all the materials used and those that needed replacing. He didn't know how to do any of that, either.

"Mr. Barnard was acquainted with Uncle Leo and was really nice," Quentin said, "He helped me for about a week and then left me with it. Actually, I got real good at my job. Two major hurricanes struck the lower part of the state that year and did a lot of damage. We were kept busy replacin' power lines all over that area. I was awful proud of my job and enjoyed it a lot. That's why I was really shook up when I got fired. Yeah, I got fired from my very first job.

"It happened like this: After I got good at operatin' the wench truck and keepin' records, I got to thinkin' about the future. What I was doin' didn't offer much challenge. I couldn't see doin' it right on and on. Line work seemed more interestin' and paid better, although the salary I was makin' wadn't all that bad. At least I was eatin' better, no more soda crackers. That's what I lived on mostly, that first week in Naples, before my first payday.

"Anyhow, as soon as I had a few bucks above livin' expenses, I bought a secondhand pair of hooks and on weekends I began practicin' climbin'. Any old tree would do. Seemed like I had a natural knack for it and pretty soon I could skinny up and down a tree like an old pro.

"Mr. Barnard was an alcoholic, I found out pretty quick. He was a climbin' foreman, meanin' he worked right along with the linemen, except on Mondays. That's when he was too hung over.

When he found out I could climb, he began lettin' me climb the poles on Monday and work the cold wires on the job. Cold wires were those on new construction that hadn't been energized. After a month or two, Mr. Barnard began lettin' me work the low side of transformers, which was secondary voltage. While I worked with the linemen, he sat in the truck and did the paperwork.

"One thing led to another and it wadn't long before he had me doin' actual line work. That was fine with me. Far as I was concerned I was just gettin' some good experience. Didn't think much about it beyond that.

"On a Friday in December, the crew was workin' in a low flat area near Naples when I noticed a green car parked a ways off. It came and went several times durin' the morning. I could see it real clear from the top of the pole where I was workin' but didn't pay it no mind. I was too busy doin' my job and thinkin' about how great my life was. Lots of good things had happened in my life that summer.

"Right after I got to Naples and for a while afterwards, I didn't know anybody outside of work. Didn't have any sort of social life at all, so I started goin' down to the pier at Naples beach to relax and do a little fishin' when I wasn't workin'. That's where I met and got to know George Miller. He was a fine man and turned out to be a really good friend. We seemed to have a lot in common, and when he asked me to share his furnished two-bedroom cottage on the beach, I agreed. It was a sweet deal for me. We divided the expenses, which helped us both out. I finally got to move out of that cramped little attic room. Me and George got along fine, never had any cross words. He was a great cook so we ate good, and then it turned out he knew a bunch of good-lookin' girls and introduced me around. We did a lot of double datin', had beach parties, and stuff like that. Had a lot of fun. I hadn't ever dated much so I got a lot of experience in things besides electricity. Liked it, too. Especially after I got my own car.

"After I made a few pay checks, I went car shoppin' and found a really great little car, a 1941 black Ford coupe, and I bought it. It had chrome everywhere, a sure sign of quality, I figured. When the sun reflected off it, you were almost blinded. I loved that car, and all the girls seemed impressed by it. Life was good . . . until things came to a head that morning on the job.

"About noon that same green car drove up and two men got out. Turned out one was a union representative and the other was from Florida Power Company out of Fort Myers. They told us that they had been watchin' us for several days because the union had heard that the wench truck operator was doing line work. Seems that was a real no-no accordin' to union rules. It sounded pretty serious but I wadn't all that concerned. I didn't know much about unions and stuff like that, even though I was a card-totin' member.

"Then, the men told all of us, the entire crew, to follow them to the Florida Power plant. When we got there we were all fired, right then, outright, on the spot, and told to draw our pay immediately. I sure didn't expect somethin' like that to happen and really hated it. Losin' my job was bad enough but causin' the other men to lose theirs really shook me up.

"Afterwards those same two men called me over and offered me a job as a lineman for Florida Power in Fort Myers. Said they had been watchin' me with binoculars and thought I did excellent work for somebody with so little trainin'. Also said I had a future in electrical work and advised me to pursue it.

"I found out later that the manager of the plant in Fort Myers was the brother to Mr. Dee Weatherly in Havana. He was our country neighbor and Daddy always thought a lot of him. I don't know if there was any connection there, but I found out they had checked the records and did some diggin' into my background.

"At the time though, what those men said didn't impress me atall. I was still in shock over losin' my job and disgusted with all that had happened. I just turned them down flat. Everything had been going' so well and I guess I blamed them for screwin' it up. That's all I could think about right then. My whole life was turned upside down in an instant, seemed like."

Chapter 10

Quentin had gained a lot of self-confidence, and even though getting fired wasn't something he took pride in, he didn't brood about it long. He was in good health, had experience in a marketable skill, and even had his own car, if he could figure out how to pay for it. He had met a lot of girls and had a lot of fun dating, getting all kinds of social experience. A lot had happened to him in a short period of time, most of it good. His situation could be a lot worse.

Another improvement was his general appearance. All that heavy labor had built up muscles in the right places, and the steady diet of good food had filled him out. His washboard ribs were no longer visible. He had acquired a nice tan, too. All in all, I thought he looked a lot like Alan Ladd, the movie star. Even my friends in nurse's training thought he was one good-looking dude. But if Quentin thought so, it never showed, because being vain has never been one of his vices. Well, there was that thing about his chest hair when he was fourteen, but I nipped that in the bud. He did always try to look his best, though. Mother set great store in appearances, and she pounded the importance of making a good impression into all of us as we were growing up. Quentin just never seemed to think his better-than-average looks were all that important.

After the big firing, and after the dust had settled, Quentin contacted the union. Strangely enough, the company he had worked for in Naples re-hired him as an apprentice lineman and sent him to work in Sarasota. Since getting fired hadn't been in his plans, he had spent all his money on dating and living expenses. Therefore, he was nearly flat busted broke when he got to Sarasota. Uncle Leo and Aunt Vermel (wife #4) were living there then and offered him a place to stay. He refused, telling them he had a place in a motel. When I asked him why he did that, he said he didn't want Uncle Leo's charity. Too proud...another Whittle trait to go along with the stubbornness.

For the next week, until he made his first paycheck, he parked his car near a park every night, slept in the back seat, and ate oranges from a nearby grove. When it got dark, he stripped down and bathed under a park faucet. One day he found some change under the car seat, two nickels and two pennies, that had probably slipped out of his pocket at some time in the past. With that bonanza jingling in his pocket, he made a beeline to the nearest cafe, had a cup of coffee and a donut for a dime, and then left a two-cent tip for the waitress. The boy was generous to a fault. His meal wasn't much, but it seemed might tasty after a steady diet of oranges.

Jerry Collins, his cousin and old partner in mischief during the summer of 1947, showed up pulling the ugliest trailer he had ever seen and wanted Quentin to move in with him. Jerry was doing line work, also, but with a different company. Apparently, Uncle Leo was working hard at getting all his nephews into the electrical business; he had also gotten Winky started after he got out of service.

Unfortunately, the Sarasota job only lasted two months. After that they worked wherever the work took them, living like nomads but making good money. Apparently Quentin and Jerry worked so hard they were too tired to cause any problems. That's what Quentin said anyway, and he wouldn't admit to any. Remembering the past, I had my doubts. It could be they were just saving up until later. I'll get to that part eventually.

One of their best jobs was with Satchel and Joseph's Electrical Company out of Jacksonville. They had been awarded a government contract to build a missile range on the east coast of Florida. The government had bought an entire peninsula. Patrick Air Force Base was on the south, and the north end was largely undeveloped, except for a small fishing village that had been vacated. Quentin, Jerry and Uncle Leo all moved to a trailer park on Merritt Island, which was within easy traveling distance to the jobsite. Since Jerry and Quentin worked on the same crew, they continued living together in Jerry's trailer. Their quiet, mannerly behavior could only have been to impress Aunt Vermel. She was a sweet, Christian lady who would have been totally shocked at what those two were capable of doing. But their demeanor at that time was totally out of character, something she didn't realize, and must have been a terrible strain on them.

The job of the electrical crews was to build a large power line from Cocoa to the Cape, crossing the Banana River and Indian River, and then running north to the lighthouse on the north end of the Cape. The purpose was to increase power to the missile launch sites where the concrete pads were being poured. They were making history and didn't realize it.

"It was hard work but I had no regrets," Quentin said, "I got some invaluable experience in new construction while I was there. The crew had to set new poles along an old existin' road and tear out the old lines. We set up transformer banks, etc, to go from a single phase to a three phase line to give more power."

As with all of them, that job eventually ran out too. Jerry returned to Dundee with his dump-on-wheels, as Quentin called it, because that's where Aunt Clora and Uncle Buddy eventually settled, sometime in the fifties, I think it was. They bought a house about a half block from the Reagan house. On the same street, too. Life can surely take some strange twists.

Quentin decided he needed a break before job-hunting again. He took off for the farm and a few days of being petted by mother and stoking up on her good country cooking. When he got around to contacting the union in Orlando, they placed him with Miller Electric out of Lakeland. They were to change out the entire distribution center for Havana, of all places. That job wasn't at all complicated. As Quentin explained, they were going from 2400 volts to a higher primary of 4160 volts to give better voltage. Doesn't make a bit of sense to me. I just repeat what he said.

During that time, Quentin lived at the farm. A lot of the kids he knew from school had moved on, either to college or working away, but they were still a few single girls around, and they began to look him over with new interest. He had changed a lot since leaving Havana. With the nice build, a nice tan, a nice car, nice clothes, and nice spending money, he was everything any red-blooded American girl could want. Getting dates was easy, so he spent his days working and his nights juking, making up for lost time. Life was good, but that job didn't last long either, and he was once again unemployed.

The electrical jobs were plentiful but sporadic. Quentin was beginning to feel like he was on a roller coaster, in the chips one minute and broke the next, and he decided he didn't want to spend the rest of his life like Uncle Leo. All that moving around was getting wearisome. He was once again thinking about joining the military. The way he looked at it, the war in Korea was going full-steam and he was bound to get drafted sooner or later. But then he couldn't decide which branch of service needed him the most. That's when he got the notion to hop over to Jacksonville and visit me before making a decision. I was in my second year of nurse's training and we hadn't seen each other in months, although we did write regularly.

Quentin left Havana early one morning, traveling two-lane Highway 90 East, and didn't get to Jacksonville until about noon. There were no interstates and driving was slow going. When he arrived there was a message from Daddy stating that Uncle Leo wanted him in Washington, D.C. immediately. It seemed there was a shortage of electricians there, Uncle Leo was making big bucks, and he wanted Quentin and Jerry to get in on the action. He also stressed that time was of the essence. Uncle Leo was still in a hurry, something that never changed.

Quentin decided straight away that the military didn't need him as much as he needed all that money. So, after a quick hello and goodbye to me, he headed back to Havana to pick up his gear. He left Havana late that afternoon, drove all night, and was crossing the Potomac River at sunrise the next day. Seeing all the sights that he had only read about would have excited him at any other time, but he had been driving twenty-four straight hours and was having trouble getting his eyes to focus. They looked like he had been on a twenty-four hour toot and were so blood-shot they looked like two cherries in a glass of buttermilk by the time he got to Uncle Leo's and Aunt Vermel's place. They lived in Alexandria, Virginia, right across the Potomac from Washington, D.C.

He almost slept the clock around, ate a big breakfast, and set out for the union hall. It was a huge office and when he arrived, there were about forty men sitting around, waiting. He was beginning to wonder if Uncle Leo had jumped the gun. With all those men trying to get work, his chances didn't look too good to him. Then he found out they were hiring both inside and outside electricians.

After showing his union card to the business manager, he was told to take a seat. He had been waiting a long time and was beginning to get the fidgets when he was called back up to the desk.

"Do you know anything about inside wiring?" the man asked.

"No, sir, I haven't had any experience in inside work." Quentin replied.

Either the man didn't hear Quentin's answer or chose to ignore it. He said. "We have several openings in the Safeway Stores Warehouse over in Bethesda, Maryland. It's a big job and they need help bad. Do you think you could handle the job of journeymen electrician at $3.25 an hour?"

At first Quentin was so stunned he was speechless. Hell, he thought, he had been picking beans all day for less than that. Since he had successfully bluffed his way through one job already, he figured he might as well try it again. There was one thing for sure, no way was he going to turn down that kind of money.

Quentin looked the man straight in the eye and said," Yes, sir. I'm sure I can do it."

He was given a journeyman ticket and sent out to the job, which was already in progress. "As it turned out," Quentin said, "the Safeway Warehouse was the largest single-story buildin' in the world and covered forty square acres. There was even a railroad track runnin' through the center, and there was a vented roof to take care of the smoke. It was awesome."

Quentin admitted he felt a little over-whelmed and intimidated by the very size of it, and he beginning to have some doubts as to what he had gotten himself into. Or, as Mother would have said, maybe he had bitten off more than he could chew. She was good with sayings and had one to fit just about any situation. At the time, though, all he knew about the place and the job was that he would be working for Bowling Brothers Electric Company. And, once again, luck or his guardian angel was with him. He was assigned to an elderly Scotsman from Hagerstown, Maryland, who had been doing inside electrical work for years. Quentin sized him up right away and knew there was no way he could fool that sharp old man. His lack of experience would stick out like a one-legged man at a dance marathon, so he decided then and there that his best chance would be to make a clean breast of it, throw himself on the man's mercy, so to speak. Which is what he did. After he earnestly explained how he got the job, and how he really wanted to learn inside work, the man...Quentin can't remember his name...studied him quietly for a few minutes. Then he said," Stick with me, Laddie, and I'll teach you the ropes. No one will be the wiser. Just keep your eyes open and your mouth shut."

He did just that and thanks to that kind man it wasn't long before he was working alongside the best of them, and doing his job with competence as well as confidence. According to Quentin, the job was very demanding and he worked his butt off. He did found the work interesting, but the main reason he worked so hard was because he wanted to make sure that Scottish foreman never had reason to regret his decision.

Quentin didn't like imposing on Uncle Leo and Aunt Vermel any longer. The trailer was just too crowded since Jerry had showed up and was living there, too. He had a job with the same company but in a different section. The two boys were thinking about getting a place together and sharing expenses until they found out how high the cost of living was in and around D.C. Then Jerry got the notion of calling Uncle Buddy and having him bring up the trailer for them to live in. Yes, that very same trailer they had shared in Florida and, according to Quentin, it hadn't improved any.

Or, as he put it, "Uncle Buddy pulled that pitiful piece of junk all the way from Dundee. It was a miracle he made it considerin' the condition it was in, but bad as it was, we were glad to have a place of our own. We pulled it across D.C. and rented a lot at a trailer park in College Park, Maryland."

That turned out to be just one of several they live in around the area. The park managers usually asked them to move on after a few days. There were two reasons for that: their rambunctious behavior...yes, they were once again up to their old pranks and other mischief... and the trailer's appearance. It gave the park a bad image.

Perhaps I should describe the trailer as Quentin described it to me. To say it was primitive would be an understatement. It was a two-wheeler, built out of some sort of hardened pasteboard instead of plywood, and painted aluminum. There was one full-sized bed, a small gas stove, an old-fashioned icebox, and a kerosene heater. In the front of the trailer, where a couch had once been, was a mattress. The boys used the community bathrooms and showers, and took their clothes to the Laundromat on weekends. The Waldorf it wasn't but it served their purpose and very cheaply at that.

Usually, when they were booted out of a park and had to go find another, they would park the trailer down the street and walk into the office. Being clean-cut, neatly dressed, and well mannered, the boys always made a good impression. They were rented a prime spot up near the front immediately. But after a few days the manager would come around and nicely ask them to move the eyesore to the back of the lot. Eventually they would be asked to move out completely.

As I mentioned earlier their on-going rowdy behavior had a lot to do with it. Not that they had drinking or wild parties or anything like that. No, their idea of fun was to one-up each other in practical jokes, and they also did a lot of roughhousing and wrestling. I imagine they got pretty noisy because nobody enjoyed a joke more than Jerry or could laugh any louder than he did. Some of the tricks they pulled on each other got pretty wild.

There was one Quentin remembers vividly and he laughed so hard in the telling that I had trouble getting it all down.

Quentin always waited until after dark to use the park's community showers because it was deserted by then and he had it to himself. He would strip down before he went to keep from hauling so much with him. After wrapping a towel around his bottom half, he would peer out the trailer door to see if the coast was clear, and then dash to the shower building which was only a few feet away.

That was his usual habit until the night Jerry decided to have some fun. He waited inside the trailer for Quentin's return, then reached out the door, grabbed Quentin's towel, slammed the door and locked him outside, buck-naked. Jerry was laughing so hard he couldn't hear Quentin begging to be let in, or pretended he couldn't. When the neighbors began looking out to see what all the commotion was about, Quentin bent over into a crouch, his hands covering strategic places, and jumped in the car. He swore it was hours before Jerry let him in, and he spent all that time thinking of revenge.

He planned it carefully and waited until Jerry was totally unsuspecting. The shower trick was but a distant memory when Quentin bought the cheapest, loudest-smelling perfume he could find in the dime store, I think it was Hoyt's Cologne, and emptied the entire bottle in Jerry's hair while he slept. Many days and many shampoos passed before Jerry quit smelling like a French whore. He got back at Quentin by peeing in his work boots. They got some strange looks and a wide berth from the men at work for a while.

There were also their many battles with aerosol shaving cream, which left them and the trailer looking like a scene from *Northwest Passage*. Afterward, they would spend days arguing over who would clean up the mess. There weren't any women around and they had both been raised to believe that house cleaning was women's work, so the trailer didn't get much cleaning. Rarely, would be more accurate. To impress the neighbors, they bought a mop and hung it out every Saturday morning.

"We took baths and washed our clothes faithfully, but I can't remember changin' and washin' linens the whole time we were there," Quentin admitted sheepishly. "And something else. We may not have done much house cleanin' and linen-washin', but we *did* clean out the icebox. Real often, too. That was because it smelled so bad all the time, even worse than the rest of the trailer. I ain't kidding. Everytime we opened the door, the stink would have gagged a maggot. Nothing we did helped any. One day I decided to take more drastic measures, and the next day our sandwiches tasted awful, like the meat was tainted or something. We couldn't eat them so we did without lunch.

"When we got home from work that afternoon, Jerry opened the icebox, thinkin' maybe the ice had melted and the meat had spoiled. The odor was so strong we had to hold our breath. Jerry reached over in the back and pulled out a small package that was hangin' from a shelf by a metal hook. When he asked me what it was, I told him it was one of those little commode deodorizers that you hang in a commode. I figured that thing ought to take care of any odor problem if it could cover up do-do stink. Seemed like a good idea at the time. After that, we had *two* odors we couldn't get rid of."

From what Quentin had to say about their cooking, it seems to me they had other odor problems as well. They agreed early on to share the cooking chores by taking turns. Neither had any experience since they thought that too was woman's work.

"Jerry always cooked the same dish over and over," Quentin said. "I think he made it up. It was a mixture of pork and beans, salmon, and lots of onions. Actually, it wasn't bad tastin', but it was the after-effects that got me. Jerry wasn't a bit bashful about passin' gas when he needed to and that was real often after his cookin'."

I imagine Jerry did that like he did all things...with great gusto. In that little trailer, it must have been over-whelming. Before leaving the subject of their house-keeping, I have to relate their Saturday morning shopping trips, or at least one of them, which serves as an example.

Trying to shop in an organized fashion, they always made out a list ahead of time. When they got to the super market, Quentin pushed the cart while Jerry filled the list. One morning Jerry apparently suffered an attack of practical-joke-withdrawal. It had been awhile. He waited until the buggy was loaded and Quentin was waiting to check out before he made his move. The store was crowded and the line before and after Quentin was long, mostly housewives. Jerry nonchalantly walked up behind Quentin and placed a large blue and white box of Kotex on top of the groceries in plain view. The was no way Quentin could get out of line to beat a hasty retreat. He was trapped, and he just stood there, his face as red as a beet, until his turn came and he paid for the groceries (including the Kotex). In the meantime, Jerry was standing behind a nearby grocery display, peeking around to watch Quentin's embarrassment and laughing himself silly.

Today it wouldn't matter, nobody would give it a second thought, but in 1951 such personal items were never displayed in public but were usually wrapped in plain brown paper and handled in a discreet manner.

"You know, such things weren't discussed or talked around but I found out later that some of the linemen used their wives' Kotex to pad their climbing boots," Quentin said. " But that mornin' in the store I could have cheerfully wrung Jerry's stupid neck. God was I embarrassed!"

Workdays passed quickly but there wasn't much to fill up the weekends. Even the practical jokes were getting old. Quentin and Jerry decided they were in a rut and needed to meet some girls, but they didn't know how to go about it. Neither would admit it but they were both a little shy. Then Quentin happened to remember that one of his female classmates from Havana was living and working in D.C. and who, as it turned out, happened to have a very pretty roommate. The four of them began spending time together, sightseeing, visiting Civil War sites in the area, and occasionally taking trips into the Shenandoah Valley. It was Quentin's first view of the mountains, and nothing he saw before or after that seemed quite as beautiful.

As usual, Quentin couldn't go for very long without playing footsy with danger of some sort. If it didn't find him, he would find it. I don't know if this attraction was just a pattern in his life or part of his destiny. At any rate, the following incident could have had serious consequences for both him and Jerry.

They took turns driving to work and usually took the back roads to the job site, which was eight miles away. On that morning they were driving through a run-down residential section when they noticed smoke boiling out of the windows of an old frame house. There wasn't a soul in sight. They slammed on brakes, ran up and started beating on the front door. Then they started yelling. When neither raised anybody on the inside, they broke down the door and ran in. The smoke was so thick they could hardly see or breathe, and the heat was scorching. They had about decided the place was empty when they stumbled across an old black man who was passed out on the floor. His back was severely burned but he was alive. They picked him up, carried him outside, and laid him on the grass a safe distance from the house. By that time people had started to gather and someone had called the fire truck and ambulance. The house was too far-gone to save, but the old man was coming around, in severe pain but alive.

Quentin and Jerry left during the confusion and went on to work. As far as I know they never mentioned the incident until many years later. They didn't seem to think it was such a big deal.

11 | CHAPTER

Quentin returned from Washington, D.C. in November of 1951, fully expecting to be shipped right out for Army basic training and then Korea. But when he reported to the draft board in Quincy, he was told that even though he was 1A status he wouldn't be called up for another six months. That was an unexpected turn of events. There he was, finally ready to go and do his duty for his country, and the government didn't even want him yet. Six months to kill with nothing to do and bills to be paid. What a bummer.

He took what money he had saved from the D.C. job and bought a small service station on Highway 27, about a quarter mile from the farm. It wasn't much, just a couple pumps, but Quentin figured he could get a return on his investment if he worked at it hard enough. He put in long hours, improved the place, and business increased, but strangely enough, he couldn't seem to make any profit. He found out why a little later; the ex-owner has helping himself to the gas pumps and wasn't paying for what he took. Quentin closed the station and salvaged what he could, which wasn't much.

The draft board finally remembered that he was waiting and notified him to report to Jacksonville for his physical in April 1952. He can't recall the exact day. As it turned out, one of Quentin's high school classmates, Guy Martin, was also being drafted, so he and Quentin traveled to and from Jacksonville together. Guy later went on into the army and only served two years. Quentin had twenty-one days of grace before he was to report back to Jacksonville, and on the eighteenth day he joined the navy.

His decision to do so was based on two things: one, army duty, lying around in mud-filled fox holes while getting shot at wasn't a bit appealing, and two, an incident occurred during that eighteen days that made a lasting impression, one he described as making him feel "very strange" at the time.

Quentin had been trying to decide which branch of the service he should enlist in but was having trouble making up his mind. One afternoon he decided to talk it over with Daddy and wandered out behind the house where he found him weeding the garden. Now, Daddy never answered any question quickly but gave it his whole attention and thought it over carefully before replying. Even when we were children and just wanted to go spend the night with a friend he did that.

On that day, Daddy leaned on his hoe and rolled a Prince Albert cigarette. After looking out over the field for a while, he finally advised Quentin to apply to the Coast Guard first and, if he couldn't get in, then apply to the Navy. The reasons he gave for this have been forgotten. It was what he said afterwards that made such a lasting impression. He looked Quentin straight in the eyes and said," Just remember this, Son. Wherever you serve, serve honorably. *I would rather you come home in a pine box that bring shame on me.*" I can't believe Daddy really meant that, even though I know he was always a very patriotic man, but Quentin believed he meant it. And I have wondered many times if perhaps those words may have influenced Quentin's future actions, especially some of the foolish risks he took.

One thing I can't leave out here is the results of his navy tests. Considering his low four-year high school average, Quentin was surprised and pleased when the navy recruiter told him his score was one of the highest he had seen, and he was really impressed. That doesn't prove anything, actually, except maybe you shouldn't go by averages in determining what a person knows or how intelligent he or she is.

On May 15, 1952, Quentin left his little Ford coupe at the farm and caught the Greyhound bus to Jacksonville. There he was sworn in and shipped out by train to San Diego Naval Base in California for basic training. The entire train carried military personnel and wasn't air-conditioned, which meant their trip across the plains states was about as pleasant as a summer picnic in Death Valley. Besides that, the engine was a coal burner. With the windows down, the soot settled into the sweat. Within a few hours, they were not only hot and filthy dirty but stunk to high heaven.

"The thing I remember most about that trip, besides bein' so dad-blamed hot, was the scenery. I always did love trains but I had never ridden one before. Also, I had never been out of the southeastern U.S. Me and two other country boys stood between the railroad cars and gaped at the scenery most of the way. I couldn't get over the flat country and wheat fields as far as the eye could see.

"In Kansas the train stopped on some side tracks to take on more inductees and the town ladies served us all kinds of homemade baked stuff. They were really nice to us and we enjoyed the food. Eventually we got underway again and finally arrived in San Diego seven days from the time we left Jacksonville. I decided then 'n there that I could get by without anymore train travel for awhile and not feel a bit deprived."

BOOT CAMP
SAN DIEGO, CALIFORNIA

At the naval training center the inductees were separated into companies with one hundred men in each company., supervied by a drill instructor who oversaw their training and inspections. As a rule, the drill instructors were extremely competitive, each wanting his company to out-shine the rest, and, according to Quentin, they were as tough as an old boot and hard as nails. Most of them were old salts, had been in service forever, and had little sympathy for the raw recruits, their theory being that the meaner you treated them, the better fighting men they made. Or something like that.

Quentin was assigned to Company 500 and his days, which seemed endless, were filled with marching and inspections. There were no laundry facilities and each inductee had to keep his white summer uniform spotless, a chore made even more difficult by the soot-filled air around San Diego and the unbearably hot weather. All that combined with the constant marching resulted in sweat-stained and very nasty caps. And those dirty caps caused Quentin some real problems.

He had a terrible time keeping his clean, and after several weeks of scrubbing his hats every day, he developed a blister on one thumb. It became infected but Quentin didn't report it after he found out he would have to fall back into the next company if he spent more than three days in sickbay. He didn't want to graduate late, among strangers, instead of with the friends he had made in his company. So he kept his mouth shut and continued marching even when red streaks began running up his arm, which nicely demonstrates the Whittle bull-headedness I talked about early on.

When they knocked off for lunch, Quentin fell on his rack (that's navy talk for "bed") and couldn't get up. His temperature was so high he became delirious. When his buddies saw how really ill he was, they took him to sick bay where he spent the next three days getting shot full of antibiotics. By the end of that time, his hand had improved a lot and he was permitted to rejoin his company.

Quentin's described his drill instructor as being a chief reservist who had been recalled and who was a full-fledged alcoholic. He had the typical red face, blood-shot eyes, and a nose that had little veins running around it like a road map. During inspections he would strut back and forth like a little Napoleon, removing and closely examining each hat. If he saw a spot, which he always did, he would slap the man back and forth across the face with his hat and yell in rhythm, "Dirty...filthy...no-good...swine!"

Quentin said, "One day I decided I had had enough and wadn't going to take that humiliation again. If the DI hit me, I fully intended to knock hell out of the sonofabitch. I knew that would bring a quick end to my naval career but right then I didn't give a damn. I eyed him as he moved along the line in my direction, slappin' faces and yellin', and I mentally braced myself. When he reached me he must have sensed what I had in mind because I just stared him straight in the eyes. It was kinda weird. He removed my cap and studied it, then handed it back without a word, just continued on down the line, slappin' and yellin'.

On the last day of boot camp, before graduation, the men were given liberty to go off base until ten P.M. On that day, also, each man was allowed to withdraw his pay and buy a bus ticket home for a two-week leave. He had to show the ticket before he would be permitted to leave the base. Quentin drew his pay and returned to the barracks where he stuffed it under his pillow. That was a common practice among sailors because there were no pockets on the navy uniform and no place to carry a wallet. The company marched to chow (that's navy for mealtime) as they marched everywhere else, and when they returned Quentin reached under his pillow to get his money but it wasn't there. He was dumb-founded at first. No one else's money was missing. Losing the money was bad enough but he was faced with the prospect of sitting on the base for two weeks while his friends went home on leave. Just saying he was depressed wouldn't have covered it. Then, a boy from Kansas went around the barracks and took up a dollar donation from the ninety-two men left in the company and gave all of it to Quentin for his ticket home. He ended up with more money than had been stolen, and he did get to go home on leave.

"I always believed the chief stole my money but had no proof," Quentin said, "I did get a little satisfaction, though. At graduation, Company 500 didn't receive any honors, much to the chief's disgust. The men didn't care. We all hated his guts and didn't want him to look good anyhow."

After graduation, and before he went home on leave, Quentin had to have a conference to see what his assignment was going to be while he was in service. He figured it was just a formality, more navy bullshit that didn't mean anything, but it was required. He told the yeoman in charge that he had electrical line experience, not thinking anything would really come of it. After all, it is an on-going joke among servicemen that they end up doing the opposite of what they are best qualified for. That being the case, setting him up as a cook or something like that would have been the norm. So Quentin was surprised when he and another man in his company were assigned to the Seabees, a unit of specialists who are essential in the construction and maintenance of airstrips, as well as electrical and communications systems on the front. They also clear right-of-ways to expedite troop movements. Quentin was real pleased with the assignment. To his way of thinking, climbing poles was a hell of an improvement over shooting at somebody or, worse yet, getting shot *at*. After his leave he was to report to Port Hueneme, located farther north on the California coast, for electrical school. He was really excited about that since he liked the work.

Another man from the company was also assigned to the Seabees. He was an Italian from Washington, PA, a coal-mining town south of Pittsburgh, and his name was Frank Rosati. He had brown curly hair, brown eyes, and was about an inch taller that Quentin's five-foot-ten inches. According to Quentin, Rosati was a good dancer, had a great sense of humor, and all the girls thought he was wonderful. Quentin was still a little shy around girls, or so he said. As it was, Rosati attracted enough attention for both of them, which worked out well, for they became good friends and spent a lot of their liberties together.

After the hell of basic training, electrical school was downright pleasant. Quentin decided the service wasn't so bad after all and actually began to enjoy himself. The chief who was class instructor didn't know beans about line work, and when he found out Quentin had a background in outside electrical work, gave him the job of teaching the other students the basic techniques of pole-climbing. Now Quentin had acquired a lot of confidence in his pole climbing and could scamper up and down poles like a veteran electrician. He *was* good at it, he knew it, and he even admitted he liked to show off his pole climbing whenever he had the chance.

"I just couldn't wait to impress all those green students with my expertise." Quentin said.

The class of fifty electrical students was taken out to the field where hundreds of thirty-foot poles had been erected for use in pole-climbing instruction and practice. There had been dozens of classes using those poles previously, and they were well worn and full of splinters from the spikes. Quentin didn't think of that when he swaggered out in front of the class and cockily began his demonstration.

"Most electricians tend to stomp their cleats into the side of the pole with each step," Quentin spoke with great authority. "That's not at all necessary. All you have to do is walk rapidly up the pole. That's a lot faster and not nearly as hard on your feet and legs. I'll demonstrate."

He raced up the pole, quite pleased with himself, and when he reached the top he locked his left leg around the pole and started to pass his safety belt around his waist to secure it. At that point only his left cleat was embedded in the pole...in a knothole, as it turned out. He felt himself slipping. All electricians when faced with this situation will automatically begin to hug the pole. It's kind of a reflex action, and Quentin grabbed hold with both arms. He slid all the way down to the ground, collecting splinters all the way.

"The pain wasn't near as bad as the embarrassment," he said." I never lived that down and it was the only pole I ever burned."

"Burned" in electrician slang is the sudden, unintended, and painful descent from a power pole. Or, as in Quentin's case, another way of saying you just made an ass of yourself. For a while there it seemed like his life was filled with embarrassments. The next one happened just a few weeks later and didn't have a thing to do with electricity.

After finishing electrical school, and before he was to be shipped overseas, Quentin was given a two-week leave. When he entered the bus station in Asheville, N.C. he was grimy, exhausted, and red-eyed from lack of sleep, but he was right pleased with himself. He had saved bus fare by catching a ride with a navy man, Joe Woods, and his wife, who were on their way to Lenoir, N.C. Joe had been in electrical school with Quentin and became a good friend. They had been on the road fifty-seven straight hours, rotating drivers and sharing expenses, and Quentin hadn't had a bath since leaving the base.

Since Mother and Daddy were visiting Myra and her family in Charleston, S.C., he decided to go directly there by bus and drive home with them. Thinking he might be beginning to smell a little ripe, like a city dump on a hot day, and not wanting to offend the other bus passengers, Quentin entered the bus station restroom to clean up and change clothes. The place was empty, to his relief.

After putting his money in the coin-activated commode stall, he deposited his duffel bag inside and stripped down to the altogether. He peeked out to make sure there was no one around, and then ventured out to take a spit bath at the sink. The stall door clicked shut behind him. There he stood, naked as a jaybird, all his clothes and money locked inside the stall, and he needed a nickel to get back in. As Quentin put it, he was in one hell of a dilemma.

He tried to approach the problem in a logical fashion. There was a hole at the bottom of the stall door but it was too small for him to crawl under. Then he searched the floor inch by inch, hoping someone might have dropped a nickel. No such luck.

He was still standing there, trying to decide what to do, when the door to the restroom started to open. He frantically looked around for some place to hide but there was no place big enough. So, there he was, cornered like a rat, living his worst nightmare. Red-faced, he finally looked up to see that it was the janitor, an old colored man, who stood there with a mop in his hand, speechless, his eyes so bugged out only the whites showed.

They stared at one another for a full minute, or it seemed like it, before Quentin began talking a mile a minute, trying to explain why he was standing stark naked in the middle of a public restroom. And all that time he was hoping the old man wouldn't think he was some kind of pervert and bolt out the door.

"I guess I musta impressed him with my sincerity," Quentin grinned. "At least, he seemed to believe my sad tale. He started grinnin' from ear to ear, showin' off his gold tooth in front. Then he pulled a nickel out of his pocket, shuffled over to the stall and opened it. Didn't say another word, just left, kinda chucklin' to himself. I can't remember for sure if I thanked him but I guess I did. Boy, was I relieved!"

I don't imagine that old janitor could find much to laugh about in his job and Quentin's predicament was probably the only bright spot in his whole day. It most likely gave him something interesting to tell his woman when he got home, like "Hey, Sapphire, wait'll I tells ya 'bout the crazy white dude I saw today!"

12 | CHAPTER

His time at home was short but Quentin made the most of it. Besides stuffing himself on Mother's good cooking, he spent a lot of time running trotlines and cat fishing on the Ochlochnee River. If Daddy didn't go, then he went with friends. Lawrence Kelly, Leon Peavy, and Ellis Harvell were usually in the group, and sometimes Reyn Durbin. I don't know if Ellis was married at that time, but the rest were, I'm sure, and they had settled down considerably. By then they were into more mature leisure activities, like fishing. But in years past they had introduced Quentin to the joys of 'possum and coon hunting...among other things. They would run the woods at all hours of the night with Reyn's seven hound dogs, named for the days of the week to keep them straight...Sunday, Monday, etc. I don't think they caught many coons or opossums but it made for good memories anyway.

Not wanting to take a chance on getting back to the base late and being caught AWOL, Quentin decided to catch the bus back to the west coast instead of hitchhiking. He knew he would be shipping out for Korea and was excited about returning to base, as well as a little apprehensive. Therefore, this was one of those times, he figured, when getting back as fast as possible was more important than the money. He could have flown but he wasn't in that much of a hurry. A bus was fast enough, thank you.

Port Hueneme was the naval debarkation port and kick-off point for many of the troops heading over-seas. Quentin was assigned to Construction Battalion Detachment #1504 which was under Mobile Construction Battalion #3. There were a total of seven construction battalions in the navy at that time, some on the east coast and some on the west coast. CB#3 was from the west coast and currently serving in Korea. So, when Quentin arrived at the base he expected to be shipped right off to Korea.

The men, most of whom were Seabees, were transferred from the base to the port by military bus and packed aboard an ancient WW II transport ship called the USNS Barrett.

Quentin described it this way: " That old bucket of rust looked like the step-child of the entire naval fleet. It looked pathetic, like it had been neglected, and it needed paint in the worst way. Most of us had some doubts that it would make it out of port, much less to Korea and the other ports it was bound for. Besides Korea, some of the men were being shipped to Japan, the Philippines, and Guam. There was a small complement of Seabees stationed on Guam. I missed Rosati and Woods and found out they had been assigned to the Seabee Base at Kwajalein."

After boarding, the men were assigned sleeping quarters in the hold (navy talk for way down in the ship). There wasn't much space. Hammocks were placed one above the other like grocery racks in a supermarket. They were so close together that turning over was a problem unless you happened to be real skinny. The big guys had a rough time of it but Quentin was still suffering the after-effects of his boot camp days and was thinner than usual. He didn't spend much time worrying about the cramped sleeping space. That turned out to be the least of his problems.

They hadn't been at sea for very long before the ship ran into some rough weather. All that bucking and rolling began to have a bad effect on some of the men, especially Quentin who got really seasick. That's not surprising since our whole family is cursed with motion sickness and all we have to do is turn around too fast and we get nauseous. With Quentin though it was much worse. He spent the entire trip heaving, wishing he were dead, and trying to figure out how to throw himself overboard.

"I would have, too, if I hadn't been so weak," he said. "Most of the other men who got sea sick got their sea legs after a few days but not me. I've never been so dad-blamed miserable in my whole life."

After seventeen days at sea with a stopover in Honolulu, the ship finally put into port. Quentin thought that solid piece of land was about the prettiest thing he had ever seen. Just the thought of going out to sea again was enough to make him turn bile green. It was obvious by then that he wasn't cut out to be a sea-faring man. For someone who had signed up for four years in the navy, he was in a pretty ridiculous situation. He might have ignored Daddy's advice and given more serious thought to joining the army if he had known what he was in for. At least foxholes don't move around like a bucking bronc.

It was night when they arrived. The men down in the hold could feel the ship slow and then the bump of the tugboats as they pushed it into port. At first light, after showering, shaving, dressing, and going to mess, they went topside for muster (that's navy talk for roll call) and were lined up along the edge of the deck according to companies.

Glancing around, Quentin's first impression of his new duty station was that it was very beautiful but awful quiet for a war zone. There were streams cascading down from the mountains and the seawater was a beautiful jade green. All kinds of trees and foliage seemed to fill every inch of the coast and looked like they were trying to shove the small coastal village into the sea. He could see huge coconut palms, breadfruit trees, banyan trees, giant fig trees, and lots of flowers and bushes he wasn't familiar with.

"It all looked so peaceful, I couldn't believe there was a war goin' on," Quentin said, "but then all the fightin' was supposed to be going on in the northern sector anyhow. Besides that, I didn't know much about Korea except that it had mountains. I sure didn't expect it to be so tropical lookin', but I got straightened out on that real quick."

As the men started down the gangplank with their sea-bags on one shoulder and a satchel in one hand, they saw a huge warehouse at the end of the pier with a sign stretching across the top that said "N.O.B.Guam." That's when they found out their orders had been changed while they were at sea, and they were to be stationed at Guam for the next eighteen months. The reason given was that the peace talks had begun in Korea, and the military authorities felt a further built-up in U.S. troops might jeopardize the progress being made there. That seemed logical but not everyone was thrilled over it.

Some of the men had served on Guam before and their remarks could be heard above the rest: "Oh shit, not again!" or "I signed on for Korea. Why did they send me back to this hellhole? I'd rather be shot at!" Quentin was puzzled about those remarks at the time, but he understood their sentiments later.

Once off the ship, the men were herded into the open warehouse. They had to report to certain designated areas of the building when their names were called. A chief petty officer from the Naval Communications Center was in charge, and he had arranged transport for the men to the different military bases around the island, according to where they were assigned.

Quentin said, "When we mustered to the chief, he called the roll and everything seemed kinda informal so we asked him a bunch of questions about the change of duty. He kept makin' sarcastic remarks, like, 'you're just gonna *love* this damn rock. I'm glad I got only two months to go,' I couldn't figure out what all the bitchin' was about. What I'd seen didn't look so bad.

"We loaded into a military truck, which had benches down each side and down the center. There were only seven or eight of us goin' to the NCS where Seabees were stationed. We drove a few miles north from the harbor and passed Agana, the capitol of Guam, on the left. It was located between the road and the sea. To our right were the cliffs. We passed through a checkpoint that was manned by marine guards, and continued to the north end of the base. The Seabee compound was off by itself, kind of isolated from the rest of the base.

"My first look at my new station wadn't what you'd call encouragin', " Quentin said. "I thought it looked seedy and neglected. There were ten Quonset huts in all. One served as the Seabee commander's operation office, and one contained the head (navy talk for the john) and laundry facilities. I was assigned to the hut next to it.

"The rest of the NCS included about fifty Quonset huts which housed the electronic technicians, or 'twidgets' as we called them. A few of the huts were earmarked for enlisted men's dependents. The edge of their livin' quarters was maybe a halfmile from ours. Between us were all the operational offices for the NCS: enlisted men's club, fire station, barbershop, galley, sickbay, and ball fields.

"Back then I didn't care much about history and I sure didn't know anything about Guam. I learned some things about it from explorin', as time went on, and I got some information from the other men. Then, I read what I could about it, which was little. Sometimes I picked up a few facts from the WW II movies they showed us about the invasion. Today I can tell you about every inch of Guam. It's thirty miles long, eight and one-half miles wide, and almost completely surrounded by coral rock. There are beautiful, white, sandy beaches, but gettin' to them was difficult when I was there. Early on I thought it was one of the most beautiful places I had ever seen; eventually I despised it and understood why it was referred to as 'the rock' by those who had been stationed there before."

Even a tropical paradise can pall after a while if a person is faced with the same boring routine day-after-day, week-after-week, and month-after-month. In time, all the men began to suffer from the on-going boredom. Female companionship might have helped but there were very few American women around. They were mostly military dependents and they were hands-off. Eventually, even the ugliest Guamanian females began to look mighty attractive.

"We didn't even get to see that many of *them*," Quentin said. "There was no public transportation and the line truck could only be used for military business. For a man to get around he had to have access to a car, and there were very few of those on the island. There wadn't that many places to go, anyway."

Maybe that's one reason a dress code and discipline weren't strictly enforced, at least for the Seabees. On the compound they did pretty much as they pleased and dressed in cut-off jeans, no shirts, and flip-flops. For work they wore brogans to protect their feet. Overall they were a grungy looking lot, according to Quentin.

Their looks probably contributed to their reputation of being rough, tough, construction workers, something they took a lot of pride in. Since they worked out of doors all the time, they were almost as dark as the natives, and their skin looked like tanned leather. So, what with their reputation and appearance, they tended to socialize within their own group and had little to do with the twidgets.

"The twidgets were pasty-faced from workin' indoors and didn't have callouses like us" Quentin said. "Some of them even acted kinda effeminate and we didn't want to have nothin' to do with no fancy pants."

As the weeks passed with each day being a duplicate of the one before, the men began to react to the on-going tedium in different ways. Some became depressed to the point of being suicidal. Some began to show signs of a mental breakdown. Many became alcoholics.

"There wadn't much to do for entertainment," Quentin said, "except for what diversion we could find at the enlisted men's club. Well, we did have movies once in a while but they weren't anything to get excited about. They were usually old black and white films and were shown out-of-doors. We had to sit on split logs. Since it rained almost every night we had to wear ponchos, and when we wore ponchos we couldn't hear the sound track.

"Most of the time we planned our own entertainment. Sometimes we had beach parties with lots of beer drinking. Sometimes we had ball games with lots of beer drinking. Sometimes we had poker games with lots of beer drinking. And sometimes we just had lots of beer drinking.

"Sadly enough, I saw a lot of good men become alcoholics while I was on Guam. The military even seemed to encourage the drinkin'. Beer was always available and we must have gone through a zillion cases of it. Only the officers could get hard liquor but we figured out a way to get that too. As electricians we were in charge of maintainin' the air conditioner and ice machine at the officer's club. If the equipment went on the fritz, it remained that way...until we found a discreetly hidden fifth in the ice machine. They caught on fast, so we had a steady supply. We could make the equipment break down any time we wanted to.

"So it wadn't surprisin' that a lot of the guys became alcoholics. But there were others in worse shape, some of them cracked up. One of the Seabees went into the latrine and tried to hack his arm off with a machete. He was found by the fire marshal before he bled to death.

"Another one started actin' really weird. At odd hours of the day we would see him outside with the water hose turned on his head. The weather was hot and muggy so we didn't pay much attention at first. Then he began goin' out at night. He would sit for hours with the water runnin' over his head and mumblin' to himself. We decided that even for Guam that was pretty far out so we reported him to the crew chief. He was shipped out right after that. We hoped he would get some treatment. I guess bein' back in the states was probably all the treatment he needed anyway."

Apparently, the men who handled the boredom best and who survived with their mental health intact were the ones who stayed the busiest. Those were the guys who tackled with enthusiasm anything they could find to fill the hours. Some of their ideas were ingenious, others bordered on the ridiculous, and some were downright dangerous. Naturally, Quentin was right in there amongst them, one of the foremost instigators, and an avid participator.

Chapter 13

There were lots of old abandoned rusted-out military equipment, both American and Japanese, from the WW II invasions, still in evidence around the island. The beaches were dotted here and there with partially submerged landing craft, barbed wire, machine gun pits, and every other kind of war matériel imaginable, reminding one of the fierce battles that had been fought there. It was obvious that back in the forties Guam had been coveted by both sides, and a heavy price had been paid for it.

While clearing a right-of-way, the Seabee crew found an old U.S. WW II tank covered with vines. Once they had hacked away the jungle growth with machetes, they found it was in pretty good condition.

"It even had a bulldozer blade on the front," Quentin said, "and we knew right off the bat that that ole tank has endless possibilities if we could get it runnin'. It was just a matter of hours before our Seabee mechanics had it goin' and then it became our own private transport. We would all pile on it and drive all over that end of the island. Couldn't take it out on the main road, though. It wadn't as good as a car but it was fun to play around with.

"Our pleasure in it didn't last long," Quentin continued. "The officers, kill-joys that they were, found out about our tank and confiscated it. Made us so damn mad. After that, pullin' something over on the officers was an ongoin' challenge. It became a game, us against them."

Not to be outdone, Quentin and crew found another mode of transportation...an abandoned 1930 Model-A Ford convertible. It was in pitiful shape, with peeling bilious-green paint, a partially rotted-off top, and a rusted-out engine. Metals rusted quickly in Guam because of the high humidity, but the condition of the engine didn't cause them undue concern, and thinking about what they could do with it once they got it running was all the motivation they needed. After hours of working on it, standing headfirst in the engine, they finally got it going. Not very smoothly, but at least it was running. Actually, it sounded a lot like a metal bucket full of pebbles. Its pitiful appearance didn't seem all that important, either. At least they were no longer stranded on the compound. But after thinking it over, they decided they had better make the most of it before the officers got any funny notions.

Quentin and his three close friends, Bazzoli, Carboli, and Lebkicker, applied for liberty and headed forth to check out the capital, Agana, which was several miles away. To prevent any chance of getting thirsty on the trip, they iced down a cooler of beer to take along. Two men sat in front and two in the rumble seat as they set out. The fact that they had neither a license tag nor a Guamanian driving permit concerned them about as much as the navy dress code did, which was not at all.

The trip took a while since the car only ran on two cylinders, and its top speed was only about forty-five miles an hour. But that just gave them more time to quench their thirst and anticipate the wild times and wild women waiting for them in Agana, a bustling port city, or so they thought.

"When we finally rattled into town, I stood up for a better look," Quentin said. "I've never been so disappointed in my whole life. There wadn't no big city there. It was just a dreary lookin' dumpy little village; a hole in the road was all. Maybe a thousand residents but no more than that. There wadn't but one main street and it was lined on each side with a few dinky little stores, bars, and cafes. As for women, all I could see were some scroungy-lookin' over-made-up prostitutes hangin' around the bar doorways. Tryin' to drum up business, it looked like. Up behind the main drag you could see some government buildin's with little narrow roads up to them. And that was it. Some capitol. "

About that time Quentin was beginning to feel a lot of bladder pressure from all the beer. So, he decided to show his opinion of Agana and relieve his misery all at the same time. As the car coughed slowly along, he sprayed the street, while Bazzoli, Ledkicker, and Carboli all hooted with laughter. They weren't in any better shape than he was or one of them might have noticed the two S.P's watching the whole show and given him some warning. They didn't, though. The S.P.'s didn't think Quentin was all that funny, stopped the car, and gave him a lecture on proper conduct for an American serviceman on foreign soil. As Quentin admitted later, he was lucky he wasn't put on report. As I mentioned earlier, discipline was very lax on Guam, and that was an example.

So ended Quentin's first liberty. His second one didn't turn out any better either.

Scuttlebutt around the base indicated there was a juke out in the jungle a few miles away that employed American girls as taxi dancers. They supposedly worked as waitresses but were actually prostitutes. It was also rumored that the girls were part of a ring controlled by the Mafia. They had been set up around the island to entertain the Philippine laborers who had been hired by the U.S. Government to help construct a new naval base. The laborers made big bucks, the Mafia wanted in on the action, and the prostitutes stayed busy relieving the workers of their wages.

Mafia or no, the temptation was just too great. The Seabees were drawn like bees to honey. They hadn't seen American women up close in months, so to be near one, talk to one, or dance with one would be mighty fine. Another more than that would be fine, too, like icing on the cake, so to speak. With all this in mind, the four men once again spruced up with great expectations, piled into the Model A and headed out into the jungle in search of good times.

With the island being as small as it was, the place wasn't hard to find, and they got there about dark There weren't any outside lights, but there was an old beat-up Oldsmobile parked near the building and they figured it belonged to one of the Filipinos. The whole place looked pretty shabby, at least what they could see in the poor light. But then, it wasn't what was on the outside that interested them anyhow but all the lights, music, and female laughter coming from within. Good times were to be had and they couldn't wait to get started.

Eager as a bunch of kids on Christmas morning, they filed inside and found places to sit at one of the tables. That's when they got the disappointment of their lives. The girls were all over those Filipinos, dancing and smooching. That was bad enough, but then they proceeded to ignore the Seabees. They might have been invisible for all the attention they got. They even had to fetch their own drinks from the bar, not once but several times. So, after drinking and nursing their grudge for about an hour, they decided something needed to be done. They filed back outside to have a conference.

As Quentin put it, "The way we had it figured, American girls who preferred to cavort with foreigners instead of us fine wholesome-lookin' American men needed to be taught a lesson. First, we pulled the outside electrical switch. When the whole place turned black as pitch, all the gigglin', whoopin', and hollerin' inside stopped real quick like. That was mighty satisfyin' but not enough.

"Next, we decided we needed to do somethin' about that car sittin' out there. We knew it had to belong to somebody inside and by then we didn't give a damn who. I jumped behind the wheel and Bazzoli sailed into the passenger seat. It was so dark I couldn't see what the hell I was doin' and I was afraid to use the lights. But I revved up the engine anyway and took off, went about twenty feet and into a deep ravine. The car was standin' on its nose, almost on end. We were shook up a little but didn't think we were bad hurt since we could move around. Quick-thinkin' Bazzoli whipped out his handkerchief and wiped off the steerin' wheel so nobody could get my fingerprints. Afterwards, we laughed about that, like leavin' fingerprints was gonna make any difference. Seemed like a good idea to Bazzoli at the time though.

"We scrambled up the side of that ravine like a couple of scalded dogs, piled into the Model A with Carboli and Lebkicker hangin' on the runnin' boards, and tore out of there at top speed, which was forty-five MPH, of course, since it only ran on two cylinders.

"We had our satisfaction, but we really expected some repercussions from that stunt. Nothin' ever came of it though, to our relief. I probably never would have done such a dumb fool thing if I hadn't been pretty well into my cups. After that, I decided I didn't care to take another liberty and didn't the remainder of my time on Guam."

The enlisted men's club wasn't bad. It had a band and it gave the men a place to congregate, play poker, chew the fat, and drink more beer. But they decided they wanted a place more isolated, with even fewer rules, where they could really let their hair down. With that in mind, they decided to build their own private club, and started making plans.

They found a spot they liked back in the jungle between the base and the coast. After they cut a right-of-way, Quentin ran an underground cable to supply electricity. Then they erected a sixteen-man tent of WW II vintage and furnished it with cots and tables. A stove and kerosene refrigerator were confiscated from the base, and in time the men began to do most of their living in the jungle.

The galley (that's navy talk for kitchen...in this case, the base kitchen) unknowingly supplied their food. Since Quentin was duty electrician, he had to keep up the reefers (meat cooling boxes). They all opened to the outside and he had the keys, so it wasn't just a coincidence that steaks and chicken suddenly became plentiful at the jungle club. They ate real well, Quentin said, and one of their favorite dishes was pileau. I imagine Quentin was the one who got that started. After all, how many northern Italians would know anything about a southern dish like chicken and rice? He probably would have introduced them to turnip greens, too, if he could have gotten his hands on some.

They had plenty of food and plenty of beer so the only thing lacking was music. That problem was taken care of when a few talented musicians were discovered within the group. They formed their own band and were quite good, according to Quentin. After awhile, to toss in a little variety, they began making tubas, an alcoholic drink. It had the kick of an angry mule but it was a nice change from beer. Tubas were made by punching the eye out of a coconut, pouring in yeast and sugar, stopping up the eye, and then letting it set until it fermented. They were very potent but he didn't say if they ever exploded.

Quentin and Bazzoli spent a lot of their time at the secret club. As Quentin described it, "We had our own little clique and you had to belong to use the club. It was kinda like a brotherhood. Most of the enlisted men on base knew about it but kept quiet. The officers didn't even suspect. That made it even more fun."

But, as someone once said, all good things come to an end, eventually. And that's what happened with the secret jungle club. It ended in a most tragic way.

One of the boys in the group was named Cantrell. He had grown up in the country near Valdosta, Georgia, which earned him the nickname of "Georgia Boy Cantrell." To live up to his name, he always wore overalls. According to his buddies, nobody knew more about the making of moonshine than Cantrell, and nobody had a larger capacity for consumption than he did. He developed a system for making moonshine out of coconuts. By taking the milky substance that coconuts give off before they nature, and distilling it, he produced an extremely powerful concoction he called an "aggie."

One night the boys were sitting around playing poker and drinking tubas. Cantrell preferred his aggies and drank one after the other until he passed out on one of the cots. About two or three hours later, the group noticed that Cantrell hadn't been moving around, and decided to check on him. That's when they saw he wasn't breathing. They had no idea how long he had been dead.

"We were all pretty well shook up," Quentin said. "Cantrell was liked by everybody. We knew his death had to be reported immediately, so we did. Some officers came out and investigated and said the cause of death was acute alcohol poisoning. Then they sent the bulldozers to flatten the tent and everything in it. Didn't take long for the jungle to overgrow the whole area. Our little camp might never have even existed."

14 | Chapter

Frustrated with the endless monotony, the men created excitement whenever, wherever, and however they could. One thing they did almost constantly was bet—-on anything, anytime, and anywhere. Usually, a case of beer was the reward, since that was about all they had of value. Their monthly salary wasn't much and didn't last long anyway.

Quentin enjoyed the betting and was always game for anything, no matter how dangerous. The more daring and exciting it became, the better he liked it. One opportunity to show his stuff and win a bet occurred at the antennae fields that were located on a bluff about two hundred feet above the sea. There were three hundred poles scattered about the fields and each was between seventy and ninety feet tall. Maintenance on the poles was provided by Quentin's electrical crew. They had to keep the grids and radio wires cleaned, set new poles, string wire, and keep the grass mowed. Replacing the poles was a major job because the ground was primarily coral rock, and the holes had to be drilled or dynamited. When an old pole was removed, the crew would use the line truck to push it over the cliff. Regulations demanded that they take the pole back to the base to be inventoried. They chose to ignore that regulation like they did most of the others.

One day, as they shoved an old pole over the edge of the cliff, the larger end became wedged under the front end of the truck with the tapered end extending out into space. Not missing a chance, the crew immediately bet Quentin a case of beer that he didn't have the guts to shinny out to the far end of the pole.

They knew from past experience that he just couldn't pass up a challenge like that. By that time he had gained a reputation for doing anything on a dare, no matter what the reward might be.

He related it this way: "I locked my arms and legs around the pole and slowly inched my way out to the end, which was smaller, smoother, and slick in places. It kinda tilted down a little, too. I started sweatin' from workin' at it so hard and that made the pole more slippery. All I had on was my cutoff jeans and brogans. I tried not to look down. All I coulda seen anyway were breakers beatin' up against those rocks about two hundred feet under me. The crew kept hollerin' and yellin all kinds of things, eggin' me on.

"Some of them were jeerin', ' Hey, Whit, don't look below. You might faint and fall off! ' and 'Yeah, I can't stand the sight of blood!' Then somebody yelled, 'Blood, hell! He has beer in his veins! '

"Then sweat started runnin' in my eyes and I couldn't see too good. When my arms and legs started shakin' from fatigue, I got to wonderin' if maybe I hadn't been a little foolish. I had to worm my way back and it was slow goin' because I was goin' backwards, uphill, from the small end to the big end of the pole. I finally made it but I didn't let the crew see how relieved I was. They all started cheerin' and whoppin' me on the back and shovin' a cold beer at me."

You are probably wondering where they would get cold beer out in the antennae fields. Well, I did too until Quentin explained how they managed to keep a constant supply of beer while at work. This was a definite no-no, of course, but they were so used to breaking rules by that time it had almost become a habit. Fun, too. Something they looked forward to. Lay awake nights thinking about, most likely.

"Every morning' after we received our work orders for the day, we drove around behind the club, out of sight." Quentin said, "The ice machine was in the rear. There was a bin on the line truck where the climbing tools were kept. We'd cleaned out the bin, shoveled it full of ice, and that's where we stashed our beer.

"The crew chief knew we were doin' this, but he kept his mouth shut 'cause he was an alcoholic. Since the club didn't open until five p.m., the line truck was his only source. You could set your watch by 'im. Every morning about ten o'clock, you could see his jeep comin' across the antennae field. As soon as he had a beer or two, he left. He didn't know power line work. All he knew was inside electrical, so he depended on me to get the work done."

Quentin won another case of beer by betting the crew that he could drop his navy hat from the top of the pole and catch it before it hit the ground. That was a trick he learned from a lineman while working at Cape Canaveral. He only made about three long steps with his cleats coming down, while his cap got filled with air and fell a lot slower, like a parachute. None of the other men could ever master that trick, according to Quentin, although they tried it a lot of times.

Quentin wasn't afraid of heights, but those ninety-foot poles were short compared to some of the heights he reached while he was stationed on Guam. On the opposite side of the island was another communications center called Radio Barragado, which served as a relay station for all military transmissions from Japan to Honolulu to the United States. Guam was situated about half way. At this complex were seven three-hundred-foot towers, and from the top of each tower was a ten-foot mast with aircraft warning lights. Those blinked night and day. When one burned out, usually about once a month, it had to be replaced.

A civilian company had a government contract for replacing the bulbs, but when the contract expired it wasn't renewed. The reason for that was unknown. However, since the burned-out bulbs had to be quickly replaced to prevent a plane/tower collision, the military authorities approached the crew chief and asked for volunteers from among the electricians.

"Foolish me," Quentin said. "I was a good climber and in charge of the seven-man crew. I was always braggin' about my climbin' so I felt like I had to volunteer and uphold my reputation. Besides, I was well into my cups at the time. Figured there wadn't all that much to it.

"They had metal ladders on those towers so you couldn't use cleats and you had to use a safety belt. I guess I was the only one crazy enough to climb the towers and I was usually drunk when I did it. One time I got sick when I was replacin' a bulb and just hung up there, three hundred and ten feet above the ground, and heaved my insides out. Never gave any thought to who might be gettin' pelted down below. Didn't really care anyhow. After I left Guam, I wondered a lot of times who they got to replace those bulbs."

Once a month the officers divided the men into groups and had military training called "war games." This was supposed to keep the servicemen in tip-top fighting shape. The Seabees thought it was much-to-do over nothing, and treated the whole thing accordingly.

They were issued green uniforms, hard hats, and blank bullets, and they were given an objective to guard and contain. The navy men from the naval air station were supposed to invade their base and seize their objective. Planes would swoop down and drop bags of flour to denote bomb hits.

"Our group didn't cooperate," Quentin said, "and we always got captured. The officers were really disgusted. The way we looked at it, the war was windin' down by that time anyway and we just couldn't see the point in all the fuss. Usually we just spent the time at the line shack, eating C-rations, and playin' poker.

"Every month we had those war games and always with the same results. There were never any reprimands. The officers in charge knew that if they squawked too much the ice machine or the air conditioner in the officers club would mysteriously quit functionin'. Actually, I guess it was a kind of blackmail, and we did use it with great enthusiasm."

As the days crept by at a snail's pace, or so it seemed, finding something to keep them busy and their minds occupied was an ongoing challenge. After much discussion over the poker table, the Seabees decided it would behoove them to take on a major project...something that would eat up a lot of time, could be done on their off-duty time, and, of course, could be kept a secret from the higher-ups. That in itself was exciting. It was finally settled. They would construct a house for one of the men in their group. At first the job looked impossible but they welcomed the challenge of it. Getting the materials they needed was no problem. By that time they were they good at stealing stuff from the base and thinking of it as a supplement to their salary.

The man who was to benefit from all the labor was a career navy man by the name of Hoffman. He was also a surveyor, a first-class petty officer, and a very devoted family man who wrote long letters home every night. Hoffman wanted to bring his family over from the states but there was a shortage of dependent housing. Officers always had first choice of the units available which meant there was a long waiting list for the enlisted men. Eighteen months was a long time to be away from his family, and Hoffman was becoming depressed. They knew the signs.

"There wadn't any shortage of talent," Quentin said. "We had seven different types of craftsmen: carpenters, mechanics, electricians, surveyors, plumbers, pipe-fitters, and heavy machine operators. We had all the help we needed and it really proved to be a joint effort.

"First thing we did was select a site off-base, up in the jungle. Nobody knew who owned the land and didn't care anyway. We just cleaned out an area and started buildin'. Me and the electrical crew hung a transformer and ran an electrical service to the site. Then the carpenters got busy with the actual construction. Everybody pitched in, worked every minute off-duty that we could, and it didn't take long. I did all the inside wirin' myself.

"It was a pretty little house, for Guam. We built it out of plywood, put on a tin roof, and even painted it. Furnishin' it wadn't no problem, either. When an officer moved out of one of the dependent houses and before another moved in, we had to check out the electrical equipment and make sure everything was in workin' order. While we were there we would confiscate a piece of furniture . . . a chair from one unit, a table from another, etc. until we had Hoffman's house furnished real nice. We found an old unworkable stove and repaired it. As for a refrigerator, well they were plentiful in Guam. They were all kerosene but did a good job so we moved one of those in.

"We finally got the house finished and Hoffman was really pleased with it. He sent for his family and they came over by civilian transport. His wife seemed to really appreciate all our efforts, but his two little girls were more excited over the wild goats we turned loose in the yard. We figured the goats would keep the jungle from takin' over the place.

"The last thing we did was get Hoffman's car in good runnin' order so his wife would have a way to get around. He had an old red 1949 Oldsmobile that was in awful shape but our mechanics got it going. Thinkin' back on it, I guess buildin' Hoffman's house was about the most satisfyin' experience we had while we were over there. We didn't have many satisfyin' experiences on Guam."

15 | CHAPTER

As you can tell from the preceding chapters, Quentin didn't like being stationed on Guam. That's putting it a little mildly, I suppose, but I can't afford to get too profane here. He did have a lot of complaints about the island, for sure, and one that we haven't even addressed yet was the food. According to him, it "wadn't fit to slop hogs with."

"We never had any fresh vegetables like I was used to all my life, and that was plumb torture to me. The worst stuff was the powdered milk and eggs we had to eat. I couldn't complain much about the meat. There was plenty of it and a good variety but, hell, you can't live just on meat by itself. I used to dream about all those vegetables Mother cooked at the farm: fresh green beans with little new potatoes cooked in 'em, corn-on-the-cob, and pots of fresh mustard and collards. But I guess the one thing I craved most, and missed most, was *ice-cold fresh sweet milk*.

"Supposedly, there were plenty of fresh vegetables, milk, and eggs shipped in but the Seabee compound got the leavin's after the other bases around Guam got their choice. Most of the time there wadn't nothin' left but California radishes. I learned to hate radishes real fast.

"One day I was assigned to chow-hall duty and was sent down to the harbor to pick up a load of 'fresh vegetables'. That's what they said. I was tickled to death and drove the truck all the way with my mouth waterin', just thinkin' about those vegetables and how they were gonna taste.

"When I got there, they loaded my truck with vegetables all right . . . California radishes . . a whole damn truck full. That was a low blow. All the way back to the base, I was so disappointed and totally disgusted that I used some words I didn't learn in Miss Moore's bible class. Then I decided enough was enough so I made a detour by the base dump and unloaded the radishes . . . all sixty cases of 'em.

"I really expected to get dressed down, up, and ever which way when I got back to the chow-hall, but it was real weird, nobody ever said a word about why I came back with an empty truck. I never could figure out the military. But I never regretted dumpin' them damn radishes. I knew Scar-Face would appreciate 'em."

Scar-Face was the name of the girl who lived at the base dump with her father. Like so many of her countrymen, she was a casualty of the war. During the Japanese occupation the island of Guam was, in essence, one giant prison camp, and the Guamanian people were treated brutally. Scar-Face in particular had been mutilated, tortured, and her tongue cut out. No one seemed to know her true age. According to Quentin, she was a pitiful sight.

She and her father lived at the edge of the dump in a primitive shack they had nailed together out of scrap lumber somebody dumped there. They stayed out of sight mostly, but when seen they were ragged and filthy. To survive, they scavenged what food they could find by digging through the dump. The whole place stunk to high heaven, was overrun by big rats, and all kinds of other varmints, and was covered with so many flies it looked like it had been sprinkled with pepper.

Quentin thought it strange that nobody tried to help Scar-Face and her father. Nobody seemed to care. But he did, and often left food as near her shack as possible.

According to available information, many of the atrocities the Guamanians suffered at the hands of the Japanese was due to one reason—-to protect a man named Tweed. He was a navy career-man who was stationed on Guam when the Japanese invaded. Instead of surrendering like the other American servicemen, he fled to the jungles and hid out until the American forces recaptured Guam two years later.

The Japanese hated Tweed because he was a communications technician, and they knew he was sending out information to the U.S. forces. They could intercept his messages, but they could never find him. The Guamanians, however, knew his different locations and sneaked him food and other essentials. His safety depended entirely upon the overwhelming hatred the Guamanians felt for the Japanese. Many were tortured and killed to protect him and, in later years, many were bitter because of the price they paid for protecting him.

When Tweed fled to the jungle, he dug a cave near the top of a high bluff overlooking Apa harbor. He constructed a radio and contacted American forces off the coast. From his lofty perch, he had a clear view of the harbor and could pass along information on Japanese shipping: the number and types of ships as they came and went. He transmitted to a submarine at predetermined times and always at night. During the day, he holed up and slept and ate. His diet was mostly mangoes, coconuts, bananas, and anything his Guamanian friends could smuggle to him. Then, two days before the American forces were to invade and retake the island, Tweed was taken off by submarine.

Quentin's interest in Tweed began when he and some friends stumbled upon his cave by accident. If they had any slack time while working the antennae fields, they would explore the area for caves. As mentioned earlier, the antennae fields were located between the Seabee compound and the sea, along the cliffs. North of the fields was the Coast Guard base. It was near there that the men noticed a depressed area that caught their interest. There were pieces of corrugated steel covered with sand and weeds that had apparently served as the roof to a manmade cave. A narrow ledge ran from the top of the cliff to below the cave site. They figured that to be a way of entrance. After studying on it, they became convinced it was Tweed's secret hideout, especially when they saw all the handmade transmitting equipment scattered about.

There was an antenna made out of a thirty-five-foot bamboo pole. A thin copper wire coiled around the pole about every one-fourth inch all the way to the top, with a piece sticking out at the end. They surmised he put it up by night and took it down before sunrise, so it wouldn't be spotted by the Japanese. Tweed later wrote a book on his experiences and called it Robinson Crusoe: U.S.N.

There was a postscript to the Tweed story. While Quentin was stationed on Guam, Tweed stopped over, enroute to Japan. Military personnel wouldn't let him off the plane for fear that some of the Guamanians might take reprisals against him. Many of the islanders still held him responsible for the brutality they had suffered at the hands of the Japanese. He flew out without incident, however.

As long as we're on the subject of the Japanese, I might as well relate Quentin's experience regarding the same. There were still Japanese soldiers from WW II holed up on Guam when he arrived there. They never surrendered after the war and hid in the jungle where they harassed the Americans at every opportunity. They never actually killed anyone but did blow out an occasional windshield and stole everything they could get their hands on, especially food. Because the Japanese were known to be armed, Quentin's crew was instructed to carry a carbine on the line truck. That provided a little fun. They shot a few doves, even a deer once, but never saw a Japanese to aim at. None of his crew ever got shot at by them, either.

Whenever the elusive Japanese holdouts were spotted, a navy plane would fly over the area and drop leaflets urging them to surrender. Those that remained, estimated to be about eight or nine at that time, were finally captured before Quentin left Guam.

The military authorities thought that ended the Japanese holdouts, but they were wrong. One lone Japanese soldier surrendered, or was captured, in 1972. He had lived alone nearly all of his life in the jungle on Guam, still believing as he was taught . . . that it was dishonorable to surrender.

The story of Quentin's Guam experiences wouldn't be complete if I neglected to include Bingo, his closest friend and constant companion during his time there.

They became acquainted when Quentin arrived on Guam, and they seemed to take to each other right away. Bingo was a mixed breed dog, mostly German Shepherd, and not much more than a puppy when they first met. When the owner, one of the other sailors stationed there, was rotated back to the states, he couldn't take the dog, so Quentin adopted him.

He spent as much time as he could with Bingo, training him and teaching him tricks. It wasn't long before Bingo was well known to everyone on the base and was accepted as one of the men. According to Quentin, he seemed to think he was human anyway and conducted himself accordingly.

"Every mornin' when the unit lined up for muster, Bingo took his place and stood at attention." Quentin said. "When each man's name was called, he would answer. When Bingo's name was called, he barked. Then, when muster was over and we had all received our work orders for the day, Bingo was the first one on the line truck. He always rode standin' up on the cab. Didn't take him long to get into the beer drinkin' either. That was one smart dog.

"The serviceman's club didn't open until five p.m. By then there was usually a long line of men waitin', and one dog. Bingo was always first in line. If I had duty and couldn't go, Bingo went by hisself and sat at his own favorite table. He would sit on his haunches on the chair and rest his paws on the table. The bartender kept a special bowl to serve Bingo's beer in and he always placed it on the table. Bingo would lap it up and keep right on, just as long as the servicemen continued to set him up, or until he passed out on the floor, whichever came first. If I wadn't there, someone would take him back to the hut when the club closed.

"One of the first tricks Bingo learned was how to open and close the screen door to the hut. He would use his paw and come and go as he pleased. When he was drunk, he had a little trouble gettin' in. He would stumble about, bangin' the door tryin' to open it, until someone roused up enough to let him in.

"Bingo always slept at the foot of my bunk. After a night of drinkin' at the club, he would usually have a restless night with a lot of gruntin' and groanin'. That wadn't all he did either. He could pass the stinkingest gas I ever smelled. He nearly stunk us out of the hut, but nobody would put 'im out 'cause we all felt sorry for 'im. The next mornin' he would be so hung-over his eyes would be bloodshot. But he never missed muster.

"If Bingo didn't show up at the club everyone wanted to know where he was. Sometimes he would be out in the antennae fields with the crew. Then sometimes he would just take a notion to go visitin' around the base. He got around by hitchhikin'. I'm tellin' the truth here, so help me! He would sit beside the road until someone passed and gave him a lift. Everybody knew him and loved him. When it was mealtime, he would catch a ride to the chow hall. Oh, yes . . . he had his own special place there, too.

"I really hated to leave 'im when my time on Guam was up, but I couldn't take 'im with me. Before I left, I decided to give 'im to a new man on base, one that Bingo seemed to like. I knew he'd be taken care of. I guess he was the only thing I really missed about Guam.

When his eighteen months in "purgatory" (that's what Guam was called by the men who served there) was finally over, Quentin received his orders to rotate back to the states. The men in his unit were transported by bus back to the Naval Operations Base at the harbor where all naval personnel were shipped in and out. They didn't get any farther than that, however, at least for a while. The military had a red-tape snafu, and the men had to wait seven days for the ship to put into port. Seven more days before they could leave, and nothing to fill the time. The authorities must have believed the old saying that "idleness is the devil's workshop." They certainly knew that a bunch of restless, idle servicemen could cause a mess of trouble if left on their own. So, as a preventive measure, they assigned them to work details to keep them occupied.

"The seaman in charge of our work detail had just gotten to Guam and hadn't yet been humbled by the experience." Quentin said. "He kinda felt his importance and tried everything he could think of to get us to work. We mostly ignored him or gave him a hard time. The way we figured it, we had been there eighteen months and were old salts and he was just an upstart. Besides which, we were all first, second, or third-class petty officers, and the work detail they assigned us seemed too much like busywork, downright silly in fact.

"Every mornin' we were picked up in a dump truck and hauled out into the jungle to clean up a Guamanian cemetery. It hadn't been touched since WW II. There were weeds and bushes head-high, and the military wanted us to whistle-blade it down; get it all nice and tidy like. First thing we did was cut us a path through the center of it, and then cleaned out an area about twenty feet square. In the center was a blown-over tombstone that was shell-marked from the bombardment. There were probably unexploded shells in that cemetery, too, but we didn't search for 'em 'cause we had more important things to occupy our time.

"We dusted off the tombstone and used it for a table to play cards on. For seven days, every day, all day, we played poker. At noon, the dump truck returned to take us to the chow hall for lunch. Afterwards, they hauled us back to work where we resumed our poker playin' until the truck returned late in the afternoon. When we left Guam, that cemetery didn't look a damn bit better."

The ship finally put into port and the men loaded aboard, yet it was another day before they could head for the states. A typhoon was headed in that direction. With the situation expected to worsen, the ship pulled out from shore into the open sea to wait it out. As the sea got rougher and the waves higher, the huge ship took a thirty-three-degree roll, which meant it almost turned over. So, not surprisingly, Quentin got seasick before he even left port.

"We were quartered in the hold again, and we could feel every movement of the ship down there." Quentin said. "Just about every man on board got sick but none of them as bad as me. There was so much puke on the floor a person could hardly walk across it because it was so slick. We only had one stairwell to get to the head and not many made it. Shoot, the smell alone was enough to make us sick without the rollin' of the ship.

"After two or three days I knew if I didn't get out of there I would die. I crawled topside and found a cubbyhole near where the lifeboats were kept. It was shaped like a horseshoe. I curled up in the fetal position in the dark and tried hard to die. I lost track of time so I don't know how long it was before some of my friends found me and hauled me to sickbay. They said I was extremely dehydrated and gave me I.V's for two days. Because of that, they put in my medical record that I had 'chronic seasickness and shouldn't travel by ship.' Afterwards, I did most of my military travelin' by plane.

"I still had bouts of sea sickness after I got out of sickbay but not as bad. The sea was calmer by then. If I felt one comin' on, I would bolt to the fantail of the ship so I could have some privacy. Unfortunately, there were other poor souls with the same idea and we would have to jockey for position. If there was a good tail wind, the ones in the rear got spattered. It was awful."

When they finally disembarked in California, Quentin made a beeline to the nearest restaurant to satisfy his eighteen-month craving. He drank three large glasses of *ice-cold sweet milk*, one behind the other, as fast as he could get them down. The waitress was shocked until Quentin explained how long he had been dreaming about fresh milk. She was the first American girl he had actually chatted with since leaving for Guam. He decided that being back in the states was mighty fine.

From California Quentin caught a plane to Atlanta, then a commuter plane to Jacksonville, making long stops along the way. He had two weeks leave coming, and he wanted to stop off in Jacksonville to pick up his car. I had been keeping it for him and using it to drive back and forth to work. After graduating and passing state boards, I had begun working for two pediatricians in the Riverside area of Jacksonville but lived in the Springfield area. Having the car was a nice convenience, but more and more often it sat in the repair shop while I road the city bus.

Maybe I'd better explain here about Quentin's car. We're talking about that sporty little 1941 Ford coupe he was so proud of. Sometimes, when it was running, I'd drive over to Havana for the weekend. Well, one weekend I got stranded there with a car that wouldn't run and no money for bus fare. This was on Sunday and I had to be at work in Jacksonville on Monday morning. Daddy's brother, Barney, the expert mechanic mentioned earlier, worked for the Dodge place in Havana. He said the Ford wasn't worth what it would cost to fix it and I trusted his judgment. That's when, out of desperation, I traded it for a 1950 Dodge. I financed it for two years and made all the payments, except for the last two and that's when I got married and moved north. Daddy made those with Quentin's allotment check. I'm not sure Quentin ever completely forgave me for trading his Ford. And, what's worse, the Dodge wasn't much better no matter how much I babied it. I guess you could say I shot myself in the foot by trading because those repair bills just kept right on coming in. Only now I had car payments, too.

Quentin stayed overnight at my apartment, and we sat up late visiting and catching up on family news. He left early the next day for Havana. At the time, Geraldine (my name for the

Dodge) was purring like new, but based on her past performance I had no idea how long that would last.

16 | Chapter

After spending nearly nineteen months on Guam, Quentin was sure he would get to spend his remaining service time in the states. But, to his disappointment, it didn't work out that way. When he arrived back in Port Hueneme, he was assigned to Mobile Construction Battalion #3, a huge outfit of about one thousand men, and they were headed to the Philippines. Since he had no say-so in the matter anyhow, Quentin just resigned himself to his fate and hoped the Philippines would be an improvement over Guam.

The men were sent by train to Allameda Air Station in Oakland, California, where they caught a MATS (military air transport) plane, a big six-engine double-decker seaplane. The trip over was divided into jaunts, and Quentin found he could handle the plane movement a lot better than the ship. One of the men, who had been stationed in the Philippines previously, said he really liked the duty there. That sounded good to Quentin.

They took off from San Francisco Bay, flew over Oakland Bay Bridge, Alcatraz, the Golden Gate Bridge, and settled down for the flight across the Pacific to their first stop, Barber's Point in Honolulu. The men had a three-day layover and were transported by bus to Hickam Field. From there they continued the trip by a four-engine military plane. Some of the military personnel on board were destined for different islands so the plane hopped and skipped, stopping at different military bases along the way.

One of the stops was at Guam where they stayed overnight. Quentin didn't leave the air base. As he said, "I didn't have any desire to see any part of that hell-hole ever again. "Maybe he had fears of getting left behind, something he wouldn't admit to, of course. He did say, however, that he really felt sorry for the guys who were left at Kwajalein, one of their stops. It was a tiny island, much smaller than Guam, only three miles long.

Overall the trip was uneventful and they landed at Subic Bay in the Philippines where Quentin was to be stationed for the next year and a half. Subic Bay was a deep natural harbor and a busy port. Ships were constantly coming and going because most of the U.S. naval fleet frequently put in at the big naval base there. The Seabees didn't stay at the naval base but were quartered in their own compound at Cubie Point, located on a mountain at the upper end of the Bataan Peninsula. Manila, the capital of the Philippines, was located fifty-five miles to the south.

The Seabee base itself straddled the crest of the mountain and was split in half by the road, which ran down the center of the compound. That was the only access. On one side of the road, building sites had been scooped out of the mountain with bulldozers. Prefabricated huts, constructed in the U.S., were put together on the sites and provided sleeping quarters for the men. They were terraced partway down the side of the mountain. The bottom of one was level with the top of another. Arranged in tiers, the huts were connected by wooden walkways that led from one level to another. The community bathrooms, showers, and servicemen's club made up the center of the compound.

The hut to which Quentin was assigned was located on the bottom level, overlooking a steep ravine that dropped off about two hundred feet. There were five huts in that row and each could accommodate twenty men. The sleeping racks were arranged around the outside walls, with the lockers, and clothes racks down the center aisle. There was no air-conditioning or heat because it wasn't needed. Instead, the huts were screened from two feet above the floor to the ceiling and shuttered to keep out rain during the monsoon season.

Across the road and staggered down the other side of the mountain were the living quarters for the operation officers and the mess hall. To take their meals, the men from Quentin's hut had to go up to the road and down the hill. They didn't complain, though. As Quentin put it, "The food was fantastic and worth the climb."

Being a much larger outfit, the Seabee unit was better budgeted than the one on Guam. Fresh eggs, milk, and vegetables were plentiful and steak was served frequently. Brunch was served on Sundays, and the men were permitted to wander in at their leisure and choose from a variety of dishes. To the Guam veterans, it was high living. There were other things Quentin liked about his new duty station, and I'll get to those later, but one thing that really pleased him was being once again reunited with his friends, Frank Rosato and Joe Woods, who had been transferred from Kwajalein to the Philippines.

The biggest complaint the men in Quentin's hut had was the location of the head. Since they were on the bottom level, they had to climb up the hill to use it. Ordinarily that didn't pose a problem, but on Saturday nights, after liberty in town where large quantities of beer had been consumed, the men found they had a real problem. During the night they had to get up often, and navigating their way to the bathroom became hazardous. They figured out a solution, though. Usually they just stepped out of their hut, staggered to the edge of the ravine, and tinkled over the side. Since the hill sloped and was covered by native shrubs and a vine similar to kudzu, there didn't seem to be any lasting odor. Or maybe they were just used to it.

As on Guam, there was an excuse to drink every night. No hard liquor was allowed on base so the men only drank beer. Quentin's personal favorite was San Miguel, a beer brewed in the Philippines and, according to him, very tasty.

One Saturday night after a drinking party, Quentin made his way back to his hut and fell out on his rack. He was feeling no pain. However, about two A.M. he woke up with a pressing need to empty his bladder. Realizing he would never make it to the head, he groped his way out to the edge of the ravine…or where he figured the edge was located. It wasn't. He found himself in open air, tumbling head over heels to the bottom of the ravine. After spending the night there, dozing off and on, too sloshed to care, he finally sobered up enough by daylight to scale the mountain. He grabbed handholds on the vines, anywhere he could find one, and eventually made it to the top. Except for being scratched and dirty, he came out of it in one piece.

Usually the Seabees wore green work clothes like the marines wore, but on Saturday nights they were allowed to deck out in civilian garb: sport shirts, khaki pants, and loafers. Being a close-knit unit, the Seabees did most of their socializing together.

Saturday night liberty meant going into Olongapo, a small village ten miles from the base, According to Quentin, it wasn't much, just one unpaved street lined with wooden sidewalks, similar to the one in the old west movies. But scenic beauty wasn't a top priority for the navy men, not right then, anyway. Sightseeing wasn't what they were there for.

Restaurants, bars, and nightclubs, one after the other, lined each side of the lone street and, like Las Vegas, they never closed. Taxi dancers, checked regularly for V.D. by the military and required to carry health cards, lounged in the doorways, flirting with the servicemen who thronged the streets, and trying to make a little after-hours money by prostitution.

The base had so many men going into Olongapo on leave that the town was under U.S. military control. The main reason was for security. There were gorillas holed up in the mountains behind the base, trying to overthrow the Philippine government. A constant ongoing battle raged between the Huks and the Philippine army, which made frequent forays into the mountains to root them out. At night, tracers could be seen and gunfire from BAR's could be clearly heard. Sometimes the Huks attacked buses of local people, robbing and killing them all. They were a constant threat. For this reason, checkpoints were scattered along the highway and manned by Philippine nationals with machine guns. All vehicles were stopped and searched. Quentin was subjected to this quite often since he was in charge of a crew and had been assigned a line truck.

One of the crew's responsibilities was to assist the townspeople of Olongapo in maintaining their generators, which relied AC/DC current. The men on the crew didn't mind for it gave them a break from their usual duties and, better yet, a chance to eyeball the local girls. Their main responsibility, however, was to help in the construction of a new airstrip, which was in progress when they arrived and still unfinished eighteen months later, when they left. They did primary-line work and high-voltage work, something they had done little of on Guam.

An entire mountain was being dug out and used to fill in one edge of Subic Bay. Hundreds of men worked twenty-four hours a day in eight-hour shifts.

"One thing we had to get used to was the constant noise of the machines," Quentin said. "There were almost a hundred of 'em and the racket they made was deafenin'. They could be heard for miles."

The men who operated the earthmovers were all military personnel from Quentin's unit. According to him, they called themselves "cowboys" and were a reckless lot. Several were killed while he was there

"The mountain was bein' chopped down at about a forty-five-degree angle." Quentin said. "The drivers would take the dozers, which weighed tons, and go free-wheelin' down the mountainside. Sometimes they would reach speeds up to sixty-five miles an hour or more, dust and clay would boil up. They couldn't see good, then, so they would run into each other and over each other. It looked like the demolition derby out there, only with big machines. Eventually, the officers who had to oversee that phase of construction, clamped down and instilled some safety rules that cut down on the fatalities."

The only time there was a break in the noise was in monsoon season. The northern Philippines held the record for rainfall—forty-eight inches in forty-eight hours. Of course it's possible the record has been broken since then. At that time, however, when the rains came, a skeleton crew was kept at the base to maintain the equipment, and the rest of the men were sent back to the states for military training.

Quentin said, "I never had to leave for that, thank goodness. With my history of seasickness I was more than happy to stay put."

While the construction was going on, and in order for it to continue at night, Quentin and his crew installed and maintained hundreds of floodlights with portable generators. They also installed the aircraft lights along the landing strip, and helped with the construction of a one-thousand-foot pier that extended out into Subic Bay to provide a berth for the aircraft carriers.

The transportation system in the Philippines was a vast improvement over what the Seabees had on Guam. Which, of course, was none. One choice they had was the local bus line, which consisted of dozens of old buses, all painted psychedelic swirls of orange, purple, and any other loud color imaginable. In Quentin's opinion, the artwork was pretty good. (I neglected to ask him if this was before or after he had liberty)

Each bus had a rack attached to the top, used for transporting the goats, pigs, and chickens of the local people. And that's how the bus line got its name. The servicemen laughingly referred to it as the "goat line." All the civilians rode those buses. The servicemen could, too, but were discouraged from doing so by the military because of the danger involved. It wasn't unusual for the gorillas to come down from the mountains, hide along the roadway, and riddle the bus with bullets.

When going on liberty into Olongapo on Saturday nights, Quentin and his Seabee friends usually road the "cattle truck" provided by the military. This was a tractor rig with a long trailer behind. The trailer had seats down each side and back-to-back seats down the center. Since there was no charge, the men were usually packed in like cattle, hence the name "cattle truck." The trucks ran every thirty minutes and shuttled the men back and for to Cubic Point.

An alternative method of transportation was by jitney (or "jeepney"), an old dilapidated WW II jeep that had the back cut off and a platform built to hold the wooden benches down each side. The back was covered and decorated with fringe. There were dozens of the jitneys to be seen around Olongapo and scooting back and forth to the base. At times there would be as many fifty jitneys parked at the base gates trying to pick up fares. They, too, were painted and decorated with wild colors and were operated by Filipino locals. That's how many of them earned their living. Each jitney could carry twelve passengers and the fare was five centavos (two and one-half cents). In town they only traveled about ten MPH. Sometimes a man could run along the side, swing up on the running board, and hop off at his destination without the driver being aware he had an extra passenger. Quentin explained all about this but never admitted to doing it…Uh huh.

Another way the Filipinos made their living was by doing laundry for the servicemen. They had passes to the base and arrived weekly in their own loudly painted jitneys. Each family contracted with the men separately, and each man was assigned a number. Their clothing was marked to prevent a mix-up. The monthly charge for laundry service was seven dollars, but this could vary according to the number of pieces.

"It was money well earned" Quentin said. "There wadn't any modern appliances and they did everything by hand, kinda like Mother used ta hafta do. The clothes were washed in a creek, beat with a stick, and hung on limbs to dry. Then they were pressed and folded by hand. The Filipinos took a lot of pride in their work. Did a good job, too."

Once a month the men were given a long weekend, from Friday to Monday, for R and R at the military resort in Bagio, one of the most scenic and beautiful spots in the Philippines. The complex, which was huge and included such amenities as a golf course, swimming pool, restaurant, and housing, was located at Camp John Hay near the small Filipino village of Bagio. It had been constructed and was maintained by the military to provide R and R for all servicemen in the East and Far East and their dependents. Quentin loved it.

He described the girls around Bagio as beautiful, with creamy skin and long black hair. They were from a race of people called Methesias(?). Quentin wasn't sure about the spelling and I couldn't find it in the encyclopedia. There were many different distinct tribes of Filipino natives and about thirty different dialects spoken, but the Methesias spoke excellent English. They seemed to be nice family-type people who were very intelligent and had high morals. In other words, the girls who worked as waitresses in the bars didn't engage in prostitution...and that meant that the men could look and admire but not touch.

The golf course at Bagio was a golfer's dream, according to Quentin.

"It was the prettiest golf course I'd ever seen," he said. " I learned to play while I was there. All the equipment was furnished free. All I had to do was tip the caddie, a little Filipino boy."

Quentin took all his R and R's in Bagio, with a few exceptions. One of those was when he decided to take advantage of his opportunity to see the sights of Hong Kong and experience a different culture. He took an LSST (a flat bottom WW II landing ship) out of Langley Point in Manila Harbor. The sea was rough and the crossing unpleasant for a seasickness-prone landlubber like Quentin. He became so sick he ended up spending his entire leave in Annie Chang's Union House—-a two-story hotel—-and never left the premises.

"I went out on the balcony a few times and looked over the scenery but never went sight-seein'." Quentin said. " It definitely wadn't my finest hour, and when I left there, I didn't have any desire to return, not as long as Bagio was available."

No passes were required to go to Bagio, and usually about fifteen men at the time went by military bus. The base made arrangements beforehand. The trip lasted six hours, with a stop at Clark AFB in Angeles for noon mess, and arrival in Bagio about two P.M.

"The resort sat on top of a mountain, really high up, and was surrounded by pines that looked like Christmas trees and gave off a sharp, clean smell," Quentin said. "The whole area reminded me of the Smoky Mountains. You could look out in all directions and see forever. The view was unbelievable."

At Bagio the enlisted men and officers all intermingled, a rarity in a military setting, and they were all treated like royalty. When the men arrived they were assigned to a cabin. There were five cabins in the group where Quentin usually stayed, and many others scattered about the resort. Each cabin was clean, nicely furnished, and consisted of a small living room, two bedrooms, and a private bath. In the rear was a patio with chairs, and a breathtaking view of the valley and mountains beyond.

The men took their meals at the club where they were seated at tables with linen tablecloths, china, crystal, and silver. They ordered and were served by waiters, and afterwards the tables were cleared by busboys. That was, in itself, intoxicating to men who were routinely shuttled through chow lines like a herd of cows . . . I guess bulls would be more accurate here . . . and ate on tin trays.

"I always ordered filet mignon with all the trimmin's and it cost me the whole sum of ninety cents," Quentin said. "There were all kinds of fresh vegetables to choose from and the villagers grew them locally. Their gardens were planted in volcanic soil, and sometimes the tomatoes were as big as man's head. Delicious, too."

After dinner he and his friends would adjourn to the bar where setups were provided and hard liquor could be purchased. There was a large dance floor, and music provided by a local band consisting of a Filipino father and his three sons, all blind since birth. They sometimes interchanged their string instruments, playing each equally well. After the club closed, the men returned to their cabins and the partying continued.

There were men from all branches of service, representing all areas of the U.S. Since many of them returned monthly, they got to know each other quite well. Sometimes they engaged in good-natured inter-service rivalry and occasionally refought the civil war. Apparently their higher-class environment encouraged higher-class behavior, for there was no rowdiness nor fistfights like they were prone to have in Olongapo.

There was a man from Tennessee, Kentucky (that's the city *and* state) in the group. He was a tall, lanky, good-looking boy who had a deep-south crackery drawl. Back home he had done a lot of coon hunting, his favorite pastime. Sometimes he would have Quentin in stitches by standing on the patio and hollering at the top of his lungs to his imaginary coon dogs down in the valley.

"Whoooeee—-catch'em, Rover! Blue's leadin' the pack! Get'em Flash!"

He was quite a character and just one of many Quentin got to know there.

Some of the local Filipino customs were hard for the servicemen to understand, especially regarding their culinary preferences. Two items of food the natives relished and considered great delicacies were fish heads and ballutes. When they ate fish heads, they sucked out the eyes before eating the rest. And they did so with the same kind of lip-smacking pleasure a southern American redneck would over a pot of turnip greens and ham hocks.

As for the ballutes, the Filipinos couldn't seem to get enough of them. They were chicken eggs but not prepared in the traditional ways. Two days before the eggs hatched, the nest was robbed. Then, the eggs were prepared according to preference: raw, pickled, or cooked. They were always served intact with the baby chicks, complete with fuzz, still inside. A hole was punched in the top and the juice sucked out first. Then, the native would peel the egg, drop the biddy into his mouth, and chew with great enjoyment.

"On just about every street corner you'd see little boys cookin' the ballutes," Quentin said. "They cooked 'em in buckets heated by pans of hot charcoal. Ever once in a while they'd yell ' Ballutes! Ballutes! Hot ballutes! Only ten centavos!' It sounded kinda like American boys sellin' peanuts at a baseball game.

"I only saw one American ever try to eat one of those things, and that was in Olongapo. There was a sailor in a bar there who was drunk as a skunk and he agreed to eat one on a bet. Didn't win, though. Before that ballute even hit bottom, he lost it all."

Another custom the servicemen had trouble accepting was how the natives disposed of their body waste. Only the wealthy had indoor bathrooms. The natives didn't even have outdoor privies. Most of them lived in thatched huts built along the creek banks. There was an open stoop extending over the water that served their purpose, so all their body wastes went into the creek where they bathed, fished, and did their laundry. The natives didn't see anything wrong with that, nor did they see anything wrong with a woman urinating while walking down the village street. According to Quentin, she would just hike her skirt, squat, and pee. There was no embarrassment.

That was the way she was raised.

There were wild chickens with beautifully colored plumage all over the Philippines. They could fly like birds. Since they were more aggressive than the domestic variety, they were often captured and trained in the national sport of cockfighting. The natives loved it and Quentin grew to enjoy it while he was there. A friend who was a local native and worked on base introduced him to the sport.

The cockfights were held every Sunday afternoon near Longapoo in a covered pit surrounded by benches. All the natives would congregate, enthusiastically bet, and root for their favorites, much like horse racing in the states. They would jabber away in their native dialect and since Quentin couldn't understand a word, his native friend placed all his bets for him.

The spectators usually consumed a good bit of liquor, home made and potent. By the time the cockfights inside the pits ended, there would be people fights outside the pits. Quentin said he had a great time.

17 | Chapter

The Seabees worked hard and when they were off duty they played hard. Since putting one over on the officers made military life more exciting, they looked on anything forbidden or any place off-limits as a direct challenge. There turned out to be another advantage to taking part in frowned-on and unconventional behavior, too...it contributed to their reputation as being tough nuts. They had worked hard for that image, were extremely proud of it, and never missed a chance to polish it.

On Sunday afternoons they would occasionally drive the line truck to the end of the point and set out on foot along a path that ran for about a half mile. Their destination was a native village on the far bank of a small creek. It had been declared off-limits because the native girls there hadn't been checked for V.D.

Once the Seabees reached the creek, they yelled to get the attention of the villagers who then paddled over and fetched them in dugout canoes. After reaching the village, they spent the afternoon lounging about, drinking the native homemade brew, and socializing with the native girls. Fortunately, the only ill effects they suffered from those trips were hangovers. There was one day, however, when they thought they were in deep trouble.

"We rounded a bend in the path and came face-to-face with two of the meanest lookin' native men I've ever seen." Quentin said. "They didn't have on anything but loin cloths and had machetes tucked in 'em. Besides the bandoliers they carried over their shoulders, each one of 'em carried a Browning automatic, a BAR WW II submachine gun. There were lots of different kinds of natives in the Philippines, includin' headhunters, and we didn't know what kind we were facin'. Besides all that, they were carryin' a long pole across their shoulders and it had two skinned monkeys hangin' on it. That was scary. Those monkeys looked just like human babies.

"None of us was feelin' very tough but the odds didn't look too bad . . . two natives against four hardened Seabees. Course they were armed and we weren't. Turned out we didn't have to worry none. They just moved over to the side of the path, looked at us out of the corner of their eyes, and let us pass. Actually, I think they were as scared of us as we were of them, but for a long time after that we avoided the village and found other ways to aggravate the higher-ups."

While taping Quentin's experiences or taking notes while he reminisced, I came to the conclusion early on that he got a vicarious thrill out of being exposed to danger, like mountain climbers, skydivers, and bungee jumpers. If it didn't come looking for him, he went looking for it. It seemed that way anyhow. Then I began to wonder if maybe he was trying to prove something to himself. Or, after what Daddy had said to him in the garden that day, maybe Quentin was trying to prove something to Daddy, too.

For instance, whenever volunteers were requested for hazardous duty, Quentin was one of the first to sign up. Like with Grandie Island, a small rock island in the mouth of Subic Bay. Ammunition was stored in caves there and closely guarded by marines. Much of the shipping in and out of the harbor passed close to Grandie Island. Therefore, work details were sent out periodically to carefully roll the shells to keep the nitroglycerine from settling to one side, which made them unstable. It was a delicate procedure and extremely dangerous. One small move and the whole place would have blown up, carrying nearby ships with it.

Quentin insisted he only volunteered because he was curious about the caves there. Perhaps. His curiosity had gotten him in trouble before. Anyway, according to scuttlebutt some of the men who survived the Bataan death march had been held prisoner on Grandie Island until they could be shipped to Japan to work in the coal mines. They had supposedly scratched their names in the caves. Since two men from Havana had survived the march and had been sent to the mines, Quentin wanted to see if their names were there. He never did, although he looked every chance he got.

There was another reminder of the Bataan death march. The Seabees had to build a road down to the bay and decided to use an old abandoned water tank to store asphalt for paving the strip. The tank was huge and was located on top of a mountain on the Bataan peninsula. The first task was to move the water tank *off* the mountain, and since it was made of solid wood, they decided to drag it with cables attached to three bulldozers.

When they went to inspect the tank and make preparations for its removal, they found it contained several skeletons and articles of rotted clothing. The authorities were notified. When they investigated they determined the skeletons belonged to American prisoners who had been put there by the Japanese and starved to death. The sides of the tank were clawed where the men had tried to climb out.

In spite of the tough image Quentin has worked so hard to get, he really is a softy when it comes to children, animals, old people, family, or just about anybody who's having rough times. The next episode shows that side of him much better than I could describe it.

Even though they had problems communicating, Quentin became friends with a Filipino native who had been hired by the military to assist the line crew. He dug holes and helped out wherever he was needed. The man was married, had five small children, and was extremely poor, a condition shared by a large percentage of the population. Time limits prevented the man from going home for lunch, so he brought his lunch to work every day. He always ate the same thing: fish heads and rice wrapped in a green banana leaf. He didn't have a sack, but he knew how to fold the leaf so it sealed in the greasy food, which he ate with his fingers.

With a lot of grunting and sign language, the native invited Quentin to visit him and his family in the village. Quentin began going there on Saturdays, occasionally, and grew attached to the whole family. Their thatched house, which consisted of one large room, was built on stilts out over the creek. Cooking was done on a small charcoal brazier in one corner of the room, and the family slept on mats. Their clothes hung along the wall. The one thing that impressed Quentin the most, however, was how immaculate the inside was. The floors were scrubbed with coconut fiber until they shone, and everyone's shoes were removed before entering.

Quentin's visits were considered special occasions, and when they knew he was coming the family cooked a pot of pork and rice. Since he knew they could only afford fish, he felt honored. The pork, which was greasy and full of chunks, was served in the same pot in which it was cooked, and a big bowl of rice was served on the side. Everyone sat on the floor around a low table with the pot in the center, and they all ate with their hands. Quentin hadn't forgotten their personal hygiene customs, but he tried not to think about it and always ate with great relish to keep from hurting their feelings.

"It was the little children I felt sorriest for," Quentin said. "They all looked malnourished and were covered with sores. I could see they didn't eat a balanced diet and couldn't afford any better. So before I went to visit I made a trip to ship's store and stocked up on all kinds of stuff. Besides that, I always tried to take a little candy for the children, some Vienna sausage which was everybody's favorite and Kool-Aid. They didn't have ice but loved Kool-Aid, especially the mama. Sometimes they mixed the drink with homemade brew and the men would get stoned."

When I asked Quentin about snakes in the Philippines, he said, "We saw pythons sometimes but they didn't cause trouble except nearly scare us to death. Like the time the Seabees had to clear a right-of-way on a curve around the mountain. We used bulldozers to push over some huge mahogany trees; some of 'em were eight to ten feet in diameter. They didn't have a tap-root and were easy to topple if you hit 'em high and hard with the blade of the dozer.

"One day a dozer operator hit a tree with his dozer blade and a python fell out of the tree, landed across the hood, then slithered to the ground. That driver, even though he had the shit scared out of him, reacted fast and dropped the dozer blade on the snake. Killed him dead. They measured him . . . coulda been a 'her' . . . at twenty-one feet long. Right away the Seabee painters put up a sign and named the road 'Python Bend'. The sign was still up when we left the Philippines."

The monetary exchange system off base was strict, but there were ways of getting around it if a fellow was smart enough and gutsy enough. When the servicemen reached the checkpoint into Longapoo, they were required to exchange their greenbacks for Philippine currency: pesos and centavos. It was against the law for an American to have greenbacks within the town limits and was a court-martial offense. This was strictly enforced. Quentin didn't know the purpose of the law and he didn't particularly care one way or the other. All he knew was that he wasn't about to let it screw up the surefire way he had found of making spending money.

He didn't smoke at that time and all the men were issued a cigarette ration of one carton a week at a charge of ninety cents. He collected his, plus that of his nonsmoking friends, and smuggled them into Longapoo by hiding six packs inside the tops of his socks. Each pack brought three pesos ($1.50) on the black market. When he left town, he exchanged the Philippine currency for American, making a profit of $1.41 on each pack. That's how he made the money he needed for his R & R trips to Bagio...a most important cause, he thought, and well worth the effort.

Sometime later, when he found out the reason for the strict greenback law, he had a few misgivings about his dealing with the black market.

After weeks and sometimes months at sea, whole fleets put in at Subic Bay and hordes of sailors poured into Olongapo on leave. They were wild-eyed and ready to party, but they needed money, which was readily available since one American dollar could be swapped for four pesos at any bar in town. That's a two-for-one rate of exchange. The sailors jumped on it eagerly and there was a whole of swapping going on until authorities put a stop to it.

Some of the servicemen on permanent duty really had a thing going. They would have their parents send them cash in their letters. Then they sneaked the money into Olongapo, traded it for pesos at two-or-one, and then exchanged the pesos for American as they left. They made a lot of money and few were ever caught, according to Quentin.

The reason greenbacks were so valuable was because of the cold war going on at that time. The communists were trying to take over the world and needed money to support their American agents. Eva, the manager of the New Life Nightclub in Olongapo, had been recruited by the communists to collect all greenbacks in town. She kept a satchel full of money in her apartment, and once a month she delivered the money to her communist contact. That person would send it to the agents in the U.S. Eva didn't really understand the important role she was playing. She was paid a percentage and to her it was just a way to supplement her meager income. She only made thirty pesos ($30) a month and struggled daily to support herself and her small son. Like most of the other girls, Eva was ambitious. She had dreams of going to the U.S. someday where the work wasn't so hard and the opportunities greater.

Eva not only ran the New Life Nightclub but also occasionally helped with the entertainment by singing, dancing, and playing the piano. Her appearance was unlike the full-blooded Filipino women who tended to be shorter and stockier. She was tall, nicely proportioned, and had a creamy complexion, brown eyes, and long curly black hair. Her looks reflected her part-Portuguese ancestry and her musical talent, intelligence, and business acumen were probably due to her affluent upbringing. Her father was a highly respected and very busy physician in Manila until the Japanese invaded the Philippines in 1942.

Eva was fourteen years old at the time. When the Japanese forces threatened the city, her father took the family and fled into the jungles where he joined a gorilla force. It was a hard life, filled with constant danger, and one to which his family was unaccustomed. They were constantly on the move, keeping one step ahead of the Japanese whom they fired upon and harassed at every opportunity.

One day an Australian pilot crash-landed his plane in the jungle near the gorilla stronghold and the gorillas pulled the badly injured pilot to safety. Eva was given the responsibility of tending his wounds and nursing him back to health. Somewhere along the way, the nurse/patient relationship became a more intimate one and Eva became pregnant. Her family was outraged and unsympathetic. Being devout Catholics, they thought her pregnancy out-of-wedlock was the ultimate disgrace. The pilot refused to marry Eva and returned to his unit when the Americans liberated the islands. After she gave birth to a baby boy, Eva was disowned by her family and banished from their sight.

She eventually made her way to Olongapo, got a job at the New Life nightclub, and rented a room in a boarding house. It was a large, crudely built, two-story frame structure that also gave shelter to several other taxi dancers from the nightclub. Each had a private room with a bare minimum of furniture and shared a communal bath and kitchen. The windows were screenless and had wooden shutters. For protection against the mosquitoes that were a constant problem, the beds were enclosed with mosquito netting. An elderly Filipino woman, who also cared for Eva's little boy while she worked, oversaw the place.

By now I'm sure you're wondering how Quentin knew so much about this woman. That's because for several months she was an important part of his life. He explained how that came about.

Quentin saw Eva for the first time not long after he arrived in the Philippines. The New Life Club had a reputation on the base as being the nicest place in town and was, therefore, very popular with the servicemen. It had fewer rowdies, and the best looking taxi dancers in town. They were hired to dance with the men and encourage them to drink. Since the girls received no salary but did receive a percentage on the drinks, they were motivated to be extra friendly.

One Saturday night Quentin went to Olongapo on liberty, and decided to check out this nightclub he had been hearing so much about. He found a corner table and sat with his back against the wall, quietly drinking beer, listening to the live band, and watching the other servicemen dance with the girls.

He spotted Eva right away because she stood out from the rest of the girls. She was very beautiful, but had the reputation of being undatable. Most of the servicemen had tried to date her at one time or another and they all failed. Even Rosati struck out, then the crew chief. Based on that, Quentin didn't think he stood a dog's chance so he didn't make the effort. Actually, he still felt shy and a little ill at ease around good-looking women.

Every Saturday night that he wasn't on R and R. at Bagio, Quentin caught the cattle truck into Olongapo and spent the evening at the New Life, sitting at his favorite table against the wall, drinking beer, and wistfully admiring the girls. Eventually, Eva began stopping by his table to sit and chat, and gradually Quentin began to lose some of his shyness. She had a little trouble with English and Quentin's name was especially hard for her to pronounce, so Whittle became "Wheetle."

It may have been his quietness, in contrast to the others, that attracted her initially. Or maybe it was the mannerly way he treated all the girls. Then again it might have been his blond good looks that appealed to her. At any rate, she began to spend an increasing amount of time at his table and sometimes bought his beer, which was extremely unusual.

One night as they were sitting and chatting, Eva asked him, "Wheetle, do you have a honeyco?" (Honeyco was a Filipino term that loosely meant boyfriend, girlfriend, mate, partner, etc) When he answered no, she casually asked, "Would you like to be mine?" Naturally he said yes. Our parents didn't raise any idiots.

His life changed a great deal after that. For one thing, he was afforded new respect by all his navy buddies for Eva was considered the pick of Longapoo. Theirs was an arrangement that seemed to benefit both equally. For his part, Quentin received Eva's fidelity, Saturday night at her place, and Sunday morning breakfast. Being Quentin's honeyco protected Eva from further harassment of other servicemen. She became strictly hands-off, an unspoken rule but one all the servicemen recognized and honored. Quentin paid half her rent and brought her goodies from the ship's store, things like Hershey bars and cosmetics that were difficult to come by and highly treasured. Once she asked him to bring her "weekly panties," the ones with the days of the week stitched on the side. He reneged on that request. The idea of going into the store where all the dependents shopped and asking for women's underwear turned him red with embarrassment. He tried to get her anything else she asked for, though, and he took her out to eat and to the movies occasionally.

After nine months of Eva's companionship, and four days before he was to ship out, Quentin received orders to return to the states. He went to Eva's that last Saturday night to break the news, expecting her to be disappointed or a little sad over his leaving. That wasn't the reaction he got, however. Although they had never discussed it, and he had never made promises or committed himself, she had assumed she would go back to the states with him. He couldn't picture her in a Havana setting, and there was no way he could support a wife and stepson on his income. But, in all honesty, he hadn't discouraged her assumptions either . . . and that turned out to be a major mistake.

When Quentin tried to explain why he couldn't take her, Eva began angry. And the more he talked the angrier she became. Finally, with a shriek she sailed on him, biting, scratching, and cursing, using words he didn't think she knew.

"She was mad as a wet settin' hen," Quentin said. "I finally managed to get the table between us, wonderin' what she was gonna do next. Then she ran across the room and grabbed a big bolo knife from under the mattress and started for me again. That knife was twelve inches long with a razor-sharp curved blade. It was a mean lookin' sucker and I decided right then I had outstayed my welcome. I dived headfirst out the window, landed in a mud hole and slid part way into the creek. She was hangin' out the window, wavin' that knife around and cursin' somethin' fierce, 'I'll cut your throat, Wheetle, you son of a beech! ' I got the hell out of there and made fast tracks to the bus stop."

The last cattle truck left at one-thirty and the usual crowd of drunken servicemen were waiting. The shore patrol was there, trying to contain the mixed bunch of sailors, marines, and air force enlisted men. Service rivalry could become pretty hot after an evening of beer guzzling so fist-fights and brawls were common at the bus terminal. Quentin, with his sport shirt in tatters, his arms and face scratched and bloody, and his loafers and khakis covered with mud, blended right into the group. He didn't draw a second glance from the shore patrol.

"I regretted the way we parted," Quentin said. "Eva was good to me and I was really very fond of her. After thinkin' about it, I kinda figured that once she calmed down a little she would understand my position and accept it. I was wrong about that, too."

The next day and every day thereafter until he left, Quentin received threatening notes from Eva. They were hand delivered by a Hawaiian named Eng, a first-class navy man. He was also a mutual friend but had no idea of the note's contents, which were pretty graphic.

"Wheetle, I have hired a Huk to slit your no-good throat. You better sleep with one eye open!" The others were just as bad, but Quentin worried more about the Huk. He knew it could be true.

"The Huks were a bloodthirsty lot. They were so sneaky they could slip past the patrollin' marine guards, creep into the huts, and steal money from under the pillows of the sleepin' Seabees. It happened more than once." Quentin said. "Needless to say, I spent three nights tryin' to stay awake and three days lookin' over my shoulder. I was plum worn out by the time we were ready to leave."

On the day of departure, all the men shipping out were transported to the harbor at Olongapo by bus, and then they marched to the waiting ship. All the honeycos on good terms with the men lined the road and yelled and cheered as they passed. Quentin knew Eva had many friends and he wasn't taking any chances, so he positioned himself near the center of the company and hoped the uniforms gave him some degree of anonymity.

When he was finally on board ship he managed to relax his guard for the first time in three long days. He thought of Eva often, sometimes with sadness, but more often with relief that she hadn't relieved him of some vital part of his anatomy. He knew he had made the right decision, would never see her again, and could get on with his life. That's what he thought, anyway.

18 | Chapter

After his Philippine tour of duty, Quentin was home on leave and feeling restless. Most of his old friends were married or had left for greener pastures, since there wasn't much in Havana to hold them. He and Daddy had made several trips to the river fishing but now he was ready for a different kind of action. So, he called his pal, Hilda Dodson.

Quentin met Hilda for the first time when he was a junior in high school. They immediately became friends, nothing romantic, just good friends. She was witty, attractive, always laughing, and fun to be around. In the years to follow, anytime Quentin was home, felt lonely, and needed fun times, he looked up Hilda. Sometimes they double dated, and sometimes she just fixed him up with a friend. He could always count on her, and she didn't let him down this time, either.

Hilda immediately lined up an evening's entertainment, a wiener roast on the shores of Lake Jackson. There were several couples there, all friends of Hilda's with their dates. Within the crowd was a tall, slim, very pretty girl with shoulder-length curly black hair and brown eyes. Her name was Thais Ann Hall. She worked in one of the state offices in Tallahassee but grew up in Blountstown, Florida. Her date for the evening was a pilot stationed at the Air Force Base in Bainbridge. His identical twin brother was also there with his date.

"All I could remember, later, about the people at that party were the two girls who had twins for dates," Quentin laughed. "They all sat on a log, smoochin', and I wondered how the hell they could tell who was smoochin' who."

Thais' memory of her first meeting with Quentin was much clearer.

"I thought he was much too good looking. But the thing that impressed me the most was that he knew how to build a fire properly, and how to sharpen palmetto sticks to roast the wieners on. He was the only man in the group who did."

Quentin might have been more attentive had he foreseen the important role Thais would play in his future. I'll get to that eventually. Try to use a little patience here.

When leave was over, Quentin took the Dodge back to California, stopping by the bus station in Memphis to pick up Rosati who had spent his leave in Pennsylvania. They reported back to Port Hueneme expecting to stay put for the remaining six months of their service time and they were counting down the days. They should have known better. One thing Quentin learned in service was to expect the unexpected, so he shouldn't have been surprised when he and Rosati were sent directly to electrical school in Los Angeles. They were paid per diem, put up in a motel, and trained in cable splicing with the Los Angeles Gas and Light Co.

There were no orders cut and no time given as to when they had to report back to Port Hueneme, so they decided to make the most of that military screw-up and stay as long as they liked. When school was completed, they just remained in L.A., spending their days tossing darts and their nights juking. They were having a grand time until their money ran out. That meant a trip back to Port Hueneme. Their plan was to slip on base, sneak over to the records department, draw more money, and hightail it back to L.A. where they would resume their life of leisure.

Sometimes the most carefully laid out plans screw up. When they arrived back on base, they discovered their company had just shipped out, headed back to the Philippines, with all their records. That meant they couldn't get money without their records, and they were in deep poop with the military authorities. The officers in charge tried to blame Quentin and Rosati with the mix-up in records and threatened them with AWOL charges if they didn't join their unit, pronto. Under the circumstances, they thought they had rebelled enough and had better comply.

Arrangements were made for them to take a military flight to the Philippines. They were to leave from the base at San Luis Obispo, one hundred fifty miles north of Port Hueneme and fifty miles south of San Francisco. With no time to spare, they jumped in the Dodge and burned rubber, and lots of motor oil, heading north. As they neared the base, Quentin saw a large warehouse sign that said, *Car Storage by Day, Week, or Month.* He wheeled in, tossed his keys to the man in charge, and said, "Sir, I'd like to store my car, and I don't know when I'll be back!" Then, they grabbed their duffel bags, ran out front, and caught a cab to the base. Unfortunately, in his haste, Quentin forgot to get the name of the storage place or the address.

The plane, which was loading when they arrived, was an old four-engine military transport, and the passengers had to sit on seats that were so hard every bump was an insult to their tailbones. The crew was made up of military personnel and the plane was loaded with medical supplies and mail. Refueling stops were scheduled for Honolulu, Kwajalein, and Guam.

The first lap was uneventful, smooth considering the seating arrangements. Then, half way between Honolulu and Kwajalein, an engine conked out. The pilot immediately feathered the opposite engine to maintain balance. Because the load was too heavy for just two engines, the plane began losing altitude, so the pilot decided to divert to Johnston Island, which had the closest landing strip.

In order to make it that far, Quentin and the others were told to jettison the cargo to lighten the load. They heaved huge crates of medical supplies and sacks of mail through the open cargo doors, but the plane continued to lose altitude. At that point, a dip in the ocean looked inevitable. They put on life jackets, sat huddled in their seats, and waited.

The pilot performed a miracle, kept the old plane in the air, and they touched down on Johnston Island intact. The island itself was nothing more than a good-sized sand bar and was manned by about one hundred air force personnel who rotated every six months. They had to or go nuts. The air base was designed especially for emergencies such as theirs, which was fortunate. Engine parts and mechanics were flown in from Honolulu, while the plane crewmen and passengers waited.

"Every day for four days, they worked on that plane. Me and Rosati would watch that plane circlin' overhead. The engine was spittin' and sputterin' with every pass. We didn't trust that piece of junk and was hopin' they'd make another plane available to us. They didn't."

Finally, the mechanics declared the plane in good flying condition, the crew and passengers reluctantly reloaded, and they continued on their way . . . for a while, at least. About half way to Kwajalein, that same engine began acting up again, popping and vibrating. Once again the pilot coaxed it along until they reached the base at Kwajalein. There, the whole working/testing routine was repeated until the mechanics once again declared it fit to fly. And once again they resumed their journey.

"Halfway to Guam that same cantankerous engine began the same damn shenanigans," Quentin said. "By this time we all figured that plane wadn't gonna get us there and we were gonna crash, sure as hell. So we were all surprised when we made it to Guam. I was about ready to go by ship the rest of the way. At least I stood a chance of surviving with the seasickness.

"We left Guam goin' to the Philippines on that same cuss-fired plane. We couldn't believe it. But the engine had caused so much trouble up till then, we figured there wadn't nothing else could go wrong. We were located at the halfway point between Guam and the Philippines, over open sea, when we ran into the worst thunderstorm I've ever seen. The turbulence was unbelievable. We would hit an air pocket and drop one-fifty to two hundred feet. The crew chief strapped us into metal racks similar to those on a bus, where belongings are stored above the seats, only we were lower down. We had on Mae West life jackets and there were parachutes stacked in the back, but we weren't told how to use them. We wouldn't have stood a chance in the open sea anyhow.

"Since our situation wasn't miserable enough, all of us became deathly seasick. Not just me, either. The whole bunch includin' the crew chief. I was wearin' my white uniform and would hold my cap over the side of the rack to barf in. I figured that was as bad as it could get, but I was wrong . . . the radio and radar went out. By that time I was too sick to care, thought I was dying anyway, so what the hell.

"We were all surprised when we made it to Manila. As we approached, we could see the lights on Langley Point, an airfield that sticks way out in Manila Bay. A small plane escorted us in. As we got closer, I could see fire boats below with lights flashing, just like fire trucks, and they were there for the same purpose . . . waiting for us to crash. Scared hell out of us but we landed O.K.".

Quentin and Rosati remained at Langley Air Field three days before catching a PBY to the base at Subic Bay. During that time, they watched with amusement as the mechanics worked yet again on that same plane. Finally, on the day before they were to leave, they noticed the plane was being loaded with dependents, women and children, about fifteen in all, headed for the states. The same military crew was assigned the flight.

"They took off smoothly enough, no problems, but about thirty minutes later we heard the fire sirens start up and here came that damn plane back with engine spittin' and sputterin'. The passengers deplaned first, then the crew, and finally the pilot. As he came down the stairwell, we could tell his face was red as a beet, and he was doing some serious cussin'. He was really pissed off. When he reached the bottom, he yanked off his old floppy military hat, threw it on the ground, and stomped it. We understood how he felt but cracked up laughin' anyway."

Quentin and Rosati were assigned the same living quarters they had previously and they settled in for another five months. It was like they had never left, except for Eva. For several weeks, Quentin didn't go into Olongapo. He was afraid Eva was still out for revenge and he didn't want to tempt her. Rosati was still in good standing at the New Life so resumed his jaunts into town. Eventually, Eva found out Quentin was back and began sending him sweet notes, asking him to come see her. He decided to stay put. But after a few more weeks, he began to go stir-crazy and decided to chance a trip to town. His intent to keep a low profile and avoid the New Life didn't work. One of the local girls saw him on the street, told Eva, and within a few minutes she was shoving her way through the crowds and yelling,"Wheetle! Wheetle!" His first impulse was to bolt but then decided he had hidden long enough, so he braced himself, expecting to see her bolo knife come flying out. She totally stunned him by rushing up and greeting him like a long, lost relative, all friendly and nice. They went back to the club and she bought him a beer for old times sake. After that, she always treated him with warmth and friendliness with no sign of hostility. He didn't know why she had changed but he was deeply relieved anyway.

"I even tried to find her a good man, but she wadn't interested. Over the years, I've thought of her occasionally and wondered how her life turned out, and if she ever made it to the states. I hope so."

Once they made it back to the states and were finally discharged, Quentin and Rosati began touring the area, trying to find the car storage business where he left the Dodge. Since he had no address and couldn't remember the name of the business, Quentin decided finding it would be about as easy as finding a black man at a KKK convention. When they were about to give it up as a lost cause, Quentin spotted a building that looked familiar. They stopped and went in. The man in charge was the same sharp-eyed old geezer who took the car keys five months before. Surprisingly, he remembered Quentin and told him he had decided the car had been abandoned He was planning on selling it the next day for the storage fees. Quentin ransomed it just in time, although the charges were probably more than the car was worth.

Now that they were free as birds, Quentin and Rosati decided to take their time going home and enjoy being back in the U.S. They had spent thirty-six months of their four years service time overseas and it was good to be back. Bill Fischer from Rochester, Minnesota, another of their navy buddies, decided to drive partway across country with them and share traveling expenses as well as the good times they anticipated.

They loaded the Dodge and headed east. Sometimes they stopped by the side of the road and had Vienna sausage, soda crackers, and cokes for lunch. Sometimes they slept out under the stars or in the car to save on motels. But when they reached Reno they decided to splurge and enjoy a little gambling before passing through. They didn't know when they would have that opportunity again, if ever, and that was excuse enough.

According to Frank Rosati, they dropped $700 along the way but their biggest expense was the Dodge. Every time they stopped for gas, they had to put in oil, and it looked like they were laying down a smoke screen along the highway. "Geraldine" was definitely past her prime.

They decided to stop in Rock Springs, Wyoming, and see one of their Seabee buddies, Jim Mehle, who had been discharged earlier. When they asked around, he was quite well known. His mother owned one of the nicest bars in town, and the Mehle family knew a lot of people, including, as it turned out, the madam of a local cat house. Prostitution wasn't against the law in Wyoming and was actually considered a legitimate enterprise. Jim immediately decided that part of the evening's entertainment should be a trip to his favorite house of ill repute.

He drove them to an attractive house in a pleasant, clean-appearing neighborhood. It looked like any ordinary house to Quentin, no outside red lights or anything else to indicate what it really was. With Quentin and Rosati trailing after him, Jim strolled up the front walk and rang the doorbell. Quentin, not wanting his two companions to know this was his first experience in such matters, was trying his darndest to act nonchalant and a little bored with it all.

The bell was answered shortly by a middle-aged fairly attractive woman who ushered them into a nicely furnished parlor that contained three couches and a jukebox. Jim seemed relaxed. He immediately started an animated conversation with the madam, while Rosati and Quentin sat on one of the couches and tried not to fidget.

Eventually, five or six girls sauntered in, dressed in negligees, and began parading around the room, swaying their hips, and looking slightly bored, like they had done the routine a million times before. Quentin decided they weren't too bad looking, maybe little shop-worn. Rosati popped some money in the jukebox and asked one of the girls to dance. The madam apparently decided enough preliminaries had taken place, walked over and said, "Well, you've seen the merchandise. See anyone you like?" She might have been discussing a refrigerator.

Quentin pointed to a short brunette and Rosati chose another. They all traipsed down a long hall lined with doors. Each couple entered a room. Once inside Quentin wasn't sure what his next move was supposed to be but he needn't have worried. The girl, as brisk and impersonal as a doctor, began to examine him for V.D. Then she started putting some sort of disinfectant in certain places.

Quentin said, "I was flabbergasted, and if I hadn't been so damned embarrassed I would have burst out laughin'. She didn't seem to notice, just asked me if I wanted a short job for ten dollars, a medium for fifteen dollars, or all night for twenty dollars. I chose the medium and paid her. Hell, I didn't have any idea what that entailed, but I figured a short job would be about like a rabbit performance and I had more confidence in myself than that. The all-nighter sounded a little ambitious and besides I couldn't afford it.

"As it turned out, I had overestimated my capabilities anyway. Or as the prostitute dryly said, afterwards, 'Swabbie, you would have lost money on the short job.' I tried to talk her into lettin' me get my money's worth, figurin' I might do better the second time around, but she wadn't a bit sympathetic.

"That whole thing embarrassed the hell out of me but I guess I shouldn't have been. It was just business as usual to her. I took as long as I could gettin' dressed, stallin' as long as I dared before goin' back to the parlor to meet Jim and Rosati. I expected a long wait, and then a lot of ribbin' from them, but to my great surprise and pleasure, there sat Rosati, all dressed and patiently waitin'.

"He looked at me and I looked at him and we both burst out laughin'. That wadn't the only laugh we had over our cat-house visit. It was an experience . . . but once was enough."

They ended up in Champaign, Illinois, where Harve and I were living while he attended the U.of I. Quentin wanted to surprise me, which he certainly did. I just answered a knock at the door and there he was...big as life. I was so excited to see him but we were just leaving for Alton, Illinois, Harve's hometown, when he arrived. It was a trip we couldn't get out of, unfortunately, so our visit together was cut short. Rosati caught a bus to his home in Pennsylvania and Quentin followed us to Alton. He decided Geraldine would never make it to Florida and, at Harve's suggestion, decided to see what kind of car deal he could get in St. Louis.

Quentin said, "I didn't realize when I dropped Rosati off at the bus station that it would be forty years before we saw each other again. He was one of my best friends in service, we shared a lot of experiences, but when he got out of the car in Illinois, we lost contact. I thought about him a lot over the years, as well as Bazolli and some of my other navy friends."

The next morning Quentin took the Dodge across the river to St. Louis and traded it for a spiffy turquoise and white 1954 Chevy Bel-Air with big whitewall tires. It had 7500 miles on it and cost him $1400 of his mustering-out pay, but he was thrilled over it. He was on his way home and he was going in style, by golly!

"I had the strangest feeling as I was cruising along the highway," Quentin said. "For the first time in four years I felt totally relaxed. I was alone for the first time in four years . . . really alone . . . and I found I enjoyed the solitude of my own company. I still do. At that time though, I found myself hatin' for the trip to end, even though I was lookin' forward to seein' the folks."

With his service obligation paid off, Quentin returned home with four years of solid, electrical experience behind his belt. His future was a blank page once again and he wasn't sure how he wanted to fill it. As a stopgap measure, he applied for and got a job with the Talquin Electric Cooperative in Quincy. The work was hard and dirty, and the pay wasn't anything to brag about, but the job would do temporarily. There was one thing he decided for sure...climbing poles until he was so old and crippled with arthritis he couldn't get his butt off the ground wasn't how he wanted to spend the rest of his life. There had to be something better.

To save on expenses, Quentin decided to live at the farm. After paying room and board, he still had enough left each payday to take care of car expenses and an occasional movie or date. Finding someone to date was his biggest problem. His rabbit-hunting girl friends had gotten married while he was overseas and there didn't seem to be many single girls his age left around Havana. On impulse he once again called his old pal Hilda for her assistance with his social life. He knew she was always ready for parties and good times. Not this time, though. Since she, too, had gotten married, she was no longer queen bee of the social scene. Her new husband was Terry Poston. But Hilda was Hilda, and sensing he was lonely, she immediately set up a double date: she and Terry, and Quentin with one of her office friends, Thais Hall. Remember her? Quentin didn't, at first.

He related their first date this way: "I volunteered to do the drivin'. I was real proud of my car and wanted to show it off to this girl, whoever she was. We were supposed to spend the day at the beach on Alligator Point so I picked up Hilda and Terry first, then we all went by my date's apartment to pick her up.

"My first thought when she answered the door was how in the world I could have forgotten a girl that good-lookin'. I was really impressed, and before the day was over I was impressed with more that just her looks. Besides bein' easy to talk to and fun to be around, she knew how to handle an awkward situation without causin' a lot of embarrassment, at least to me.

"When we got back to town that afternoon, I was flat busted broke. I had bought all the gas, snacks, and beer durin' the day. Then Hilda suggested we stop by KFC and pick up a bucket of chicken for supper at their apartment. I didn't know what to say. I figured anything I said or did right then wadn't goin' to make me look good, and I did want to impress this girl. But Thais, bless her little heart, saw what was happenin' and loaned me the money to pay for the chicken. She was real nice about it, too, kinda smoothed it over. Come to think of it, I don't think I ever did pay her back." Quentin laughed.

He has never been a shallow person, his feelings go deep, and so when he finally fell in love he fell hard. The day after their first date, Quentin told Daddy point blank that he had met the girl he was going to marry. It was a statement of fact. Daddy, being Daddy, proceeded to give him a little counseling on marriage and the pitfalls thereof. That was a given, because Daddy usually had a spontaneous lecture tailored for any subject, and he wasn't at all bashful about sharing his wisdom. Mostly, he just shoveled up a lot of common sense and since we all respected his opinion, we listened. Many times we would seek him out, especially if we were faced with a tough decision. This wasn't decision-making time, though. Quentin knew what he wanted. After listening through all of it, he said firmly and without hesitation," Yes sir, I'm sure. She's the one I want to marry."

Thais wasn't as sure, more cautious you might say. He had to do some wooing before she was ready to take the jump. I've wondered at times what would have happened if Thais had refused his proposal. He probably wouldn't have ever married, just turned into a crotchety old bachelor. As it was he had his work cut out for him. Courting Thais wasn't always easy. There were times when things didn't go well at all, like that night in August of 1956.

We had all congregated at the farm to spend time together for a couple weeks. The old house was overflowing with adults and children, and there was still no indoor plumbing. That meant a serious lack of privacy, of course. Quentin had a heavy date with

Thais that night and wanted to spruce up and make a favorable impression. He thought he had matters well in hand

When he drug in from work, he was hot, sweaty, bone-tired, and smelling so bad he could have given a polecat competition in a stinking contest. He decided an all-over bath and shampoo was an absolute necessity before he could pick up Thais. With that intent in mind, he filled the old cast iron wash pot with water, piled wood around the base, and heated it to a comfortable temperature. Rather than transfer the water to a washtub to bathe in, he decided to eliminate the middle step to save time. It was dust dark already and he didn't want to be late. Deciding he was far enough from the house for privacy, Quentin stripped off his clothes and stepped into the wash pot. Just as he was settling down with a grunt of satisfaction, the three-legged pot tipped over, dumping him and the water onto the ash and mud covered ground.

He didn't get burned, but he *was* late for his date. When he straggled to the house, covered with mud, a towel wrapped around his waist, and grinning sheepishly, we all cracked up laughing. It was sympathetic laughter, of course. But, even though things didn't seem to be going so well in his love life, Thais continued to show interest. It could be, at that time anyway, that she was just fascinated by a man who could get himself in such ridiculous situations.

School Days *1941-42*

1937 • Edwina, 7 years old
Quentin 5¹/² years old

1937 • Quentin & Edwina

1938 • *Back Row:* Myra, Wintston.
Front Row: Quentin, Edwina

1946 • Jerry & Quentin in cane field

1948 • Quentin & "Janie"

1943 • Quentin(11¹/²), Edwina(13), & "Rodie"

1948 • Quentin & "Jerking Josephine" (1930 Model A Ford)

"The Farm" (after renovation)

1944 • *Left to right:* Myra, Edwina, Winston, Quentin, Verda Mae & Cecil Whittle

1950 • Quentin at the beach Naples, Florida

1950 • Quentin and his date for high school prom, Betty Kelly

Working in Naples, Florida (Quentin on bottom)

1950 • Quentin's first job in Naples, Florida

1950•Quentin & Jerry's trailer, "Ye Ole Harpoon House"—Washington, D.C.

"Geraldine" • 1950 Dodge Wayfarer

Quentin and his "Pride & Joy", a 1941 Ford Coupe

*Front Row(left to right):*Cunningham, Woods, Rosati, Markowski, Zander, Maziers, Cobery, Bird, Day, Dent, Richardson, Hendrix. *Middle Row:*Phleger, McIntire, Dunne, Duncan, Dunn, Vassalo, Pleleps, Whittle. *Top Row:* Bizzaro, Fischer, Granet, Ross, McSwain, Lebkicker, Burrows.

1953 • Quentin and friend, "Bingo"-Guam

1953 • Quentin and "Transportation" on Guam

1954 • Quentin and Dad on leave after Guam

1953 • ("Georgia Boy"), Cantrell at Guam

1953• Quentin with friends and "Transportation" at Guam

1953• Guam Antennae fields

1953• Quentin and Sea Bee Hut

1954• Construction Battalion #1504, New Year's Eve party (Quentin and Bingo in center)

1984 • "The Taco Times" Wed., Aug. 1

1957 • *Quentin*

1970's • Highway Patrol School in Tallahassee. (Quentin, first row, third from left)

1955 • Thais before Quentin

1955 • Eva, Philippines

1965 • Head of petroleum corporation presents Quentin the first Trooper of the Year Award.

1965 • Lt. Gilbert, left and Capt. Cosson, right, admire Quentin's Trooper of the Year Award.

1958 • Quentin and Thais with 1st born, Mark

Quentin Whittle family
Naval Academy **1976**

19 | CHAPTER

With marriage in mind, if he could convince Thais, Quentin began giving some serious thought to finding a better job, something with a future and more money. He was definitely motivated.

Late one afternoon he stopped at the Truck Terminal Diner on highway 27 north of Havana to grab a bite to eat. As usual, he looked and smelled like he had spent the day in a hog wallow. He hesitated about going inside but his hunger pangs won out. After he seated himself in a booth and ordered, he looked around to see if he knew any of the other customers. Sitting up at the counter was one of his old classmates, Joe Peavy, and Joe spotted Quentin at about the same time.

"Joe came right over and sat down," Quentin said. "He started tellin' me about the Highway Patrol School in Tallahassee, where he was goin'. Then he started tellin' me I ought to apply. He said the patrol was expandin' and actively recruitin' young men. I sat there and compared my nasty, sweaty clothes to Joe's neat, clean appearance, and decided to give the idea some real serious consideration."

A few days after talking to Joe, Quentin received the same advice from Sgt. Ralph Strong, who for many years had been the only trooper in Gadsden County. Everyone either knew him personally or knew *of* him. Quentin met Sgt. Strong for the first time in the fall of 1951. That meeting didn't happen under the best of circumstances.

Just after Quentin returned from Washington, D.C. and before he entered service, his 1941 Ford Coupe quit running. I was a senior in nurse's training and taking my psychiatric affiliation at the Florida State Mental Hospital in Chattahoochee.

Quentin took a notion to pay me a visit there so he borrowed Daddy's old Dodge pickup truck to make the sixty-six-mile round trip. On his way back home, about midnight, the truck headlights suddenly went out.

"It was so black I couldn't see anything, not even three feet in front of me. I just stomped the brakes and they automatically locked up. The tires started squallin' and I skidded all over the place before I finally hit the right shoulder. I was scared to death, so I just sat there awhile tryin' to calm down and figure out what to do. There wadn't any traffic and I couldn't see a light anywhere. By my calculations I knew I had to be near the airport on State Road 12 going toward Havana, since I had just left Quincy. There wadn't a telephone at the farm then so I couldn't call Daddy for help, and it was a mighty long way to walk. I didn't have money for a wrecker either.

"I was just sittin' there tryin' to decide what to do when Sgt. Strong drove up. His house was nearby and he had already gone to bed when he heard the brakes screamin'. He thought there might be an accident and came down to see. I'll never forget how nice and courteous he was to me and how helpful. He knew Daddy and Uncle Barney and he drove me all the way to the farm in his patrol car. I was totally impressed. He talked to me even then about gettin' on the patrol, and I remember thinkin' how satisfyin' it must be to have a job like that, where you could help people in trouble. I knew I would be goin' in service soon so I didn't give it anymore thought.

"Just after I talked to Joe at the diner, Sgt. Strong showed up at the farm one day. He heard that I had been discharged from service, and he came out to talk to me again about applyin' for the patrol school. They had the older troopers out lookin' for applicants.

"It was hot as blue blazes that Saturday morning and I was mowin' the lawn, barefooted and wearin' nothin' but a pair of jeans. We stood out under one of the big oaks, slappin' gnats, and talkin'. He told me that the patrol was lookin' for two hundred good men and he thought I would make a good recruit. He urged me to apply."

Even afterwards, Sgt. Strong continued to encourage Quentin and, unknowingly, gave him the inspiration he needed to succeed. "In my mind, "Quentin said, "Sgt. Strong was the ideal lawman and I tried real hard, always, to pattern myself after him."

A few days later Quentin filled out an application in Tallahassee. He thought it was a simple matter, cut and dried, but he found out that getting accepted was an involved process. His background was thoroughly investigated. When his supervisor at Talquin was interviewed, he immediately called Quentin in and offered him a twenty-five-cents-an-hour pay raise. He was making $1.25 an hour at the time, which seemed almighty cheap for working with hot wires and risking his life daily.

"I refused their big offer. Told the man that if I was worth twenty-five more cents an hour, why weren't they already paying me that much. No, hell, I didn't want nothing more to do with Talquin."

Quentin was accepted into the Florida Highway Patrol in October 1956. School was held in the barracks at old Dale Mabry Field in Tallahassee. (DMF was a busy airstrip during WW II but was closed after the war ended). Since Quentin had just completed four years in the military, and the training was much like boot camp, he adjusted quickly. Some of the other students didn't fare so well. Out of a class of one hundred prospective troopers, divided into two classes of fifty each, running simultaneously, eighty-four graduated.

"We had to get up every mornin' before daylight, do calisthenics, and march. There were classes in defensive warfare, defensive drivin', and marksmanship. Classes lasted all day and sometimes we had night classes. Our instructors were from the patrol and FSU. The university professors taught us points of law.

"We had to purchase our khaki uniforms and the coveralls we used for defensive trainin'. There was a bed check every night. If a student failed a test, he had to make it up on Saturday evenin's. No one could get leave to go off campus durin' the week, but we could stay out until eleven on Saturdays and then we were off on Sunday."

Road Patrol School lasted two months and Quentin graduated in December 1956.

In the meantime, Quentin's courtship of Thais was hindered by the little time he had to pursue it. On weekends they sometimes went out to eat at the Corral Drive-in on South Monroe Street, or Thais would fix dinner at her apartment.

"Thais was a great cook, even then," Quentin said, "which helped since the only income I had was the $50 a month I was paid during trainin'. By that time, she had agreed to marry me and was savin' all she could out of her salary."

Thais looked at it a little differently, "I wasn't impressed with what he had or where he carried me to eat. It was just him. I was happy as long as we were together, but I didn't really trust him at first. I had learned from past experience that good-looking men would feed you a smooth line and end up hurting you. He acted like he was crazy about me, but I didn't really take him serious until he gave me the ring."

"I ordered her ring from Sears Roebuck," Quentin said, "and paid for it on time. That's the only way I could get her one. Actually, it was pretty nice, one fourth carat, and cost about $125, which was pretty expensive back then. I decided she was worth it, and a lot more. I really had it bad."

They made plans to have a small wedding the last of December, after Quentin graduated and knew where he was to be stationed. Troopers were never assigned to their home counties, so he decided to apply for Leon County, since it adjoined Gadsden. His application was approved, and their plans moved forward. They paid a month's rent on a small apartment on Tennessee St.

Quentin figured he had it made—-he had a girl he was crazy about and a job with a future. All he had to do was work hard, do a good job, keep his nose clean, and the promotions and pay raises would follow. That's what he thought, but that's not how it worked. He became disillusioned before he had been on duty a month, and was ready to throw in the towel almost before he begun. It all came about with his wedding. That's when the poop hit the fan, so to speak.

"I was workin' six days a week and I had only been turned loose with my own patrol car for two weeks, "Quentin said. "I never had a weekend day off and naturally Thais wanted to get married on Sunday. So, I went to the troop commander, A.D.Cosson, and asked him if I could swap my Monday off for a Sunday, so we could get married. I didn't think the request was so unusual and he agreed to it, although he did look kinda funny."

On Sunday, December 30, 1956, Quentin and Thais had a private ceremony at a preacher's house in Tallahassee at two o'clock in the afternoon. Their attendants were Hilda and Terry Poston. Thais' mother, Mellie Hall, was there from Blountstown. (Mother and Daddy couldn't be there because they had gone down to Leesburg for Grandma Carter's funeral) After a small reception, Quentin and Thais drove down to Panacea to spend the night at the coast. That was all the time they had for a honeymoon, since Quentin was working the evening shift and had to be on duty at three P.M. the next day.

"When I checked in by radio on Monday, I was told to report to the patrol station. That wadn't all that unusual so I wadn't alarmed. Capt.Cosson was sitting there, also Gilbert, the trooper from Chattahoochee. Gilbert had just been promoted to corporal and transferred to Perry. Cosson introduced me to Gilbert, who I already knew. Then he told me I was to ride down to Perry with Gilbert in his patrol car, find a place to live, and report to work on the day shift there the next mornin'. I was totally flabbergasted. That was my first exposure to the dirtiness in the patrol, but I soon found out it was a dog-eat-dog political jungle. I was heartsick. It was many years before I understood that Cosson resented my request to swap days to get married . . . and that was his vindictive payback."

They hadn't driven many miles toward Perry before Gilbert pulled the car off the road and stopped. He said, "You don't really know that SOB back there, Whittle. I'm going to be honest with you. He told me that when you got to Perry, I was to do everything I could to run you off the patrol. He said you couldn't follow instructions, or apply the rules and regulations of the patrol, and he didn't want you. Well, I want to tell you this . . . don't quit. Come on down to Perry and work for me. Do your job and we'll have no problems. Between us we'll show that SOB."

(Quentin found out later that the two places troopers were sent when the big wheels wanted to run them off were Perry and Key West, generally considered the worst duty stations in the whole state.)

"I decided to follow Gilbert's advice, "Quentin said. "He had been honest and straightforward right from the start, and I didn't see where I had much choice anyway. As it happened, Gilbert turned out to be a good friend, but right then all I could think about was the mess I was in. Hell, I had only been married one day. All our money had been spent on rent, deposits, and groceries. Thais had been workin' hard tryin' to make a home out of that dinky little apartment. How could I go tell her we had to leave Tallahassee, and she would have to give up her job? Everything had been going so great. Now I didn't know what to expect.

"I knew Thais would have to give two weeks notice before she could come on down to Perry, so the first thing I had to do was find me a place to stay. It was freezin' cold, being winter and all. The Buckeye plant was open but under construction. There were a lot of workers in Perry, and all the motels were full. I looked and looked but couldn't find a place to stay. Finally, way after dark, I found a boardin' house run by an old woman. It was full of construction workers, too, but I guess she felt sorry for me because she let me stay even though I didn't have any money. She hung up some sheets on a screened-in porch and made a place for me to sleep. I nearly froze to death, but that's where I stayed until Thais came down."

Gilbert took Quentin back to Tallahassee that first night about midnight so he could break the news to Thais and pick up his gear. He got up before daylight, picked up his patrol car and drove back to Perry to work the day shift. Thais turned in her notice, and for the next two weeks drove Quentin's car to Perry on weekends. They were given a place to stay and warmly welcomed by the other troopers and their families. To them that was the brightest spot in the whole miserable mess. In Perry, the troopers were all one big extended family. They all looked out for one another, sharing the good times and supporting one another through the rough times.

"I didn't feel so good those first few days. I was a nervous wreck. New job. New marriage. And the day before the bottom fell out, I had my first high speed chase on Highway 90. If it hadn't been for Gilbert I would have surely quit, just as Cosson wanted me to."

Things eventually got sorted out and the nightmarish beginning settled down to a routine of sorts. Thais found a secretarial position in Perry, and they used her savings to purchase an eight-foot-wide by forty-foot long trailer to live in. They parked it in a small mobile home park south of town for a while, but eventually moved to a privately owned lot where they, and three other troopers, were allowed to park their trailers for free. In time they saved enough money to buy their own lot south of town. Since Thais was pregnant, they figured it was a safer location for children.

In the meantime, Quentin was quickly becoming a seasoned law enforcement officer, learning how to catch the bad guys without getting himself killed. It was close many times. But he worked hard, never goofed off, and totally devoted himself to the job. He was definitely motivated. As he said, "I was aimin' for better-than-average evaluations and, in spite of A.D. Cosson, a promotion someday."

His beginning salary was $250 a month. That was for working six days a week with one day off, and that day had to be taken during the middle of the week. On weekends and holidays he worked twelve-hour shifts with no overtime pay nor comp time given. It was to be twelve years before he could spend Christmas Day with his family.

"The patrol was small when I joined," Quentin said, "only three hundred troopers state wide, and most of the troopers knew each other. Now there's probably over sixteen hundred. There was a certain esprit de corps, especially among the smaller counties like Taylor. We were a close-knit group, our families all socialized together, and helped each other out in times of trouble."

20 | CHAPTER

Troopers were offered incentives to accumulate extra time off. Additional days were given for: apprehension of a stolen car with the driver, apprehension of a load of moonshine with the driver, and apprehension of a hit-and-run driver where there was a fatality or serious injury. A trooper who wanted extra time so he could take a vacation or just spend more time with his family would concentrate on one of those things. Quentin, however, concentrated most enthusiastically on all three. In the first five years he was on the patrol, he led the state in felony arrests. Most were escaped prisoners, moonshiners, or drivers of stolen automobiles.

To rack up such an impressive record, Quentin had devised an almost foolproof system.

There were no interstate highways then, and most north and southbound traffic had to pass through Taylor County. Since there were only two service stations in Perry that stayed open all night, Quentin theorized that anyone on the run would have to gas up in Perry no matter in which direction they were headed. So . . . he cultivated friendships with the people who pumped gas. (Self-service stations were still in the future.) As soon as he checked on duty, he went by the patrol station and wrote down all pertinent information regarding escaped prisoners, stolen cars, etc. Then, he carried that information around to all his friends at the service stations. They were his eyes and ears, and it paid off.

That's how he caught five AWOL servicemen from Canada. They had stolen a car, driven down to South Florida, robbed several service stations, and then headed back north. They hadn't shot anyone, up until then anyway, but they were known to be armed and were considered dangerous.

"I was the only trooper on duty and patrolling on Highway 98 west out of Perry about three A.M. when I spotted the car." Quentin said. "They didn't give me any trouble or threaten me when I pulled them over. It could have been a sticky situation, since they were armed. I arrested them and took them to jail in Perry to wait for the military authorities."

The next day, Quentin changed shifts and worked from three P.M. until midnight. As soon as he started patrolling, he apprehended two armed robbers south of Perry and took them back to jail. Just as he started to have their car towed in, he met another car northbound with three men in it. They were escapees from Fort Myers, and driving a stolen car. He stopped and apprehended them, too, making a grand total of five felons he had captured in one hour—-all armed and considered extremely dangerous. His total count jumped to ten in the next twenty-four hours. He didn't say whether that set some sort of record. To Quentin it was just a job, and he usually downplayed the danger involved.

"There are ways a trooper handles himself in certain situations, "Quentin explained. "A lot just depends on instinct."

Not all situations, even though similar, could be handled in the same way and a mistake in judgment could be fatal. Normally, if he was working at night with the nearest backup miles away, Quentin would make the prisoners lay face-down by the side of the road, and keep them covered until help arrived. That was his usual procedure, but there were times when the situation varied, and Quentin had to adjust his thinking in an instant. The following incident is a good example

Three criminally insane patients escaped from the state mental hospital in Chattahoochee, after someone smuggled them a pistol. They kidnapped a white nurse for a hostage, stole her Pontiac, and took her north of Tallahassee where they left her tied to a tree. She wasn't sexually assaulted and freed herself shortly afterwards. The alarm was out as soon as they left Chattahoochee but they were traveling back roads and had eluded capture up to that point.

"I was workin' the day shift and patrollin' north of Perry when I spotted a car going southbound which fit the description. They were speeding which was unusual 'cause it drew my attention to them. Well, they were supposed to be crazy so maybe they didn't know any better," Quentin grinned," but I turned around and gave chase. Sometimes we'd be up to 110 MPH, and I'd be within ten feet of their bumper, but they wouldn't stop. Had my lights and siren goin'. When I got up close enough, I could see the nurse wadn't in the car and figured they had either put her out, killed her, or she had gotten away. I could only see three male passengers.

"At one time our cars were so close they were almost locked together, and we were still going 110 MPH, heading for Perry which was about fourteen miles away. I knew if we continued into town at that rate of speed there would be one hell of a pileup. Somebody would get killed, possibly innocent people. There were no other troopers on duty at that time, and no county deputies out. The only other officer on duty was the county sheriff and he was in the courthouse in Perry."

When Quentin initiated radio contact, the dispatcher at the Perry patrol station monitored the chase as follows:

"This is 234 (Quentin's I.D.) Perry. I'm in high-speed pursuit. Signal 18 (felony) and signal O (armed and dangerous) out of Chattahoochee."

The dispatcher knew immediately the meaning of the brief transmission and went on *emergency traffic,* which was patrol lingo for keeping all the stations clear. No one else could transmit so that only Quentin could be monitored.

Quentin gave his location as "fourteen miles north of Perry. Southbound on State Road 20." Then, he kept the dispatcher informed with periodic updates as the chase continued.

The restrictions on law enforcement officers were not as rigid then as they are today, Quentin explained. If an officer saw someone acting in a way that endangered the lives of others, he could take whatever action he felt was necessary to stop that person. Quentin, in that instance, had to rely on his own judgment, act accordingly, and hope to God he made the right decision.

On that day, as usual, he had a carbine with a thirty-round clip in the patrol car. He had also taped another clip upside-down to the side of it. That way, by using a little ingenuity, he could shoot thirty rounds, turn it over, and shoot another thirty. The carbine was a good preventive measure in some situations.

It could penetrate metal, leaving just a small hole, and it was especially effective in shooting out tires. Now, having their tires shot out usually made a big impression on the felons...most of the time, anyway.

Quentin considered blowing out the tires as he was flying along, nearly kissing the back of that stolen car. But then he reconsidered. Those men were crazy, armed, and eager to shoot, so a blown tire wasn't about to stop them.

"When I got right up behind them, the man sitting in the front passenger seat, turned half way around, held up the pistol and waved it at me. Then he nodded his head as though we were talking," Quentin said. "I picked up my carbine, showed it to him, and nodded my head also. The other two men musta realized about then that there was gonna be a gunfight because the back seat passenger slid down out of sight, and the driver slid so far down he had to look through the steerin' wheel to drive.

"Old Bravo cocked his pistol and pointed it at me. I figured his back window and my windshield would deflect his bullet a little, so I decided to let him shoot first. After he got off his first shot I planned to jam my carbine through the windshield and shoot it like a machine gun." Quentin continued.

Just as the man took aim, Quentin backed off a few feet. At that precise moment, the driver who had slid down so low he couldn't see the road, ran off onto the right shoulder, hit a small washout, and the car bounced, just as the passenger pulled the trigger. He shot the back seat passenger through the leg.

"I didn't see the back window shatter, but I knew the gun had gone off 'cause I saw the flash and smoke. When the man in the back seat began screamin', the driver thought I had shot 'im so he immediately sat up, stuck his arm out the window, and began flaggin' like crazy, lettin' me know he was goin' to stop and give up."

The car slowed and pulled over on the shoulder, and Quentin pulled the patrol car up behind. He got out with the carbine but stood behind the car door. The driver fell out on his hands and knees, and Quentin yelled for him to lie face down on the grass between the two cars.

"There were lots of sandspurs there and that seemed like a fine place for 'im." Quentin said. "The one who was shot was still screamin' so I figured he was out of action. I was more worried about the one with the gun, so I thought maybe I'd better bully him a little and make him get out of the car. So I yelled, All right, you sonofabitch! I've had enough of your shit! Do as I say or I'll fill you so damn full of holes yore own mama won't know ya!"

Quentin admitted he was plenty mad, but explained that part of his tough front was to intimidate and let the man know he meant business. His theory was that you should show a burst of temper to give the felon the notion that you just might lose control and shoot hell out of him. It usually worked, too. That time it did, anyway. The man was so impressed he fell right out of the car into the ditch.

"Where's the gun, you bastard!" Quentin yelled. "Put the gun in sight where I can see it!"

"I ain't got a gun!" he said. (Apparently the man meant he didn't have it on him for it was later found tucked into the nurse's shoe on the floorboard.)

Quentin made the man roll toward him along the ditch for several feet, and then stopped him while he, too, was facedown in the sandspurs.

"Put your hands behind your back! Now!" Quentin yelled.

In the meantime the driver who was still lying between the cars had continued screaming, "Don't shoot, Officer! I give up! I give up!"

About that time, the man in the ditch got to his knees and started to rise.

Quentin yelled, "Don't get up! I'll shoot hell out of ya if ya get up!"

He stood up anyway, about five feet away by that time, acting tough, and sneered, "You don't look like you'd shoot anybody, you sonofabitch!"

Quentin raised the carbine and shot off four or five rounds just above the man's head, nicely parting his hair. The man froze, started shaking, and his eyes popped about an inch out of their sockets. Then he fell flat of his face in the sandspurs again and began begging for his life. I asked Quentin if the man messed his pants but he said he didn't check.

Just after he handcuffed the two men, the sheriff drove up and helped him transport the injured man to the hospital in Perry and the other two to jail.

As Quentin said, the men had been declared criminally insane, but they had enough sense to know nothing would happen to them. There were never any reports on the incident, except for the ones Quentin had to fill out, and there was never a trial. They were shipped back to Chattahoochee the same day. It was just another episode in the life of a trooper...and Quentin's guardian angel was still on duty.

Taylor was a dry county at that time, and so were most of the surrounding counties. Anxious to get some more extra days off, Quentin and Raker, another Perry trooper and a good friend, became experts on moonshiners, how to recognize them and how to catch them. The two men worked closely together and with the Beverage Department. Long before law enforcement officers came up with the idea of "profiles" to identify specific lawbreakers, Quentin and Raker had already devised their own system.

"One of the first things we learned was that cars transportin' moonshine usually had overload springs to carry more weight," Quentin said. "When it was empty, the car looked like it was scootin' along the highway on its nose. And when it was loaded with shine, the front and back ends were even. On a rough stretch of road, the car would bounce, which was unusual for a passenger car. Now, if a suspicious car passed headin' south, one that had it nose on the ground and its tail in the air, and a few hours later it came back north all evened up, then an observant trooper could apprehend the driver with a load of shine and earn himself a day off. It got to be a bit of a game. They were always tryin' to outrun us, didn't often succeed though. When we did catch'em, they didn't usually give us any trouble. Me and Raker got to know a lot of 'em by name." Quentin laughed.

Moonshining had become a lucrative business around Taylor County. Many of the behind-the-scenes financial backers were church-going pillars-of-society types. There were big bucks to be made and they all wanted a piece of the action. The higher-ups were pretty well insulated from arrest by the small potatoes on the lower end of the ladder, the brewers and transporters. They were usually the ones who were caught, arrested, and had to serve time in prison. So they devised all kinds of ways to elude Quentin and Raker.

"One thing they did was run interference for each other," Quentin said. "They would use two cars. The first car would fit the profile and everything about it would indicate a load of shine. It would go first, ahead of the loaded car by about a quarter mile. We would spot the bogus car and give chase and he would try to outrun us. After runnin' at around 100 MPH for ten miles or so, the driver would pull over. He would get a ticket for reckless drivin' but he didn't give a damn. While we were messin' around with him, the loaded car would quietly pass and continue on its merry way. This didn't happen but a couple times before me and Raker caught on, then we began waitin' for the second car."

During the years Quentin was busy making moonshine arrests, he turned over all evidence to the county sheriff. It was stored at the county jail. A court order would be obtained and the homemade brew would be poured out or destroyed. At least, that is what was supposed to happen. Of all the shine turned over to the sheriff, Quentin couldn't recall ever seeing a single tin or jug being poured out or destroyed. One can only surmise what happened to all that evidence.

Apprehending the driver of a stolen car was a lot different from catching one with a load of moonshine. There was a lot more danger involved, for one thing. So, to give themselves an edge, Quentin and Raker came up with a profile for this type of felony, also. A license tag that was wired on or held in place with one screw caught their attention immediately. Those tags were stolen off other vehicles, supposedly to throw off the law enforcement people, and were usually attached carelessly. Another thing Quentin and Raker watched closely was the tag number itself. At that time, and until in recent years, the first number always designated the county, running from the highest populated to the lowest. Dade County was number one and the smallest county was sixty-seven. The next letter indicated the weight of the vehicle. Most felons weren't smart enough to know that and would sometimes steal a tag from a heavy car, such as a Pontiac, and put it on a Volkswagen. That was like waving a red flag to a trooper, and gave him a legitimate reason to stop the car. That led to the arrest of a felon, the recovery of a stolen car, and earned the trooper extra time off.

"One thing I would watch, when I was patrollin', was the driver himself. "Quentin said. "A lot of times his manner would give 'im away. If he looked straight ahead when we met on the road, I got suspicious. A man with a clear conscience would always turn his head slightly as he passed and glance at me. Then, if I watched a suspicious driver through my rear view mirror, after we passed, and saw *him* watchin' *me* to see if I was gonna turn around, I knew I had him.

Usually they observed the speed limit so as not to draw attention to themselves, too. But there were a few exceptions, and they usually resulted in high-speed chases. Those could get dangerous. Most of the time I didn't know who was drivin' the stolen car, whether he was an escaped convict, on the run, or a mental patient. So I had to always be alert...my life depended on it."

Quentin had only been on the patrol a couple years or so when he had to take his patrol car over to Pensacola to have the speedometer calibrated. Since the farm was on the way, he stopped by to check on the folks. It was on a Saturday and getting on toward dark when he got there, so he decided to stay overnight and drive on to Pensacola the next day.

Now, I believe I mentioned earlier about the Negro juke creating a disturbance during the summer of 1967, when Jerry spent his vacation with us. Well, the disturbances had never stopped but had continued all those years, every Saturday night, just like clockwork. Only now the juke had been moved closer, just down the lane in front of the farm. The illegal liquor business was still going strong, as was the Bolita.

After Quentin, Mother, and Daddy had retired for the night, the loud partying began and went on for hours. Quentin had my old bedroom, which protruded out in front of the house, so he could hear it the loudest. He finally dozed off but was awakened about two A.M. by a Negro man and woman, cursing one another in loud voices. When he looked out, he saw they were right near the front gate, which was about a hundred feet from the road. They were obviously drunk as skunks.

Quentin put on his pants, grabbed his sawed-off shotgun, and went out the front door. The man saw him coming and started staggering back toward the road, but the woman just stood there.

"Get out of here now," Quentin told her. But she just glared at him and didn't move.

When he told her again, she started cursing him, turned her back, stuck out her fanny, and said, "Jes put it in theah anywheah, Sherff!"

So he did. Right in the butt. Over 300 buckshot. She fell down on the ground and started yelling, "Lawdy , Lawdy, I'se been shot!" Then she crawled off down the road and Quentin went back to bed.

Quentin found out later that she worked for M.D.Peavy, a neighbor. When M.D. took her to the doctor the following day, he spent hours digging out all the buckshot. She recovered. Nothing was ever said about it. And peace reigned at the farm thereafter.

21 | Chapter

The following incident occurred sometime in the early sixties. Quentin's not sure about the exact time, but he hasn't forgotten a single detail. This one is in his words, exactly as I recorded it. He's better at telling tales than I am so I decided to let him run with it.

"We were still livin' on the south side of town, and I was workin' the evening shift, from three until midnight. Raker was on days. One afternoon, as I headed for the patrol station north of Perry to check into service, I stopped at the highway, waitin' for the traffic to pass so I could pull out. That's when Raker passed by, followin' a 1957 light green Pontiac. They were goin' north at about forty-five to fifty MPH. He waved at me and I could see he was talkin' on the radio, checkin' out the tag number of the Pontiac. There were a couple cars behind him when the traffic cleared, and I could pull out. He told me on the radio that the Pontiac had an improper tag, one for a lightweight car instead of a heavy car like the Pontiac. There was no record that it had been stolen, but a trooper could stop a car just on suspicion. . And Raker was suspicious.

"One of the cars between us got on by, and I could see there were two white males in the Pontiac. About that time, Raker said, 'He's runnin',' and both cars took off. Raker pulled up even with him in the inside lane and they were neck and neck. Then, all of a sudden, the driver cut over and sideswiped Raker, knockin' him over into the median. We were in town by then, near Perine's Gulf station and some motels. People came runnin' out and gatherin' to watch the action.

"After he hit Raker, the driver skidded around and started back south toward me. I was still several hundred yards from him. Raker backed off, floor-boarded it, and hit him in the rear. The front grill of the patrol car was mashed into the radiator and steam started boilin' out. That disabled Raker's car but the impact had spun the Pontiac around, knocked it backwards across the median, then back into the northbound lane, and finally head-on into the car that was between me and Raker. It was an out-of-state car with a couple in it. Hit him in the grill, knocked *him* off to the right and disabled *his* car. Raker had a high temper and he was startin' to get mad.

"In the meantime, I was watchin' what was goin' on and tryin' to slow down. When I saw all this happenin', I braked, skidded over and hit the concrete curb on the right, so hard that it bent in the tire rod. Knocked it to about a forty-five-degree angle, which screwed up the steerin'. It was beginnin' to look like a demolition derby out there, and all the folks watchin' were enjoyin' the show.

"The Pontiac driver put his car in gear, then, and floor-boarded it. He and his passenger had slid down in the seat, totally out of sight, and he couldn't see where the hell he was goin'. He just did it. The car jumped up onto the dirt median, but the impact knocked the right rear tire off the rim. When he hit the dirt, the car paused.

"Raker had run on foot about fifty yards from where he became disabled and had traffic blocked in the southbound lane. I jumped out of my patrol car and we ran over to the Pontiac. Raker ran around in front just as the car began to get traction and gather speed. Almost ran over 'im, and that really made him mad. I pulled out my pistol and shot out the right front tire. I was right beside the car and could see them lyin' in the seat. All this time I was hollerin' at them to stop and get out. The driver was still mashin' the accelerator, the motor was whinin', and the wheels kickin' up dirt. Raker ran around to the driver's side, pulled out his pistol and shot three times into the door in a pattern about five inches apart. At that close range, the driver shoulda been hit, but he wadn't.

"About that time, the car caught and ran out on the hard road. Even with two flat tires he shot across the highway and hit the curb on the other side. The right passenger door flew open and the passenger fell out on the dirt. The driver, who would raise up now and then to get his bearin's, yanked the wheel of the Pontiac and started back south. I emptied my pistol into the back of the car but that didn't stop him either.

"I ran over to the passenger, dragged him over to a telephone pole and handcuffed him to it. Raker couldn't chase the Pontiac, so I got in my car and tried to catch him. The tires were squallin' and smokin' because they were at an angle, and I was havin' a hell of a time keepin' it on the road. We were headin' south. I could see 'im but I couldn't gain on 'im. When we started around a curve, I lost sight of 'im, but I could track 'im 'cause his bare rims were runnin' on the asphalt. I saw where he turned in by the airport, headin' west. There were people there at the Vo-Tech school who flagged me on, pointin'. They had heard the commotion and figured out what was happenin'.

"When I got about halfway through the airport, roughly a mile, my tires were so bad I couldn't steer on that unpaved road and just bogged down in the dirt. In the meantime, Trooper Wendell Ivey, who was patrollin' on the north end of town, heard us on the radio and headed our way to help out. While I was sittin' there, tryin' to get my car goin', Ivey overtook me. I grabbed my 12-gauge sawed-off shotgun and my carbine and jumped in the car with him. We kept on trackin' the Pontiac.

"We made a left on Tuckett, a paved road going south toward the coast. The Pontiac was out of sight, but he was still eatin' up asphalt with that rim, so trackin' was easy. We reached a rural area, and saw where he had turned a corner. From the car tracks, we could see he went about a hundred yards, turned off through a ditch, then right out through some planted pines that were about twelve to fifteen feet high.

"Now, Ivey had a sort of nervous twitch, and it tended to get more pronounced when he got nervous or excited, which he was right then. He was holdin' tight onto the steerin' wheel with both hands, and every time he twitched, the car swerved.

"The Pontiac's knockin' down the broom sage, goin' between two rows of planted pines, while I'm directin' Ivey...Go, man! Get on with it! Go! We were bouncin' off pine trees 'cause Ivey's twitchin', bendin' fenders, knockin' off the rear view mirror. Finally we hit the swamp adjoinin' the Fenholloway River. That river was really bad then, so polluted it stunk to high heaven and nothin' could live in it.

"I told Ivey to stop. He wadn't drivin' fast enough to suit me anyhow. When he stopped, I jumped out with my shotgun and started runnin' ahead of him. Ran up on the Pontiac where the pines met the swamp, and when I broke through the sage I could see him outside the open car door. He was bendin' over and rummagin' through a suitcase with his right hand, and holdin' a knife in his left. He was lookin' right at me, so I just threw up my shotgun, cocked it, and emptied both barrels at him . . . double-ought buckshot. Hit the car, I could hear it pingin'. Then limbs and twigs started fallin' out of the trees all around him . . . but not one damn shot hit him. He just turned around and ran.

"I followed, loadin' my shotgun with the extra shells I had in my pocket. But then he started runnin' faster, and flat outrun me into the swamp.

"Ivey radioed for the trackin' dogs from the prison, once we knew the man had abandoned his car and would stay on foot. In the meantime Raker had caught a ride and got there about the time the dogs did. I put up my shotgun and got out my carbine 'cause I loved to go with the bloodhounds. By that time it had gotten personal, and I wanted to catch him bad.

"So, we picked up his tracks and started out, just me, Raker, and the dog boy, who was unarmed, him bein' an inmate himself. The tracks led down to the edge of the river where he had apparently jumped right into that old stinky polluted water. That's when Raker got leg cramps and had to quit. Me and the dog boy and the bloodhounds kept goin'. We could see where he came up on the other bank, and we knew we were right on his tail 'cause the water was still runnin' down the bank into the river. It's thicker there in the swamp, but we picked up his trail again.

"He crossed a little ole creek that feeds into the Fenholloway and seemed to be following the river along the edge of the swamp. By that time other officers were surroundin' the area, which is encircled by a road.

"We chased him, runnin', for maybe a mile, right on him. I was soakin' wet, hasslin' worse than the dogs. My gun belt and pistol were wet, but I still held onto my carbine. We tracked him to where Buckeye had pushed up wind-rows and cleared the land to plant pine trees. It was at the edge of the swamp. Right out in the middle of that wide-open field was a big ole brush pile, about as high as a house, and the dogs went right to it. I ran around on the other side and could see he hadn't come out that way.

"I hollered, Come on out, you SOB, I know you're in there! If you don't come on out, I'm gonna empty this thirty-round clip right in there!

"He yelled, 'Wait! I've had enough! I'm givin' up! I'm comin' out!'

"At that time, we thought he mighta armed himself when he was rummagin' around in that suitcase, earlier. But he came on out, and when I frisked him, he didn't have a gun on 'im. I handcuffed 'im, and then had to walk 'im to a road where the other officers were waitin'.

"The news media had gotten on the scene by then. I have a picture somewhere. Raker is leadin' him up the road, and I'm draggin' along behind them with my carbine, soakin' wet, and stinkin'.

"Turned out the prisoner was allergic to the chemicals that were pollutin' the river, and he turned as red as fire, his skin was that irritated, and he was some kind of miserable. That river water didn't bother me none, but it totally destroyed my new pair of shoes I was so proud of. Eat the stitches out of them in a few days and the soles fell off. Destroyed my gun belt, too.

"After we got him in the car, I finally remembered that there were two of 'em. I told the other officers to wait a minute...we don't know what they've done yet, but there's another one up yonder in town handcuffed to a pole.

"Well, the city police were on it, but they had no authority outside of town so they were just sittin' there with 'im. They didn't know why he was wanted, but then neither did we, at that time anyway. So I got on the radio and told them to take him on into jail. We got there a short time later and started tryin' to sort it all out.

"We found out the Pontiac had been stolen in Fort Myers, and the tag was stolen off a Volkswagen. The driver was one of three escaped convicts from a state road camp in LaBelle, Florida. They had split up and one of them drowned tryin' to swim a canal. Never did find out about the third one. Turned out the passenger in the Pontiac was just an unlucky hitchhiker. He was scared literally to death. We cleared him and he took off, probably walked the rest of the way to wherever he was headed.

"The Highway Patrol wadn't too happy over the messed-up cars and came to investigate the incident. It didn't amount to much. I think they may have given Raker a reprimand for rammin' the car. He *did* have a temper. Mostly, they were puzzled as to why none of our bullets were effective. The three shots Raker put in the door penetrated the outer layer of metal but didn't go inside the car. When I emptied my gun in the rear of the car, none of them penetrated, just flecked off the paint. That incident was one of the decidin' reasons the Road Patrol went from 38's to 357 Magnums right after that.

"We later found the prisoner's gun hidden in that big brush pile, but never did find the knife. The gun was a snub-nosed 38 Special. There was no record of it bein' stolen. I never could figure out where he got it, but I kept it for several years. Finally sold it to a dispatcher at the Madison Patrol Station for $50. Well, I thought I sold it, but the check bounced so I guess I just gave it to 'im.

"Nowadays we probably would be suspended or fired for wreckin' out cars and shootin' our pistols. Back then we could use whatever force we thought was necessary to apprehend a felon. It was called protectin' the public. We based our moves on suspicion and we had that pretty well honed. We were seldom wrong in our judgment calls. Far as I'm concerned a police officer who isn't suspicious is worthless.

"Raker was the best I've ever seen at bein' suspicious . . . at any and everything. He was better than I was, but I was probably second! His judgment couldn't be faulted. I learned a lot from Raker."

CHAPTER 22

The security at the Taylor County Jail during the early sixties was rather loose so jailbreaks weren't all that difficult or all that rare. The outside door wasn't kept locked and the only locked doors on the inside were the master door to the cell area and the cell door itself. At night the only person on duty was an elderly jailer by the name of Wright. Noting all this, three prisoners, incarcerated for armed robbery, hatched a plan to make a jailbreak. The night they chose, in the winter of 1962, was bitter cold, a fact that apparently didn't cross their collective minds. After all, the inside temperature of the jail was pleasant.

One of the prisoners pretended to be sick and began moaning, groaning, and rolling around on his bunk like he was in awful pain, while the other two began calling out to Mr. Wright for help. When he hurried back to check on his sick prisoner, he left the cell door and master door open. The men immediately jumped him. One man grabbed his pistol, and then tried to shoot him with it but couldn't. That's because Mr. Wright reached out and grabbed the gun. When he did the hammer came down, caught his hand between the index finger and thumb, and prevented the gun from firing. One man jerked the pistol away, and then shoved Mr. Wright down on the cell floor. Before he could try another shot, the other two began urging him to forget it. They were anxious to leave before someone came. In their haste they forgot to tie up Mr. Wright. Obviously, the three were not the brightest prisoners to come down the pike.

Naturally, as soon as they were clear of the building, Mr. Wright alerted the law enforcement officers by radio. Since all lawmen operated on the same radio frequency, everyone knew of the escape within twenty minutes and had all congregated at the jail. The group included county deputies, city policemen, and state troopers. Quentin was working the three P.M to midnight shift but ended up working all night, which wasn't unusual.

When the three prisoners left the jail, they ran across the street and then separated, two going in one direction and the third traveling alone in another direction. The bloodhounds were immediately brought in and put on the scent of the two traveling together.

"We knew one of the three men had Mr. Wright's gun but we had no way of knowin' which one, "Quentin said. "So we had to proceed with caution. Didn't figure they could be very far ahead of us, either. We were all dressed for the cold weather but they were wearin' their lightweight short-sleeved prison clothes. We knew they had to be miserable in that freezin' weather.

"The hounds got on the scent and took off, trackin' them through Perry, headin' in a northerly direction. Some of the officers tried to stay about a half mile ahead of the dogs, especially if the trail seemed to be headin' toward a highway. You could always tell if the dogs were getting' close by the way they acted.

Eventually, they ended up at a cypress mill northwest of town. Across the paved road from the mill was a planted pine forest about six acres in size. The trees were real thick and about ten to twelve feet tall. There was a graded road around the forest and a fresh-plowed fire line runnin' through the center and around the perimeter. We figured for sure they were in there somewhere.

"We took our flashlights and walked the fire-line first, to see if we could spot their footprints. We could see where they had gone in, but we couldn't see any prints comin' out, so we knew they had to be in there somewhere.

"Grady Murphy was chief deputy at that time but later became sheriff of Taylor County. He and I decided to spread out and walk through the area, staying about two hundred yards apart. We kept our flashlights off, walked real quiet, and stopped often and just listened. It turned out to be a pretty good plan 'cause I walked right up on 'em, threw on my flashlight and arrested 'em. Neither of 'em had the pistol so we knew the third man had it. He was the most dangerous and he was still at large.

"It was close to three A.M. by the time we had the prisoners back in jail, and they were almighty glad to be back, believe me. They were exhausted and nearly froze to death, but we were all in the same boat. Some of the officers decided to go home and get some rest before continuin' the hunt. Havin' an armed fugitive on the loose around Perry bothered me so I decided to stay out until he was caught.

"Even though his trail was cold we decided to try the dogs anyway and were surprised when they picked up his scent near the jail, where the men split up. This one headed through the eastern part of Perry and was tracked two miles to the schoolyard. He lost one of his shoes when he traveled through some thick briers, but he found an abandoned tennis shoe near the school and used it as a replacement. We noticed then that his shoes had two different kinds of tread which made trackin' him a whole lot easier.

"About five A.M. I drove to a quiet subdivision about a mile ahead of the dogs, parked on a side street with my lights out and engine off, and just sat there and listened. It couldn't have been more than five minutes before I heard a Volkswagen crank up a block away, then drove off down the street with the lights off. I knew it was him. I cranked up, kept *my* lights off, and slowly overtook him. He was obviously lost because he circled a block or two, tryin' to find the main highway.

"Finally I eased up behind him, turned on my lights and my top blue light. He stopped in the middle of the road. His windows were all frosted over, but the driver's window was down and I knew he was armed. I ordered him to throw the gun out and put both hands out the window so I could see them. He did everything I told him to, as meek as could be.

"That ole boy was plumb relieved to be caught. He said, 'Officer, you won't believe this but if I knew which way it was back to that damn jail, I'd have done went back myself. I'm freezing to death. I give up.'"

Quentin handcuffed him, and then took him back to the patrol car. He was in pitiful shape: skinned up all over, exhausted, and shaking all over from the cold. One foot was bare. He had lost the borrowed shoe.

"If he hadn't been such a mean SOB I might have generated a little sympathy," Quentin said, "but I couldn't forget how he treated Mr. Wright. I was just glad to get 'im locked up again so I could go home and get some rest. The people followin' the dogs couldn't believe I had 'im. It was just a shot in the dark. Actually I had no idea he would go that way. It was just a hunch."

During his career in law enforcement, Quentin seemed to have an uncanny ability to read criminal minds. He explained his success in apprehending so many criminals this way: "I tried to put myself in the prisoner's place and decide what he would do under the same circumstances. It usually worked, most of the time, anyway."

The following incident also occurred in the early sixties.

There was a state road camp in Perry and the prisoners were often used to clean out ditches and the road right-of-way. They were transported to and from the work area in a dump truck fitted with a cage on the back. One day there was a work crew on the beach road, about fourteen miles south of Perry, working under two guards, each armed with a shotgun and pistol.

"The prisoners overpowered the guards," Quentin said, "took their guns and locked them in the cage. Then they flagged down the first car to come by. Turned out to be Constable Jim Bodiford, a big, ole, heavy-set fellow. They took his car and locked him in the cage with the two guards.

"There were seven prisoners in all, and they couldn't all go in Jim's car, so two of them took his car and headed south towards Steinhatchee. The other five flagged down the next car to come along, and lo and behold it was the overseer for the D.O.T. He was in a state car with the decal on the sides. His name was 'Mule' Campbell and he was locked in the cage, too. Mule's son was the trooper from Perry who was later kidnapped and murdered in Georgia by a serial killer.

"They took the truck down to the swamp near the beach and left it. It was pretty isolated down there and they didn't worry about anybody findin' the men for a while. They must not 've planned their escape too well, though, 'cause after they left the beach they wandered around the back roads tryin' to get out of the state. Them ole boys was plumb lost. Of course, nobody knew there had been an escape or what was goin' on.

"In the meantime, I was workin' traffic on the highway north of Perry. I had just stopped a car in the mouth of a road leadin' off the 4-lane. He had pulled over and I pulled in behind him with my light goin'. I don't remember now if I had written him a ticket or was talkin' to him or what. Anyway, we were standin' there when this man came drivin' down the side road and stopped. He said, 'Officer, there's been an accident right down there. Did you hear it?' Then he gestured back down the side road. When I told him no, he said, 'There was a state car comin' down the road and it just ran off the road, ran through a fence, and then the men in it just got out and ran down toward the woods.'

"I got in my patrol car and drove down there. As soon as I saw the car and thought about the man's story, I knew right off the bat that some inmates were on the run.

"I got on the radio and started doin' some checkin'. Called the D.O.T., tried to get Mule Campbell on the radio, tried to get an answer in the truck but couldn't get any response. Then we began to look for the crew. We knew by then that they had been workin' on the beach road. D.O.T. was out lookin' for 'em, too. Captain Johnson was in charge of the inmates.

"They had some good trackin' dogs at the prison and they brought 'em out to track the ones on foot. I stayed with them. All the other officers were called in to help with the search. We tracked 'em till real late, back through the woods and swamps to the north end of the county near Shady Grove. They seemed to be followin' an old railroad bed.

"The dogs lost the scent about two A.M. so Capt. Johnson and his men started ridin' up and down the dirt roads lookin' for tracks of the prison brogans. It was awful dark out there, no moon atall. But those brogans all had distinct type soles, which helped with the trackin.

"Joe Peavy was helpin' with the hunt and we walked down the railroad a ways and were just standin' there talkin'. I don't remember what about but probably about how to catch 'em. We found out later that the prisoners were hidin' in the bushes nearby and overheard our conversation.

"Since I was workin' the day shift, I went on home and went to bed. They found the tracks again early the next mornin' and put the dogs out again. They seemed to be goin' in a circle. The dogs tracked them through Perry, through the suburbs about a mile behind the patrol station on 27, and then they headed back north again. There's a lot of swampy places around there and the dogs lost their trail again about midmorning

"I was patrollin' the 4-lane again about a half mile north of where they had wrecked the state car. I backed off the road and was just sittin' there watchin' traffic when I happened to notice this old Jim Walter type house sittin' over in the field, vacant. It had been there ever since I had been in Perry and nobody had ever lived in it. It was just partially finished, had old jalousie windows, and the yard around it was all growed up in waist-high blackberry briers.

"I got to lookin' at that house and thought...they were comin' this way...usually they squat somewhere in the daytime...that would be a good place to hide. I drove straight across the median and into a little driveway. The house set about a hundred yards back in the field. I got out and started walkin' to it. Got about half way and the briers got so thick they were grabbin' those old gabardine patrol pants and just stickin' and shreddin' them. Course I couldn't help but think about how many rattlesnakes were in those briers, too. That helped me convince myself the prisoners weren't in there. I turned around and went back to the patrol car and left. I found out later, after they were apprehended, that they *were* squattin' in that house and watchin' ever move I made. Had the shotgun trained on me and was just waitin' until I got within range.

"That night they left the house, went behind it, crossed a field to an old house and forced their way in. There was an old man and woman livin' there, and they made her cook them something to eat and then tied them up.

"The old man was an ex-constable himself from Lafayette County. He still had a pink and white 1956 Ford from his job and he had never taken his siren out from under the hood. Sirens back then were the old type that was activated by a foot pedal on the floor, like the dimmer switch was. Our patrol cars were the same before we had electronic sirens.

"They took the old Ford, what money they could find, left the couple tied up in the house and headed out of state. They stopped at a service station in Valdosta, Georgia, to gas up. Nobody knew exactly what happened then except one of them got nervous or excited and accidentally hit the pedal on the floorboard. That set off the siren and it started blowin', makin' a god-awful racket. All the commotion caught the attention of a city policeman and he captured them right there.

"They caught the other two escapees up near Lulaweeki for basically the same type of foolish mistake, probably for speedin' cause Lulaweeki was a right famous speed trap. They were all brought back to Florida and charged with a bunch of stuff and they confessed to all of it.

"Prisoners escaped right often from the road camp. Ordinarily I would go with the dogs, if they could spare me and weren't short-handed. I liked followin' the bloodhounds."

(Before I go on to the next chapter, which also takes place during the sixties, I want to make sure one important event that took place during that time is given its proper place in the sequence of events. In 1966, at the age of sixty-seven, Daddy died suddenly of a heart attack while visiting Lill, Mother's youngest sister, and her family in Leesburg, Florida. There's no way to describe the impact on the entire family so I won't attempt it. But we still miss him; always will, but especially around election time. That man did love to argue politics.)

23 | CHAPTER

Once Quentin got his brain in gear, so to speak, he could dredge up a bunch of old "war stories" from his days on the patrol. Usually, when he came for a visit, it became our routine to sit back, prop our feet up, and just talk. Some days he was more expansive than others. Sometimes a little toddy was all he needed to loosen his tongue and his memories. That's when I would whip out my trusty little voice-activated tape recorder and get it all down...if I remembered to turn the darn thing on, that is. There were a few times when I became so engrossed in what he was saying that I would indeed forget. Then, a couple hours later I would remember, and call myself a few bad words because I missed some good stuff that way.

One tale he related involved a wild car chase he had back in the late fifties, or around that time.

"I was called out one night about one or two o'clock, along with Sheppard, a trooper who lived next door to me," Quentin said. "There was a Cross City trooper who was chasin' a car into Taylor County. He hadn't been able to stop the man who had out-run everything for miles down south: constables, deputy sheriffs, two or three troopers, and a couple road blocks at the Suwannee River. The Cross City trooper, the only one still in pursuit, actually worked at one of those weight stations for trucks. He was driving a 1957 Chevrolet, dogging the guy's tail, and was getting' pretty close.

"When Shepard and I got down near the beach road, south of Perry on 27, we stopped a semi truck and had the driver pull it across the highway. Highway 27 was still a two-lane road then.

Sheppard was in front facing north towards Perry, and I was backed down so I could go either way in a chase if he made a U-turn.

"We barely had time to get our patrol cars in position and put out a couple flares before we spotted them comin', a light blue 1959 Ford convertible being chased by Slim in his old patrol car with his little ole dinky light on top. The guy pulled up to the semi and stopped, then did a donut with tires smokin' and squealin' and headed back south again, movin' on. I took off after him.

"There was a closed barbeque place about a quarter-mile south, the only buildin' along that stretch of road. He pulled into a driveway near the buildin', turned off his lights, and stopped under an oak tree, then just sat there with his engine idlin'.

"I pulled up behind 'im and threw my spotlight in the back window but couldn't see anything. The window was made out of some sort of plastic material like convertibles had back then. I got out and started toward his car. He hadn't opened his car door yet so I hollered for 'im to get out. Then, all of a sudden, he threw the car in gear, turned on his lights, and took off. He jumped a ditch about three feet high. Threw dirt and gravel all over me. Sheppard drove up about the time I jumped back in my car and we took off after the convertible again. Bounced over that same three-foot ditch, and started chasin' him back south again, runnin' about 110 MPH. After a couple miles we passed one trooper sittin' by the side of the road with a blown-out motor. I was drivin' in the left lane and Sheppard in the right. I kept tryin' to get up beside the guy but he kept swervin' back and forth.

"All of a sudden I looked up and saw we were meetin' a Greyhound bus. That's about the only vehicle we saw on the road that night, thank goodness. Sheppard dropped back and I pulled in behind the Ford, just in time. All of a sudden that boy swerved into the left lane and tried to hit the bus head-on. The bus driver got totally off the road onto the shoulder. We used him as a witness later. As soon as we passed I got back into the left lane again.

"By that time we had been notified by radio that it was a stolen car, and we were allowed to shoot at those. In fact, the whole back end of that car was already peppered with bullet holes from pistols and shotguns. I always carried my carbine with a 30-round clip and was right anxious by that time to use it.

"Sheppard and I were talkin' back and forth on the radio. He was in a good shootin' position and was goin' to try to shoot out a tire, but then he lost his gun. When he stuck his arm out the window to brace the gun on his spotlight, the wind, goin' at that speed, just pulled it right out of his hand. So he dropped back and I pulled in behind the Ford and in front of Sheppard again. Got my carbine, stuck it out the window and braced it real tight, like I had done many times before. Usually, I could fire it one time and it would reject the shell, but the wind was so hard against the reseater I couldn't put another shell in the chamber. So, I had to pull it back inside to reseat the rejecter before I could fire again.

"I shot at him twice that way, goin' 110 MPH, tryin' to hit his tires. Saw one shot hit his bumper and one the road, I think. Hadn't done no good that I could see so I just raised the damn thing. Shot twice through the canvas-top, about where I thought he would be.

"We were in Salem by then, twenty miles south of Perry. Passed some more patrol cars along the road, out of gas. They had started chasin' him down about Crystal River. He hadn't run out of gas because he had been pullin' out of a service station when they got to him. He had gassed up and left without payin'. That's when they routinely ran a check on his tag and found out the car was stolen in Bradenton.

"He pulled over and stopped after I shot at 'im. The window on the driver's side was down about half way. I grabbed my pistol and flashlight and ran up there. He was turned partially around, reachin' into the back seat. When I threw my light into the car, in an instant I could see somebody on the right front floorboard, and somebody in the right rear floorboard. In seconds you could see that. There was also a rifle lyin' on the back seat and he was reachin' for that.

"His old hippy hair was right near the window so I just reached in, grabbed a good handful of it, and yanked him out through the window opening, body, feet, and all, and onto the road. The rifle was just a 22 but that will kill you and he was tryin' to get to it. He cussed a little, didn't want to be handcuffed, so I threw 'im across the hood and was frammin' him around a little bit 'cause he was resistin'."

(Quentin kinda grinned at that telling, and he didn't say so outright, but I got the feeling that he and Sheppard were getting a bit annoyed).

"Sheppard ran up about that time," Quentin continued. "Can't remember his exact words but he was pretty excited and yelled something like, 'Now don't kill him, Whittle! Don't kill him! Let me have 'im.' Well, when I gave him to Sheppard it got even worse. He lost his cool completely and I had to take him back. We didn't really bloody him up; just kinda hit his head on the hood a few times and kinda knocked him senseless.

"Turned out the other two people in the car were runaway juvenile girls. Nobody knew they were in there durin' the whole chase. He was a seventeen-year-old juvenile himself. We got the girls out and I put him in my car. Other troopers began to show up then. Ole Slim, he's dead now, came up, as well as a few who'd run out of gas and had some brought to 'em

"We took the juveniles to the Taylor County jail and had to get the sheriff's wife to sit with the girls. Didn't have HRS then. It was a lot different than it is today.

"The boy was charged with reckless drivin' and other things but he was a juvenile so we couldn't do much. Turned out his daddy was a county commissioner down in Bradenton and he was a typical spoiled-brat-type. Look how many lives he jeopardized, but he was released and went back to Bradenton to get in more trouble.

"The Sarasota or Bradenton paper wrote up the incident, watered down his part in it, but had my name since I wrote up the ticket. Said when I got him out of the car, I kicked and stomped him, handcuffed him, and threw 'im in my trunk to take him to jail. I didn't do it...but I was tempted. In the first place my trunk was too full of radios and equipment to put him in there and I sure didn't kick or stomp him. A reporter or two came up to Perry but they didn't call me or ask me anything about it. They just took his word for it and printed the damn thing.

"Actually, the patrol just laughed about it. They knew it was lies. We figured that was the end of it, but about a month later I was called to Cross City for a hearin' since Cross City was where he tried to run the roadblock. Runnin' a roadblock is a felony charge but nothing ever came of that either. Since his daddy was a commissioner he got out of most of it.

"That same boy, several years later, shot at Trooper McDaniel. I wish I could remember his name. He was doin' time in Alabama for somethin' I guess his daddy couldn't get him out of, and he escaped, stole a car, and came back to Florida. That time he was on Highway 90 when Mac stopped him. He had a 30-30-lever-action rifle and just got out of his car and started shootin' at Mac. Missed 'im but hit his radio, then jumped back in his car and took off again. They finally tracked him with dogs and caught him later down at the football field, hidin' in the booth. I wadn't that familiar with all the details since I wadn't there at the time, but I've wondered a lot of times about that boy and how he ended up."

"Then, there was that time, probably around 1963, that I was workin' the midnight shift when I got a radio dispatch to be on the lookout for a 1960 Chevy that was northbound. The tag number was given and a description of the white male driver. He'd been hitchhikin' and had been picked up by an old man near New Port Richey, goin' north on Highway 19. That was about midnight. He knocked the old man in the head, stole his wallet, and pushed him out into a ditch of water to die. The old man came to and staggered over to a nearby dairy and spread the alarm.

"I started crusin' south and met the car just south of Perry, not far from where we were livin' then, which was about two-hundred yards off the highway. I turned around, verified the tag number and put on my lights. He slowed down as if he was goin' to pull off the highway, but he didn't. Just sped up again and turned into the road up to our place. The road makes a T and he turned right on the dirt road, and dead-ended in a neighbor's yard. He didn't stop, just kept goin', right through a field of ten-foot black volunteer oak trees and occasional stumps. I didn't stop either, stayed right behind 'im. We ran through Joe Maddox's and Earl Johnson's yards, right by their bedroom windows. They all got up and looked out. I imagine all the noise and flashin' lights got pretty scary. Not to Thais though, she slept through it all.

"We knocked down a few clothes lines, then ran through Lloyd Wood's back yard and through his chicken yard. Chickens were squawkin' and flyin' all over the place. The driver finally hit the four-lane again and headed north towards downtown Perry. I called the station and told them to notify the city policemen. We ran eighty all through town, ran two red lights, and never did see the first policeman.

"After we got north of town, the highway patrol station notified Tallahassee that we were headed that way. Trooper Gillis headed south to meet us. In the meantime, I was right behind the Chevy and tryin' to get along side. We met Gillis just north of Lamont and we decided to try a runnin' roadblock. Before we could get it goin', the man ran off the road and skidded into the dirt median. It was boggy and he started spinnin' mud. I had my headlights on him by that time and shot out his right front tire.

" He threw up his hands and started yellin', 'I give up'. I ran to the back of the car and came up from behind. Made him step out of the car and padded him down for a weapon.

"Gillis had been in front so he turned around, came back, and put his headlights on the driver's side. Then he came runnin' up, pulled his revolver, cocked it, and said, 'Run, you son-of-a-bitch, run now!' He was pretty mad. I told him he might better put his gun down; he had it pointed at me, too.

"We found the old man's credit card in the car. The driver was AWOL and had used it to gas up in Chiefland. He thought he had killed the old man. Figured he was safe. He went on trial in Dade County before a circuit judge. That judge was about the craziest man I've ever seen. A disgrace to the court is what he was. He and the prosecutin' attorney would cuss each other in open court. I had to appear down there three times because the judge kept post-ponin' the case. When it finally came up, he reduced all the man's charges to one misdemeanor and let him go. He looked over at me, slammed the gavel down, and said, 'Officer, justice has been served' and I was so damn mad, I said 'like hell it has.' That's when the prosecutin' attorney kicked me under the table. I could have been held in contempt but didn't much care at the time."

(That same judge was caught taking bribes or something, was relieved by the governor, and later elected to the legislature. Go figure.)

Lest you think Quentin's life was nothing but endless days and nights of high-speed chases and other sorts of life-threatening stuff, I have to correct that here by telling of his leisure time activities. It's true he didn't have much leisure time, but he made the most of what he did have. He and his neighbors—-Lloyd, Joe, and Earl, mentioned in the above tale—-often spent time together at an old hunting camp about eight miles south of Perry. It was a mile west of US 19 on an island in a swamp. When it rained the camp was totally surrounded

One day they had to been to Cypress Lake fishing and had started back to the camp in Quentin's '49 Ford pickup. Billy Maxwell, the HP dispatcher, was also in the group. It was about three o'clock in the morning and pitch-dark when they missed a turn in the road and got lost. Quentin didn't say as much but I got the notion from the telling that they were all feeling mighty fine. That's why being lost didn't concern them much, I'm sure. They stopped every so often to have a "song fest", using a bunch of old, country church songbooks they had come by. Quentin said they harmonized but he couldn't remember who sang what part, just that they sang "real good" since they had been practicing a lot of the camp.

They finally stopped in a thickly wooded area under a big oak tree, where they had a more prolonged concert, giving it all they had, when a nearby porch light suddenly popped on and a male voice drawled, "Y'all are real good, about as good as I've ever heard, and I appreciate y'all serenadin' me and all, but I've got to go to work tomorrow and I need some sleep!"

The night was so dark they hadn't realized they were sitting in somebody's yard. They recognized the man as a local fellow who was suspected of making moonshine. He also had the reputation for shooting first and asking questions later, a real mean dude. So they high-tailed it out of there, thankful they weren't full of buckshot.

It was probably around that time that Quentin nearly had his arm cut off by a boat motor. He, Lloyd Wood, and his brother Doyle, were trout fishing at the coast. They were about three miles out when they had a report from the Marine Patrol to head back to shore because "there was a bad storm coming." The wind had already started to pick up and the water was choppy with waves about two feet high.

They made it back to shore and started into a creek to unload the boat, when a big wave came up under the front end, pushing it straight up. Quentin was running the motor and he fell out the back into the water. The water wasn't deep there and

Quentin could stand with just his head out of the water. The boat was full of water and Doyle started bailing with his shoe while the boat was running in a circle. As it passed by, it hit Quentin before he could get out of the way. Doyle or Lloyd finally got the motor turned off.

When Quentin looked down, the water was turning red all around him. He hadn't even realized that the boat prop had hit him, much less sliced his left arm all the way to the bone.

When he got home, he changed clothes, wrapped his arm in a towel, and went to see Dr. Dyal, who put twenty stitches in his arm. That's the way Quentin told it.

(Mark says he remembers this incident real well, because he had broken his arm and was at home when his dad got there. He said Quentin came in, as calm as could be, with blood dripping off his fingers, and told Thais he reckoned she needed to take him to the E.R.)

24 | Chapter

A man making a career in law enforcement usually does so for the satisfaction he gets out of the job—-protecting the public and all that noble stuff—-and not for the financial advantages thereof. Quentin accepted that, but he did think his salary should cover the basics. It probably would have, too, if they hadn't insisted on doing foolish things . . . like eating. Even with Thais' best efforts at stretching their dollars, and she was good at it, their money always seemed to run out before the month did.

They were still living south of town in the eight-by-forty-foot trailer, and two children had been added to the family: Mark, born January 1, 1958, and Donna, born April 30, 1960. Living was cramped. Either they would have to find a way to supplement their income, or Thais would have to go back to work. Neither of them considered that an option. Quentin wanted better for his children than he had experienced as a child, so obviously some adjustments would have to be made. His options were limited, though, because the patrol was strict about what the troopers could do in the way of moonlighting.

"You couldn't just go out and get a part-time job," Quentin said. "You had to have their approval. As a trooper, you couldn't open a business that was competitive with other businesses in the county. And you couldn't work anyplace where alcohol was sold, like a Jiffy store or fillin' station. There was the limited time off to consider, too. I was workin' six days a week with twelve-hour shifts on the weekend. That was about 1963 and we didn't go on a forty-hour workweek until 1967. Still, I knew I had ta come up with some way to make a few extra bucks."

That's when Billy Maxwell figured out how to get rich real fast and needed Quentin's help.

Billy was dispatcher at the patrol station at that time and one of Quentin's good friends. There wasn't anything about Billy to dislike. He had rust-colored hair, a ruddy complexion, was always laughing, and had rather fish than eat.

He grew up in Cairo, Georgia, where his dad owned a bait and tackle shop. The farmers thereabouts would catch rattlesnakes and bring them into the store where they were stored in barrels. Ross Allen would pick them up, take them back to his place at Silver Springs in Ocala, and milk them for the venom. That's what they make the antidote for snakebite out of.

Billy got all excited when he heard snakes were bringing a dollar a foot, and decided he and Quentin needed to go into the rattlesnake trapping business on the side. Getting Quentin to agree proved a little difficult, though. That's because he hated rattlesnakes. On the other hand, it didn't sound all that complicated and it was a lot of money...so Quentin agreed.

Billy had gotten all the instructions on snake trapping from an old experienced farmer in Cairo. Since Taylor County had a zillion gopher holes and that's where rattlesnakes like to bed, they figured they were all set to make a fortune. They gathered the equipment they would need: A length of PVC pipe with a plug in one end, a funnel, a pint of gasoline, a stick with a loop of wire, and a galvanized garbage can. On their next day off, they got up early and went out into the scrub oaks and palmettos, looking for gopher holes. They parked near a dirt-logging road, and started out on foot, carrying their equipment. Eventually, they found a hole that looked promising and dropped their gear on the ground nearby.

First, they took the PVC pipe, cut a few small holes just above the stopper, and eased that end down into the hole as far as it would go. Billy was giving instructions all this time and demonstrating.

"Now," he said, "you have to blow down the pipe. Snakes are attracted to heat, and the heat of your breath will make him rattle and you'll know he's down there, just waitin' to be caught.

"Next, we take that little funnel and pour exactly one teaspoon of gasoline down the pipe. If you put too much, it'll put'im to sleep and he won't come out. Then, you blow down the pipe and that pushes the gas fumes out through those holes at the bottom, and that'll make him groggy. If you listen at the openin', you should be able to hear'im. He'll come out then. When he does, we'll take that stick with the loop on the end, snag 'im around the neck, and drop'im in that galvanized garbage can and put the lid on it. We oughta be able to put a dozen or more in that can. At a dollar a foot, Whittle, we're gonna be rich!"

Billy leaned over and put his ear to the opening of the PVC pipe. That's when he threw everything down, jumped back a few feet, and hollered, "GOODGODAMIGHTYDAMN!" and took off running. He jumped behind an abandoned rusted-out car body a good distance away and peeked out. Quentin, in the meantime, had taken off in a different direction.

Billy said later he had never heard so much rattling and figured there was a whole nest of snakes down there ready to crawl out. He didn't want to be anywhere around when they did. Quentin certainly didn't. They went back to town without even bothering to collect their equipment. Just left it lying there. So ended their grandiose plans for making a quick fortune. Billy later became a deputy sheriff in Live Oak and he hasn't changed much over the years. You still can't be around Billy for long without finding something to laugh about.

As for Quentin, he decided there had to be a better way to increase his income than pussyfooting around with rattlesnakes. Getting a promotion would work nicely, so he decided to apply himself to that end.

If I had to choose a title for this part of Quentin's bio it would have to be: "You Can't Climb the Ladder of Success If They Nail Your Feet to The Ground."

When he enrolled in the Patrol Academy, Quentin was pretty much of an idealist. And when the instructors gave their motivational lectures on how to get ahead in the patrol, he listened . . . and he believed.

"All you have to do," they said, "is do your job well, keep your nose clean, keep your bills paid, stay married to the same woman, guard your reputation, and the promotions and raises will be yours." Quentin swallowed it all and was so filled with enthusiasm he was prepared to give his all for the glory of the patrol. Man the torpedoes and full speed ahead!

He got a more realistic indication of how the patrol actually worked when A. D. Cosson, the troop commander, tried to force him out of the patrol. That was the day after he and Thais got married. But he thought that was an isolated incident. He still couldn't believe it was *all* a crock, so he hung on to his dreams of promotions and worked hard toward that end.

After awhile, he began to take stock. When he started on the patrol, the average time to be promoted from trooper to corporal was about eight years. After five years he noticed that some of the men were being promoted prematurely. And that's when he realized that there were political aspects to some of those promotions. Like old silver, his idealism began to show signs of tarnishing.

"Still, occasionally, you would see someone get promoted on their own merits," Quentin said. "That's what kept you goin'. It was awfully hard to support a family on a trooper's salary so you just kept workin' toward that promotion and raise. You did anything you had to, at least what you could stomach and live with."

Quentin had never had a disciplinary problem, his record was spotless, and his evaluations were always outstanding or above average. So he figured he stood a good chance.

More time passed and Quentin began to get discouraged when he saw he was being passed over by men with less seniority. Then, out of the blue, something happened to rev up his engine and give him renewed hope.

Major Simmons, the number two man in the State Highway Patrol structure, called to tell him he had been selected to represent the state of Florida at the World's Fair in New York City. There were only eighteen troopers in all, so to be chosen was considered a feather in a trooper's cap, and it carried a tacit understanding that a promotion was assured.

Thinking that his hard work over the years was finally going to pay off, Quentin decided to make whatever sacrifices were necessary to insure his promotion. Financially, it would be a tight squeeze. Out-of-state per diem was only $18.75 and he knew living expenses were high in NYC. To be on the safe side, he went to the bank and borrowed two hundred dollars. With the promotion to corporal and a 10 percent raise, paying off the debt shouldn't be a problem. It was the other sacrifices he had to make that gave him a problem. He would be away from his family for three long months, and he wouldn't be able to see Mark begin first grade. But he didn't see that he had a choice.

The fair was open nine months out of the year and closed during the winter months. Each trooper served a three-month stint, with three troopers—-two from the regular patrol and one from the turnpike—-going up at the time. Quentin was assigned the fall slot, leaving the end of August and returning the end of November.

On the day he left, the on-duty troopers between Taylor and Duval counties relayed Quentin to Jacksonville. When he reached the airport, he met the man who was to be his roommate: Glen Blocker, a safety education sergeant from Miami. The HP paid for their flight to N.Y., but after arriving, they had to foot the bill for a cab to the hotel where they were assigned.

During the first year, the HP was the only organization represented at the fair that didn't provide transportation for its employees. The following year an unmarked car was provided, but it was too late to help Quentin and Blocker. They found out real fast that getting around a city the size of NYC was very expensive, much more than they had expected. Since the forty-second street subway was only five blocks from their hotel (the Sherburne in downtown Manhattan), it became their primary means of transportation to the fairgrounds on Long Island. The trip took an hour each morning and evening, and the tokens were twenty-five cents each. That wasn't so bad, but added to the bus fare it was. They had to pay fifty cents (each way) to go from the entrance to the fairgrounds to the Florida exhibit.

Their biggest expenditure, however, was housing, which they expected. According to Quentin, the hotel was a "real dump" and the rates were $18.75 a day, the exact amount of their per diem.

"Our digs weren't much," Quentin said, "a room with two double beds, a small adjoining sittin' room, and a bath. We moved a small table into a closet and set up a hot plate so we could cook some of our meals and save on food. There wadn't a light or vent in there, but we made out. Glen still laughs about my pots of stew, when I talk to him.

"Another expense was laundry. We had to wear a fresh uniform every day because soot and grime was everywhere. That was $1.50. Then we found out that while we were pinchin' pennies and nearly starvin' to death, the turnpike trooper was livin' like a king. He had a large two-bedroom suite, with kitchenette, in an apartment complex near the entrance to the fairgrounds. The Turnpike Authority picked up the bill so he had his per diem to party on, and believe you me, he did a lot of that.

"Major Simmons tried to get permission from Col.Clifton for us to move in with the turnpike trooper, but he refused. All the Florida employees except Blocker and me lived in that complex. It had been leased by the state. Accordin' to Simmons, Col. Clifton was afraid we might be tempted by all the young, good-lookin' women livin' there. Hell, we worked with those same females every day. That was just his excuse, so we stayed in our flea-bag and commuted."

The Florida Pavilion, which sat in the middle of seven acres, was truly beautiful and turned out to be one of the most popular attractions at the fair. Outside, there was a mock Everglades display with alligator wrestling and other attractions. Inside, there were priceless paintings and other art objects, such as gold coins from recovered, sunken Spanish galleons. Part of Quentin's job was to patrol and help guard that area. Another duty involved PR work; answering questions any tourist might have regarding Florida. He had to do some boning up for that job, but he liked meeting and talking to the people. All the Florida people working at the pavilion took a great deal of pride in it.

Outside of work, Quentin and Blocker had little entertainment, mainly because they couldn't afford it. One Sunday, however, they went sightseeing to several of the famous NYC attractions. Quentin said, "I would've enjoyed it a whole lot more if the family could've shared it with me. Truth is . . . I was homesick as hell."

"Bein' at the fair wadn't all bad, in spite of the miserable livin' conditions and nearly starvin' to death," Quentin said. "There were some positive experiences. I got to talk to troopers from all over the U.S. and found out the problems we had in the Florida patrol were pretty much the same all over. Some of our duties were different, though. We found out first-hand about one of them while we were there.

"On two occasions, Glen and I had to rent a car and pick up the Florida governor at the airport. Had to pay for it out of our own pockets, too. One time we had to borrow from the turnpike trooper. Anyway, Gov. Ferris Bryant was a pilot in the National

Guard and he flew a military jet to the airport on Long Island. One day we picked up a car at Hertz and started to the airport to meet 'im. We were both in uniform and Glen was drivin'.

"It was late afternoon, everybody was gettin' off work, and traffic was a nightmare. The route we had to follow was a broad parkway divided by a grass median. Ahead, we saw a woman had pulled up over the curb onto the grass and was tryin' to change a flat tire. In Florida we were trained to help motorists in trouble, so we did what came naturally: we pulled up behind her onto the grass and proceeded to change the tire for her.

"We didn't realize it at the time, but New York troopers didn't do that. As it was, we nearly caused a traffic jam. People were rubberneckin' tryin' to see what we were doin'. Then, a news camera crew happened to be passin' and they stopped and commenced takin' pictures. Glen, bein' a sergeant, did all the talkin'. We didn't understand what all the fuss was about. We were just doin' the job we'd been trained to do."

When the three months were over, Quentin returned to Perry, a few pounds lighter, and resumed his old routine with the patrol. Then he waited for his promotion to come through. And he waited and waited...

In the meantime, he continued doing his job, chasing the bad guys.

The next summer, five prisoners escaped from the state prison road camp. They over powered the guard in the recreation area, took his pistol, pistol whipped him, and then climbed the fence and jumped over. The top of the fence didn't have razor wire back then. They headed for a big cypress swamp, which happened to be located between Quentin's house and the prison road camp.

The bloodhounds were brought out and all the law enforcement officers converged on the scene. Quentin was off duty when the station called him out. He put on Levis and his short-sleeved patrol shirt (so he could be identified), then grabbed his carbine and headed into the swamp, going towards them from the south. He would go a few yards and then stop and listen.

"There was a pond about thigh-deep just ahead of me," Quentin said, "and I noticed there were ripples on the water. I thought to myself, well, lookie here...shit, they're coming right towards me! I crouched down behind a cypress stump and there they were, comin' single file, right towards me. The first one had the pistol and they'd stop once in a while and listen.

"I made a quick decision. I had the carbine and thirty rounds, so I decided to shoot right over their heads, first, to scare the hell out of 'em and let 'em know I meant business. But I forgot I hadn't put a round in the chamber and when it clicked, they heard it. Then things started happenin' fast. The prisoner with the gun fell off to his right while the one behind him fell to his left. The third man just stood there lookin' around, like he was addled or something. He made a good target so I aimed at 'im, intending to shoot 'im in the leg at about the water line. But, just as I pulled the trigger, he dropped down in the water and I shot 'im through the jaw, knocked out most of his teeth and part of his tongue. I yelled at the men to drag 'im out 'cause I wadn't going in after 'im. I knew one of 'em still had a gun."

The other lawmen and dogs caught up about that time. Grady Murphy, one of the deputies, heard the shot and ran up to help Quentin. His legs were all gashed and bleeding where he had gone through some barbed wire. He grabbed the second prisoner around the legs, as he was trying to crawl into a hollow log, and pulled him out. The one with the gun got away.

They made the two prisoners lock arms, marched them to the highway, and then had them sit on the ground by the side of the road while they waited for Captain Johnson to arrive. He was in charge of the road camp, and a fine fellow, as Quentin described him.

When he got there, he said, "Whittle, dammit, why didn't you kill the SOB? Do you know how much its gonna cost to fix his jaw?"

Gilbert took the injured prisoner to the hospital to get patched up and the third man was caught later in a boxcar on a siding north of Perry. They never did find the pistol.

Quentin said later that was the only time he ever shot a man, although he was sorely tempted many times.

25 | CHAPTER

The summer of 1964 was busy time for Quentin. On June nineteenth he was working the evening shift, the only trooper on duty in Taylor County. When he checked in at three P.M., he was told of a robbery/kidnapping that had taken place in Panama City earlier that day. An APB (all points bulletin) had been issued alerting all law enforcement officers in North Florida, Southwest Georgia, and Southeast Alabama. He began patrolling south of Perry on U.S. 98. Since all southbound traffic from the west had to pass through Taylor County, he figured they would take 98 if they headed south.

All troopers are required to monitor their radios when on duty, and Quentin did so that night with increased interest as additional information became available. Two white prisoners had escaped from a maximum-security prison in Orange County, stole a black Lincoln Continental convertible and made their way north. Around noon they robbed the Western Union office in Panama City, kidnapped the female clerk, took her to an isolated, wooded area, northeast of Panama City, where they brutally and sexually assaulted her, then tied her to a tree and drove off. The woman, forty-three and the mother of three children, freed herself about five P.M., made her way to the nearest road and flagged down a car. She was taken to the police department, where she amazed personnel by giving a cool-headed, detailed description of the incident, the two men, the car, and also the tag number.

She also informed the officers that the men were armed with an automatic pistol, a Thompson submachine gun, and had repeatedly bragged about not being taken alive. An APB (all points bulletin) was posted advising all law enforcement officers to use extreme caution and not try to apprehend the men without backup assistance.

Quentin was about twenty miles south of Perry at ten-thirty that night, patrolling four-lane Highway 98. The shift had been rather boring until then, nothing much happening, so monitoring the big manhunt on the radio helped pass the time. The latest transmission indicated the two men had been spotted by a police officer on the Apalachee Parkway in Tallahassee. Their black Lincoln Continental convertible had a flat tire near the Parkway Shopping Center and they were in the process of changing it. The policeman, following instructions, had radioed for back-up assistance and a large segment of trained officers were scrambling to get to the scene. The plan was to surround the felons and close in rapidly, before they could get to their guns. The radio was then on "emergency traffic," meaning no other transmitting was permitted. Tallahassee had an open channel because they were in a dangerous situation. All other transmissions ceased.

The night was hot, humid, and pitch black. The patrol car wasn't equipped with an air conditioner, so Quentin had the windows down, trying to pick up a little breeze. There was no traffic, and no sounds other than the radio, the hum of the car engine, and the rush of air past the window. He was cruising south at about 45 MPH when he noticed twin headlights suddenly appear in his rear view mirror, moving up at a high rate of speed. He figured whoever was driving that car had it wide open, at about 100 MPH. He cursed his luck that they were behind him instead of in front of him. There was no way to clock their speed, and no other way to prove they were exceeding the speed limit. The charge wouldn't stand up in court, otherwise.

Oh well, he thought, as soon as he gets up close enough, I'll pull him over and give him a warning ticket for speeding and reckless driving. At least I'll have something to show for the shift.

Just as he whizzed past, Quentin hit the siren and threw on the top lights of his patrol car. The man tried to brake, nearly lost control, and with tires squalling, skidded to a stop on the right shoulder of the road, throwing gravel and dust everywhere. Quentin pulled his patrol car close up behind and flipped on his bright headlights. That's when Quentin recognized the car and tag number. It was supposed to be in Tallahassee but it wasn't. There it sat, big as day. Apparently the Tallahassee police officers were getting set to scare the poop out of two, innocent, stranded motorists.

Quentin sat there for an instant, trying to decide what to do. He was definitely in one hell of a predicament. There he was, on an isolated road, with two armed and dangerous criminals, and no back-up help available. Just him and them. The nearest on-duty trooper was down near the Suwannee River, too far away to help. He quickly decided his only chance, and it was a slim one, was to bluff it.

He pulled up close to the rear of the black, Continental convertible, left on his high-beam headlights and turned off the top light. Now he could see them clearly but they couldn't see him. In the few seconds of darkness he had, he grabbed his microphone and called the Cross City patrol station, which was nearest to his location.

"I'm 1050 (stopping) signal 18 out of Panama City. South of Salem."

That's all he had time to transmit because he wanted to be out of the car first. He took his service revolver in his right hand and stepped out behind the open car door. In a laughing, jovial tone of voice, he called to the driver, "Hey, Ole Buddy, are you trying to see how much you can get out of that crate? Whatcha tryin' to do, see how fast that ole piece of junk will go? Step on back here and let's discuss the speed limit in these parts."

Both men sat there for a few seconds. Quentin could hear them talking, it was a quiet night and their voice carried. The driver was telling the passenger that they were being stopped for speeding, and they were laughing about it. And that's exactly what Quentin was hoping for.

The driver got out with a big grin and sauntered back toward the patrol car, squinting his eyes against the bright lights. When he was within a foot of the door, Quentin stepped out with the pistol at waist level, where the driver could see it but the passenger couldn't. He motioning him forward, turned the man around, handcuffed him, then pressed his pistol against the man's spine and cocked it.

"Even breath hard and you're one dead sonofabitch." Quentin spoke softly, "Cooperate or this gun may go off. I might get a little nervous. Understand?" The prisoner nodded.

Quentin laughed out loud occasionally and mentioned speeding. That was to give the passenger, who was craning his neck trying to see through the plastic rear window, the impression it was all fun and games.

"Now tell your buddy to come back here, that I want to talk to him, too. Do it right or you're dead meat." Quentin said.

The prisoner called out, "Hey, Joe, the man needs to talk to you, too." Until then, he hadn't spoken at all, just looked totally stunned, like he didn't believe what had happened to him.

The passenger climbed out the right car door, grinning, and approached the patrol car. Since he, too, was blinded by the headlights, he didn't see Quentin until he stepped out with his gun cocked and told him to turn around and back up. He handcuffed the two men together by interlocking their arms, which further immobilized them. Troopers were only issued one pair of handcuffs, but Quentin carried an extra pair that he bought himself, just in case he needed them. It was a good plan.

The passenger got over his shock about then and began to get mouthy. He started swearing and ran through his entire vocabulary of curse words, Quentin said. That took a while. Then he ended his harangue with: 'I'll tell ya this, you goddamn pig, you've got guts! If we'd knowed you was stoppin' us for anything but the way we were driving, ya damn sure wouldn't uv took us so easy!"

(I might mention here that I had to use literary license and a little imagination in regards to the curse words. When I pressed Quentin as to the <u>exact</u> language used in these situations, he just said it was to rough for my tender ears. So I tried to remember how Daddy used to talk to the mules, and improvised.)

Quentin radioed again, requesting help, stating that he had apprehended the two fugitives, but it was twenty minutes before help arrived. That's because the nearest trooper had to come from below Cross City. Tallahassee officers hadn't yet arrested their suspects but had them surrounded and were getting ready to close in. When told that Quentin had arrested the fugitives, they didn't believe it, and a radio argument followed. Tallahassee reminded Perry that they were on a 1033 (emergency transmission) and to shut up. It took a while to convince them.

When Trooper Pye arrived from Cross City, he waited with the stolen car while Quentin transported the prisoners to the jail in Perry and returned. Then they had to wait for the law enforcement officers and investigators to drive over from Panama City. When the car was searched, the Western Union moneybags were recovered, as was both weapons and one dead rabbit. The rabbit remained a mystery.

Quentin said he wasn't at all afraid during the affair, but he got a little weak-kneed afterwards. His emotions didn't catch up until after the fact. I suppose that's what they call post-stress syndrome.

Law enforcement officers frequently have to make quick decisions, as Quentin did, based on their training usually, but often just on their instincts. It's that unique ability, to act without in-depth thinking that can mean the difference in making an arrest and being shot dead. So it was in this case . . . and in many others during Quentin's years on the patrol.

The two felons were convicted in state court and sentenced to life terms. Quentin figured that was the end of it, but the following Christmas he received a note in the mail from one of the inmates. "Have a Merry Christmas, you sonuvabitch. Remember me. When I get out, you die. Bet on it!" Whether the men are still serving time, Quentin doesn't know. He hasn't heard from the man again and says he hasn't worried about it. That wasn't the first threat on his life, nor the last.

The Florida Petroleum Council is a large lobbying and politically powerful organization in the state. Known for its work on behalf of the intrastate oil companies, the FPC is also well known for its pro-law enforcement stance. Beginning in 1965, the FPC began recognizing one state highway patrolman each year for an act of outstanding heroism the preceding year. Supervisors from all over the state were encouraged to send in recommendations for any trooper within their jurisdiction who they felt qualified for the Trooper of the Year Award. The recipient was to be decided upon by the hierarchy of the highway patrol, all troop commanders statewide, and the representatives of the FPC.

Sgt. Gilbert, Quentin's supervisor at the Perry patrol station, felt Quentin had met the criteria by his coolheaded action in the preceding incident. He sent in his recommendation. In 1965 Quentin was notified he had been selected from a field of several troopers. The highway patrol flew Quentin to St. Augustine for the annual FPC banquet. The highlight of the affair was the presentation of the first Trooper of the Year Award. Quentin received a badge to wear on his uniform and a wall plaque. The press attended and there were many newspaper articles praising him for his valor. He felt honored by all the hoopla ... at the time anyway...and he hoped he had gained some brownie points towards a promotion.

The following year, the trooper of the year received a badge and a plaque, plus an all-expense-paid cruise to the Bahamas. For his entire family, yet. Sgt. Gilbert, who had been promoted to lieutenant and transferred to Panama City, remained Quentin's good friend and decided he had gotten the short shaft. He notified the FPC, who agreed. By his action however, Gilbert stirred up a hornet's nest with the highway patrol's head honcho, Col. Clifton, and Quentin was caught in the middle. For a trooper who preferred to keep a low political profile, he sure had the knack for finding himself right out front.

So ... when the FPC notified Quentin that he and his family were to receive a belated, all-expense-paid, three-day weekend at a Sarasota resort, he politely thanked them and refused. A couple days later, a highway patrol bigwig called Quentin in and urged him to accept. It seemed the FPC had become perturbed by the whole affair and was applying pressure in certain high places within the patrol.

To defuse the situation, Quentin agreed to the trip. By that time, it was 1966 and Thais had just given birth to their third child, Ronnie. She couldn't go but Quentin took the two older children, Mark and Donna, for a vacation at Lido Beach in Sarasota. It would have been a more enjoyable time, Quentin said later, had it been under pleasanter circumstances.

As I mentioned earlier, a lot happened to Quentin in the summer of 1964. Some of it certainly wasn't pleasant, but all part of the job. Like the following event, which definitely had historical significance. Quentin got to be a part of it, but, to be honest, I think he would have preferred chasing armed bank robbers.

In June, civil rights activists decided the public beaches should be integrated. Whether they picked St. Augustine because it was a hotbed of KKK activity was unknown, but certainly probable. The bigger the fuss, the more national attention the movement would receive, and that was the goal of the civil rights leaders.

Besides having strong KKK sympathies, St. Augustine was also a center of certain other illegal activities—-dog fighting and cock fighting, to name a couple. Consequently, there were lots of rednecks in that geographical area, and it was rumored that the local sheriff depended on their support at election time. So ... St. Augustine, that summer of 1964, was a tinderbox just waiting for something to set it off.

Tension heightened with the arrival of Martin Luther King, Jr., all his allies, other national civil rights leaders, and even the wife of the Massachusetts governor, Mrs. Peabody. Then, to add fuel to the already combustible situation, the Alabama KKK showed up in force. All the North Florida and South Georgia staunch segregationists, who began arriving by car, bus, train or anyway they could get there, egged them on. Altogether it spelled big trouble with a capital T. To record all this were hundreds of news reporters who showed up with T.V. cameras. St. Augustine wasn't a very large town, and it was beginning to get mighty crowded. It was also beginning to get lots of national attention.

Confrontations began to flare up between the two opposing factions almost immediately. M.L.K. wanted to integrate the beach; the local people decided he wasn't, and the situation got nastier every day. Fights broke out. There was sporadic gunfire. Injuries happened. And law enforcement people were called in from all over the state.

The highway patrol commander called Quentin at home and said, "You get to St. Augustine 10-18 (as fast as you can get there)." He was on the riot squad but hadn't had any official training. Nevertheless, Quentin loaded up all his riot gear and took off for St. Augustine, or as he put it, "I hauled buggy, wide open."

All the law enforcement people had been instructed to congregate at the National Guard armory for instructions and assignments. In addition to the HP, there were marine patrol officers and game wardens from all over Florida.

Quentin said, "Just as I pulled up in the parking lot of the armory, this unmarked white Pontiac come skiddin' up beside me. There was a trooper behind the wheel and his face so pale he looked like he was gonna pass out any minute. I wondered if he was in shock, or close to it, anyways. When he jumped out of the car, I recognized our troop commander, Capt. Cosson. He reached in the back seat, shoved a box of tear gas grenades in my hands and said, 'Take this in the armory, Whittle! These sons of bitches are crazy over here! Watch yourself! You're gone get killed!' He sailed in his Pontiac, squalled his tires, and laid down rubber getting' back to Tallahassee. He left me standin' in the parkin' lot holdin' his box of grenades.

"I went on in for my assignment and was pleased to find I had been grouped with Lewis Shelfer, a marine patrol officer from Havana, and Trooper John Sheppard, currently from Troop H and originally from Greensboro. He was the navy man I met in Guam, the one we gave a hard time the week we shipped out. We became good friends after joining the patrol."

There was mass confusion at first for there were no specific codes or laws to govern such a situation, and the law enforcement officers took a lot of abuse from both sides. The officers themselves resented having their state invaded by a bunch of critical, outspoken northerners. However, it was their job to protect them, so they set about doing that. It didn't matter how distasteful they found the job, nor how dangerous.

Just before dark every afternoon, the demonstrators would gather at a big Negro church in St. Augustine. Quentin, Shelfer, and Sheppard would meet the blacks there to begin the parade downtown.

"Before they removed our nameplates, the demonstrators picked out Sheppard's name and made up a ditty to march by." Quentin said. "Every night, without fail, they would sway, clap their hands, and sing their song about Sheppard, 'Everybody loves Trooper Sheppard, he's our brother, etc.' It was to the tune of an old hymn, but I can't remember which one. Sheppard hated that song. He was from Greensboro, a small, predominantly black town in north Florida, and it just didn't set well.

"Leadin' the bunch was MLK and many black reverends from all over the U.S.," Quentin said, "and they all wanted to march around the old slave market, which was symbolic to them. By the time we reached downtown, it was nighttime. Now, people tend to do things in the dark they wouldn't think of doin' during the day, so the taunts, insults, and missiles began to get worse.

"We had two lines of officers, two abreast, on each side of the marchers who were four abreast. It seemed to take forever to walk that distance. The streets weren't well lit and the T.V. cameras were there by the dozens. On the third or fourth night, we began to hear shots, fired in the air, at first. By that time, we had been issued hard hats . . . solid white ones. So we made good targets. Later on they changed those to blue and issued us a baton.

"Some of the white rednecks would break through the line, pick out one of the white demonstrators, pop him good and run out the other side. It would happen in just a couple seconds. I saw some of them knocked out cold as a bat.

"I was caught on T.V. grabbin' this ole boy when he ran in front of me, and as he started out the other side. I put my baton around him and pinned him to me. He looked up over his shoulder and said, 'Officer, let me go! Officer, let me go! I'll leave! I'll leave if you'll let loose.' I said, 'Get your damn ass out of here, now!' and I turned him loose. When I dropped my arm, he took off like a scalded dog. The patrol used that incident later as part of a trainin' film at the academy. Used it for several years, I think. It wadn't meant to be critical but to show the danger of the situation.

"It was during one of our nightly jaunts escortin' the demonstrators that McDaniels got shot. He was marchin' just behind me when I heard him say he had been shot in the arm. There was blood ever'where. We found out later it wadn't serious, just from an air rifle, but it could have blinded him or worse.

"There was a bunch of white, college, student sympathizers who arrived for the big show. One was from Gainesville and he was hobblin' around with a bum leg, one eye bandaged, and one arm in a cast. He was there every night and got the devil beat out of him regularly, but he always showed up the next day. The white segregationists would pick the white sympathizers out of the crowd and beat them up the worst. Their bein' there was enough to infuriate the segregationists.

"Then, every morning the blacks and their sympathetic supporters would hit the beach. There were hundreds, and a big majority were white women who had been imported for the occasion. That in itself was an agitation back then.

"They would go arm and arm way out in the salt water. In front of them would be hundreds of whites who had preformed a line out to neck deep. Sometimes they were three or four deep, circled like a horseshoe. There was a place about fifty feet in diameter for the blacks to swim. Our job was to protect both contingents. Considerin' the circumstances, it was an almost impossible task.

"We locked arms with one line of defense, probably 125 officers in the water, facin' outward, in water up to our shoulders, with the blacks swimmin' behind us. Some of the rednecks would congregate on the beach and throw rocks and missiles at us. I never got hit by a rock, but I sure got some cussin' aimed at me. There was this one white gal who came down every day to harass the blacks. She was a beautiful girl, but she had a mouth so filthy I couldn't believe it. And she wore a skimpy, little, green, polka dot bikini, just a halter and a brief bottom. I had never seen one before then, and I sure never heard any woman talk like she did. We had to wear our nametags at first and she started lookin' for me everyday. Then she would position herself on the beach in front of me. I don't know why she singled me out but she did and she laid a flat cussin' on me everyday. Most of it was racial, like 'How do you like that nigger stuff, Whittle?' Only it was doctored up more.

"Now, in that day and time, we didn't like what we were havin' to do anyway, but we did it because it was our job. What she was yellin' at me irritated like hell. God, that was miserable duty!

"There were a lot of other officers trying to keep the on-lookers from comin' too close to the water's edge so the rocks and stuff they were throwin' wouldn't hit a target. That beach scenario was repeated every afternoon as well.

"We didn't get much rest durin' that time. We worked day and night. After escortin' the demonstrators back to the church every night, we had to patrol until one or two o'clock. We stopped and checked cars and recovered guns, brass knuckles, dynamite, crowbars, and about anything that could be used as a weapon. Anything movin' was searched, even without a warrant. The situation got so bad they had to declare martial law.

"We carried all the stuff we confiscated, and all the ones we arrested, to the armory. The sheriff and his deputies would sit on the steps of the armory with a cooler of beer and hand the ones arrested a beer as they went in. The sheriff popped the tops himself. His name was Hoss Manusi. He ran a crooked outfit and the governor later replaced him. Rumor had it that he was a big dude in the KKK.

"Eventually things settle down after all the demonstrators left. It seemed ironic that old lady Peabody made such a to-do about coming down here to show us how to integrate. Wadn't only a few weeks later that they had race riots in Boston that made what we had in St. Augustine look like child's play."

CHAPTER 26

In 1965, when Quentin received the first Trooper of the Year award for an incident that occurred in 1964, a lot of press coverage and positive PR was generated for the patrol. With that, and his stint at the World's Fair, Quentin felt his chances for moving up were good. Colonel Clifton submitted promotions to the cabinet, and they were announced the second Tuesday of every month. But time began to pass, and Quentin began to get impatient.

"Some of the men who were at the fair began to get promoted. Troopers made corporal, and corporals made sergeant, etc. There wadn't all that many of us, and there was a teletype every time somebody got promoted, so I knew what was goin' on," Quentin said.

"One Friday night, Captain Cosson and Major Simmons drove down to Perry and came to the house. They tooted the horn and I went out to talk with them. They told me they had come down to give me the good news—-I was to make corporal the followin' Tuesday. They told me to watch the teletype on that day. Before they left, they made some complimentary remarks about the good job I'd done and had me all puffed up.

"On Monday night they came back and told me I wouldn't get the promotion after all. They had argued all weekend with Col. Clifton. It boiled down to me and another trooper. Simmons wanted me, and Clifton wanted the other man because he belonged to the Masons and I didn't. He had gone through the initiation ritual with Clifton in Tallahassee.

"They made it clear that if I wanted to get ahead I should consider joinin' the Masons. That didn't set well with me. I told them if that's what it took to get anywhere on the patrol, then I guessed I'd just stay put. I didn't believe in that kind of doin's. To me, a trooper's promotions should reflect the kind of job he did and not his ties to some organization that didn't have nothin' to do with the patrol.

"It was about then I gave some serious thought to resignin'. They did a lot of drivin' back and forth tryin' to get me not to. They even tried to convince me that what had happened was just an isolated incident, and if I held on, my chances for advancement were good. Seemed to me like those isolated incidents were happenin' too damned often. But I liked my work, so I stayed.

"The man who got the promotion was transferred to Tallahassee where I wanted to go, and he was a two-time retread. He had left the patrol twice and returned, which was unheard of. That, in itself, indicated to me that he had some political power behind him. Actually, he was a good man, but I figured I was a good man, too.

"So, I was still a trooper, still trying to make ends meet, only now I was having to pay off the bank loan for the money I borrowed to take to New York"

Things rocked along. Then, the patrol began getting a lot of criticism because the promotions were so obviously tainted by politics. Some of the higher-ups decided that to pacify the critics, a fairer method of promotion had to be developed. An independent committee was formed to study the issue and draw up some guidelines. They decided that a competitive test would be given to all who qualified. In addition to the test score, a man would also be given percentage points based on his efficiency evaluations during his entire time on the patrol. Extra points were added for each year on the patrol. This gave a man with more seniority a slight edge, which was only fair. The patrol was going to expand and hire a lot of new troopers, meaning a lot of promotions were coming up.

Quentin had about nine years in by then, and good evaluations, so he studied hard for the test. He was confident he would finally get that elusive promotion. A list of twenty-five names was to be compiled from the highest test scores. There would be many promotions awarded, spread out over a year with some chosen each month. Any names left on the list at the end of the year were just out of luck. If the list ran out before the end of the year, a new list of twenty-five names would be compiled from the next high scorers.

Quentin got all excited over his prospects. He figured the upper echelon of the HP had finally wised up and was going to promote in a totally fair manner. Around the last of January, the test scores came out by teletype and were posted on the bulletin board. Quentin wasn't on it but he still didn't give up hope. He knew if all the men on the first list were promoted before the end of the year, he was bound to make the second list.

However, once he had a chance to study the first list, he knew his chances of promotion were zilch, and he knew the HP was up to business as usual. Out of the original twenty-five men, eight were from Troop B in Lake City, the second smallest troop in the state. Not the first trooper from Troop H had qualified for corporal. Troop A from West Florida was larger than Troop H and they had no one on the list either. That should have raised a few eyebrows, and it did.

As the year progressed, promotions were made and in late fall, the entire original twenty-five candidates had been promoted. At headquarters, they pulled the next twenty-five names and compiled a new list with plans to make more promotions to corporal. That's because the quota for sergeants and lieutenants had been filled. Or so they said.

On that list, the trooper's exact test score was placed next to his name— 92.7 for example. If two men had the same score and their names were coming up, they had to go to Tallahassee and take a tiebreaker test. When the second list come over the teletype and was posted, Quentin noted that he was #34 and tied with another trooper, Joel Pigue, from Lake City. Out of the next ten names, there were still more from Troop B. December came and Quentin knew it was going to be close. He kept waiting for them to call him to Tallahassee for the tiebreaker test with Pique.

"He was a good boy," Quentin said. "We went through the academy together. Before the test, he was disgusted with the system, too. We used to talk about it a lot at night when we were both on duty and would meet at the county line.

"Late in December, we got a teletype from Tallahassee that #34 on the list was Joel Pique and I was bumped to #35. It seems they had made an error in his *evaluation*. He got a fraction of one tenth of 1% added to his test score, which put him ahead of me. The last week of December, Joel made corporal and I was left hangin'. I didn't go back to retake the test in January. I knew by then it was a crooked setup.

"There was a trooper from Perry who was stationed in Lake City. I won't use his name for obvious reasons. I knew him well and helped him get on the patrol. He came to visit relatives in Perry occasionally, and we'd meet and talk. It was from him that I found out how the tests were rigged. The night before the tests were to be given in Lake City, he and seven other candidates for promotion sat up all night in his house and studied the test questions. I never asked him how they got access to the test and he didn't say.

"I never said anything to anyone about the cheatin' on the exam. Hell, here was a bunch of poor troopers like me, who had no political clout, and had been tryin' to get promoted any way they could, and still couldn't make it. My friend had a family and was strugglin' like me. I couldn't blame them after what I had been through. The only way I could deal with the situation, and resolve the matter with my own conscience was not to take the test anymore, and I didn't."

As far as the competitive tests were concerned, there were so many complaints the first year that changes were made the second time around. The tests were given on the same day all over the state. That should have taken care of any cheating. That wasn't the case, however. Within a few years, the HP bigwigs had already figured out how they could bypass the top men and promote someone who had political pull, or was just a good ole boy—-a Mason, as Quentin described them. He was still bitter about that.

"They finagled around and promoted the ones they wanted to, just as they did before. I knew some good men who deserved a promotion but were bypassed . . . like me. So, nothin' really changed. It still burns me up to hear them tellin' the new recruits in Tallahassee the same ole hogwash they dished out to me when I went in. They're still preachin' the same ole sermon, too. 'The opportunity is there, men. Just do your job, pay your bills, and stay morally straight . . . you'll move up. Just look at me. See what good hard work will get you? ' He's usually a captain or major' It was a bunch of crap then and it still is today.

Godalmighty! How the young people eat it up. It's what they want to hear, so they believe it all. What they don't realize is that at least 75% of the higher ranks of the HP didn't get it that way, but because of who they knew in a position of power."

This part I would title: "As a Last Resort, Just Buy the Sucker!"

Quentin had decided a promotion just wasn't in the cards for him, and he was thinking seriously about going into the bee business on the side as a way to supplement his trooper salary. That was about the time he became privy to some interesting scuttlebutt. It seemed a man could actually *buy* a promotion in the HP if he went about it in the right way. After what Quentin had been through, he wasn't surprised, nor did he even question it.

As I probably mentioned earlier, Quentin was his father's son and could have matched him for stubbornness. He decided that since he damn well deserved a promotion, and obviously couldn't get one the legitimate way, then he would damn well buy one. So it came about this way:

The governor's chauffeur, Nathan Sharon, was a friend of some of the troopers in Perry, and he enjoyed a certain amount of political power. He had the governor's ear, in other words. The governor sat in with the cabinet to approve promotions, and that made only five or six people who actually had the say-so on whether a man moved up or not.

"I decided to go for it," Quentin said. "I borrowed $500 from the bank again. That was a lot of money then, probably what I made in salary in a month, if that much. There were four of us: me, Trooper McDaniels, Trooper Joe Peavy, and Gilbert, who was already a sergeant. He wanted to make lieutenant and go to West Florida, since he was from Chipley and had a farm there. Peavy wanted to make corporal and stay in Madison, which was unheard of then. A man wadn't permitted to stay in the same county after being promoted.

"McDaniels, like me, just wanted a promotion, and neither of us cared where we were transferred to as long as we got it. He was the only one on duty the day we made our big move, and he was in uniform. The rest of us were either on our day off or had taken a vacation day, so we were all dressed in civilian clothes.

"McDaniels conveniently developed radio trouble in his patrol car, which made a trip to Tallahassee necessary. The repair shop, unfortunately, was located right behind patrol headquarters, so we were forced to do a bit of sneakin' around in order to pick him up without being seen.

"We drove on down to the Capitol and met Nathan. He had a small office of his own just across the hall from the governor, who was Hayden Burns then. Nathan had set up an appointment with the governor for us. We sat in his office until time to walk across to the governor's office.

"We had all the money in a plain white envelope and it was to be presented to the governor as a birthday present, even though it wadn't his birthday. Hell, we didn't even know when that was! But the word 'birthday' was the key.

"Sgt.Gilbert was a silver-tongued skeester and he was going to do the talkin' for us. It was decided ahead of time what he'd say. We filed into the governor's office and Gilbert gave his speech. We were all standin' fanned out in front of the governor's desk. Nathan introduced us all and Burns recognized my name because of the Trooper of the Year award I received in 1965. He told Nathan to write down all our names for him, and then he took the envelope without openin' it and poked it into the right, top, desk drawer.

"We were only in there a few minutes because Gov. Burns had a press conference followin' our meetin'. It regarded his road project, which later defeated him.

"About the first person we ran into as we left was the chauffeur for the road board chairman. I knew him when he was a dispatcher, and I knew him to be a back-stabber and a toadie. He knew us all, shook our hands, and acted so nice it was plumb sickenin'. You could almost hear his bells start clangin'... what were we doin' in the Capitol in street clothes? We took bets after he left on whether he had gone straight out to headquarters to blab.

"Cosson didn't know we were there, naturally, since we had gone to such pains to hide it from him. The reason for that was because we were forbidden to go to the Capitol without authorization from the troop commander. They didn't want you getting any political tit they weren't aware of. That was one of the unwritten rules of the HP, but understood by all the underlings.

"The next day I got a call to come to Tallahassee immediately, this was before I could go on duty at three P.M. I knew what it was about: My dinky attempted bribe to get a promotion. I was totally disgusted. Havin' to borrow money I couldn't afford to buy the promotion I was entitled to anyhow really stuck in my craw. By the time I got to Tallahassee and walked into Cosson's office, my mental state wadn't too good. I never had kissed anybody 's hiney and I wadn't about to start. Besides, everybody knew how Cosson had gotten his. He was a trooper for four years, based in Madison County. Then he was selected as a governor's chauffeur. After the governor served, Cosson was never demoted back to trooper, as he was supposed to be by law. Politics, right?

"Louisa May Ott, Cosson's secretary, knew what was comin' when I went in. She made all kinds of facial expressions and pointed towards his door. I went in.

"He started right off the bat, 'Whittle, goddammit, don't lie to me! I know you, Peavy, Gilbert, and Mac were up here yesterday at the Capitol! ' The only way he could have known was from that little suck-ass lieutenant chauffeur.

"He didn't wait for me to answer but kept on ranting. 'I found out Mac didn't have nothing wrong with his radio either. He lied and y'all came over here. What in the hell were y'all doing in the Capitol? Don't you lie to me! '

"I don't really know what I said, I was so mad. Basically, what happened was I got up from my chair, walked around the desk, grabbed Cosson by the front of his shirt, lifted him off the chair, got right in his face and said, ' you sonuvabitch! I was up here tryin' to get ahead anyway I could! I was tryin' to buy myself a promotion. All of us were. We went directly to the governor and I gave him money to be promoted to a little ole corporal, like you and everybody else has done, either through kiss-ass, or through political connections, or buyin'!'

"He went berserk. He turned white as a sheet, started shaking his head, threw his arms up over his head, and said, 'I ain't heard that! Don't tell me no more! '

"He knew if there was ever any type hearin' he would have to testify that he had knowledge of the affair. The very thought threw him into a panic. Also, knowin' that a lowly trooper even had knowledge of the corruption within the political structure of the highway patrol was just too much. He knew I had been beaten out of two promotions previously.

"After that, he began to calm down, get himself under control. He apparently decided the wise thing to do would be to sweep the whole thing under the rug. After all, with what I obviously knew, if I got mad enough I could cause more stink that a pissed off polecat.

"Cosson said, 'Just go back to Perry. Don't say nothin' about this to anyone. I knew I could get you up here, Son, and we could discuss this thing like civil people'

"Well," Quentin said, "I came on back to Perry and waited to see what would happen. Gilbert made lieutenant and was transferred to Panama City, as he wanted. Things didn't happen all at once. We had to be promoted gradually because the cabinet only met once a month. Eventually, Joe Peavy made corporal and stayed in Madison, as he wanted. That left McDaniels and me. It was gettin' on towards the end of the governor's term in office and he was to run again.

"What happened was, he got defeated. Claude Kirk won. Me and Mac didn't make our promotions and we retired as troopers. I guess the governor used our money to have a big celebration when his birthday did arrive. As for me, it took a hell of a long time on my salary to pay off that $500 I borrowed. Actually, I guess not being transferred with a promotion turned out to be the best thing that ever happened to me, but I didn't see it at the time."

27 | Chapter

Living in a town the size of Perry, a person can become acquainted with most of the residents in a fairly short period of time. But being in law enforcement speeds up the process a good bit. So, by the mid sixties, Quentin had either met, knew personally, or heard of most of the people in the area. Among them was an elderly man by the name of Vern Davis. He was a beekeeper, had more hives than anyone else in Taylor County, and was considered the expert on beekeeping, at least locally.

Quentin took a liking to Vern and whenever he was in the vicinity and had a few minutes, he would stop by the Davis home to chat and have a cup of coffee. Their conversation usually revolved around beekeeping. In time, they became good friends and the more they talked, the more interested Quentin became in beekeeping. He picked Vern's brain, and then read all he could find on the subject.

One day it finally dawned on him that beekeeping might be a good way to supplement his income, at least while he was waiting for that promotion and raise. For one thing, it met all the criteria of the patrol in regards to moonlighting…no selling of booze, no competition to local businesses, and no infraction of all those other rules they laid down. Besides that, it had another advantage, one he really liked; he would be his own boss. Not having anything for an initial investment didn't worry him unduly.

"I began to help Vern out once in a while, whenever I could," Quentin said, "and found out I really liked workin' with the bees. I learned to rob and extract honey, and it wadn't long before I took over that part of Vern's bee business, while he was siphoning-off and going strictly into queen-raisin'. He couldn't lift much, his back was hurt, and he was getting' older.

"Then, very slowly, I began to buy bees from him. He would sell me bees with nothin' down and I would pay him by workin' it out in labor whenever I could find a few hours. And that's how I got my start in beekeepin'—-very slowly.

"Then, anytime I heard of a swarm of bees in the area, after they had attached themselves to a tree limb, I would go capture 'em. That didn't always turn out too good.

"In 1967, I heard of a swarm down in Athena, about ten miles south of town, so I got all my equipment and took off down there. The swarm was right near the highway where some D.O.T. people were working on the shoulder. They found out what I was going to do so they all came over to gather round and observe.

"Since the bees were on a high limb, I drove my pick-up under it and put up my five-foot ladder in the bed of the truck. I climbed up the ladder, put the swarm in a cardboard box and started down. That's when my foot slipped. I fell, and the box of bees turned upside down on my head. There wadn't many places on my face, scalp, and arms they didn't sting me. I yelled for the D.O.T. people to gather some pine straw and start a fire but they all took off runnin' in every direction. Couldn't blame 'em. So I kicked up some straw and started my own fire. The smoke made the bees stop stingin'. I was rakin' them off my arms in bunches. Had over a hundred stings on my face and neck, even in my ears. I was so swollen and sore the next day, I couldn't go to work, one of the few days I missed. Couldn't even turn my head. I reckon I musta built up an immunity from that episode 'cause I never had a problem after that.

"Another time I tried to capture a swarm that was even higher up in a tree so I used my extension ladder. That time didn't turn out too well either. I climbed to the top of the ladder and just as I put my right foot on the limb, the ladder fell. I hugged that pine tree and slid all the way to the ground. Took a lot of bark off that tree. Spent the rest of the day diggin' splinters out of my arms. Made me so mad, the next day I went back and got that damn swarm of bees.

"In about 1968, I think it was, we had the chance to buy a house and two acres of land on Millinor Road north of Perry. It was in a good section north of town and we needed more room for the children. I sold the place south of town, and then borrowed enough money over the mortgage to have a honey house built at the new place. Afterwards I began to get my extractin' equipment, one piece at the time.

"I decided about then to go whole hog and go into beekeeping in a big way. Bought two hundred hives of bees at one time from Vern Davis, then paid him off as I sold the honey. That was a good deal for me. When we only had one day a week off, and if I was on the evening shift, I would get up early in the mornin' and work the bees. Then, when we went to a 40-hour week, I had more time to spend on the bee enterprise.

"Eventually, I built up to three hundred colonies. We had to move them, of course, back and forth, around the state. That started in the late sixties when Mark, our oldest son, got old enough to help me with the liftin'. He was about ten or so and he got real good at helpin' me rob. Then all the family helped me extract. It turned into a family business and, out of necessity, gave us more time together.

"I had acquired a panel truck by swappin' the old pickup for it, but it wasn't big enough for my needs. So I turned around and swapped it to Winky for a 1963 Ford flatbed truck that he had gotten from Tampa Electric. He wanted to go into the cable splicin' business on the side and he needed a panel truck. Worked out good for the both of us.

"First, we moved the bees to South Florida for the orange flow, then from there to the Apalachicola River for the tupelo and ty ty flow, then back to Taylor County for the gall berry and palmetto. You couldn't pick your time to move 'em; they had to be moved when the blooms came on. Then we had to extract after each move. Sometimes we had to do it at the same time and that kept us all busy.

"I had to take most of my vacation time each year to work the bees and there were lots of times when we had to haul the bees and work in the rain. We would rob the hives when the orange flow was over. We'd take a load of supers down to Dade City and, since it was so far, there wadn't much time to do what we had ta do once we got there. We would leave before daylight and get there at the crack of dawn and start robbin'. We had to have heat so I'd use a blowtorch to heat the top of the acid boards on top of the hives. The heat created the gases, which drove out the bees.

"We replaced the full supers with empty ones so the bees wouldn't swarm, and then stacked the full ones on pallets on the truck until it was loaded down with honey. By the time we drove all the way back to Perry, it was about dark. Thais, Donna, and Ronnie would be extracting while Mark and I were gone because we had to make two or three trips. By the time we unloaded the honey at the honey house, it would be eleven or twelve o'clock at night.

"We'd get two or three hours sleep, then start out again. We did that usually three days in a row. The tupelo flow follows the orange so we had to move as fast as we could. After the robbin' was over, the hives of bees were moved and this was done at sundown. It took all night to move bees from near Dade City to West Florida. They had to be unloaded before daylight or the bees would boil out. It usually worked out good, time-wise, unless there was a delay due to something like a flat tire.

"Then we would head back to Perry and start extractin' again. We had to get the honey out of the supers as quickly as possible to get them back on the hives so they could be refilled. We only had a limited supply of supers anyway. All this went on day and night durin' the season but we seldom had to keep the kids out of school to help. Well, maybe Mark a time or two.

"It was exhausting work. One time me and Mark were comin' back from one of those long moves from Dade City to Liberty County and back to Perry, and we were comin' home by way of Bloxham Cut-off below Tallahassee. It was just after daylight and we were facin' the sun. I couldn't get my eyes to focus I was so tired, and Mark was too young to drive. We were both exhausted so I just pulled over on the shoulder, and we just rolled out of the truck into the ditch, and fell asleep. Me and him both. Didn't give a thought to how much doggy-do we might be lyin' in, or how many chiggers and ticks might be feastin' on us. Didn't even give a thought to how many snakes might be crawlin' around. We slept real sound in that ditch until about noon and nobody ever did stop to see if we were drunk or dead.

"One time we were comin' back from Liberty County when we stopped at the Big Bend Truck Stop on the old truck route around Tallahassee to gas up. The price had just gone up from

27 cents to 31 cents a gallon. I said, 'Looka there, Mark. There's no way we can move bees to South Florida with the price of gas bein' what it is!'

"Workin' the bees was rough at times but we all loved to do it, especially the children. They still talk about that being some of their happiest childhood memories. We spent a lot of time together as a family back then. If we didn't have to work the bees and had a little extra time, we'd go lookin' for Indian arrowheads and artifacts.

"Anyway, after a while I hired a fellow named Leon to help us out part-time. He was good help. He and Mark did the heavy liftin' while I supervised. We didn't have a bee loader so everything had to be done by hand. One time they were liftin' a hive down from the truck and dropped it. It was awkward and heavy, and they could only use the tips of their fingers to hold each side. The bees come boilin' out and started stingin' through the veils they wore. Getting' stung happened pretty often but we got used to it. Eventually built up immunity. If you're not allergic to bee stings you won't even swell up. That's true. Actually, a bee sting doesn't hurt as bad as a mosquito bite either, after you work around them awhile." (That's what Quentin says, anyway. There are some things I'd just as soon take his word for, thank you very much. Besides, Mark said he never did get used to being stung in the face!)

Thais added one of her memories here: "One time Mark and I were extracting and we were talking away while we were working. We could always talk about anything under the sun, and it was awhile before we realized the whole floor was covered with honey. When you spin the extractor, the honey goes into a settling tank and then into a barrel. Well, when the barrel filled up, the honey ran over the side and all over the floor. We weren't paying attention and had forgotten the faucet going to the barrel was open. Major Phieffer from the Highway Patrol was supposed to stop by to see our operation and Mark and I were frantically trying to clean it all up before he arrived. It was a mess. We didn't tell Quentin about that until years later!"

"The price of honey was better then than it is now," Quentin said. "I sold my honey to Cal's Tupelo, owned by Alton Langston. He was originally located in Tallahassee but later moved his operation into the old LeKoe Canning Plant in Havana, just a few blocks from where Mother lived. Later, David Langston took over from his dad. I sold all my honey to them.

"When I first started in the bee business, the price paid for honey was fifteen cents a pound for gall berry, and about twenty-five for tupelo. A barrel contained about six hundred to six hundred and sixty pounds of honey. Then it started to go up in price. It peaked out around sixty-three cents a pound for tupelo. At that time we were producin' about thirty-four thousand pounds yearly. That was our best years. We paid off the house mortgage in seven years by doublin' up the payments.

"Something else I did along then was pay each of the children for their labor. They bought their own clothes with their earnings, which helped out, and they learned to manage money that way.

"After Mark finished high school and left home to enter the Naval Academy in 1976, Ronnie was old enough to take over his job. Our financial position had improved a lot so I let Ronnie take over part of the bee business to work on his own. He did a lot of the robbin' and heavy liftin' because I was startin' to have some back problems myself.

"Then, when Ronnie graduated and got an appointment to the Air Force Academy in 1984, I started cuttin' back on the bee business. The kids said it was because I had lost my 'slaves'. They were sure of it when I bought the ridin' lawn mower. Anyway, I quit beekeeping totally and sold all my equipment, to Lloyd Woods.

(Besides losing his cheap labor, Quentin had another reason for throwing in the towel on the bee business: he had other irons in the fire, or plans to put some there anyway. I'll get to that later.)

"I started other people in the bee business, too. One of them was Jerry Wells, a friend of mine, who owns a jewelry store in Perry. It was years after I quit, about 1990 I think, that he had a swarm of bees in his yard and didn't know what to do. He knew I had been in the bee business for years so he called me. I fixed up an old box I had left over and went on down to Jerry's.

"Since the bees had pitched on a limb right near the ground, I just sat the empty hive under them. You have to do everything in slow motion because jerky motions irritate the bees. I took the top off the hive, sawed off the limb, and then laid the cluster of bees, which weighed about four or five pounds, near the entrance to the hive. There were already preformed bars in the hive, with a drone cone. It was a ready-made home for them. That's why they swarm, they're lookin' for a home. Nine times out of ten they 'ill go right in. Then they start makin' a droning noise, which draws all the bees in the vicinity into the hive. There's usually hundreds flyin' 'round and it draws them all down.

"Sometimes, in a situation like that, if you can't get to the limb to saw it off, you have a problem. You can throw a rope over it and try to shake them off. That's not too successful because the queen has got to go in the hive, too. The big glob of bees will fall to the ground, but if you have your hive close by sometimes they will go on in.

"Jerry's girlfriend, who is a schoolteacher, had a camcorder, and she took a video of me hivin' that swarm as I explained to them what I was doin'. Wadn't no problem.

"Afterwards, she took that video tape and used it as a teachin' tool in school. They made copies of it and it ended up in two or three surroundin' counties. If I had known they were gonna do that I'd have polished up my presentations a little more!

"Jerry got so interested he went into the bee business himself. Built up to about fifteen hives, eventually. There were a lot more people in Taylor County into beekeeping by then but it got a lot harder. More diseases that were harder to treat and not as much profit either. I got out at the right time. "

There's another little tid-bit I want to toss in here that had nothing to do with bee keeping. In the early years of living on Millinor Road, Quentin got the kids a four-wheel dirt bike. They had two acres to go whizzing around on. Sometimes while Quentin was still on the patrol and had the evening shift, he would come home for supper. Before the kids saw him, he would sneak up behind a tree, turn on the garden hose and spray them as they zipped pass on their dirt bike. They would squeal, giggle, holler and generally raise a ruckus until Thais stuck her head out the back door and yelled, "Quentin Whittle, stop aggravating those children!" But she was laughing when she said it. She knew Quentin wouldn't mind anyway.

CHAPTER 28

After Quentin had given up on getting a promotion and had his beekeeping enterprise moving along nicely, a chance for promotion presented itself from an unexpected direction. This time it all sounded legitimate, above board, and too good to be true. About time, by gosh.

Charlie Ware, a Perry resident, was head of Phillips Petroleum for the area. He was also head of the local Republican Party and, because of his work during the campaign, carried a bit of weight with Claude Kirk. After Kirk was elected, Charlie Ware thought it would be nice to have a Perry man on Kirk's staff and recommended Quentin for the job of governor's chauffeur. Quentin only knew Ware casually and was surprised he had a chance at getting the position. According to Florida statutes, that meant he would have a promotion to a rank not less than a lieutenant and with an equal raise in pay. He figured he could handle that kind of promotion...yes indeedy!

Quentin lived at home and commuted to Tallahassee. During the day, he shared the basement security room in the governor's mansion with two troopers who patrolled the grounds, and a couple people assigned there from FDLE. Quentin was on call at all times during the day and that took some getting used to.

"I had to open his car door for 'im and drive 'im any place he wanted to go. I knew that eventually there would be other duties, like havin' to travel with him anywhere he went. That meant bein' gone from home a lot. Didn't take me long to figure out the job called for a lot of sacrifices I wadn't totally sure I wanted to make. On the night of the inaugural ball, somethin' happened that settled the matter once and for all, to my mind at least."

Quentin's job was to man the door of the mansion. He didn't have much to do, just stand to one side at semi-attention and look pleasant. Mostly he was window-dressing, which was what Kirk wanted, for the new governor was a man who enjoyed the bowing and scraping and homage paid to him as the chief state potentate. The press called him flamboyant, a fairly accurate description. It was obvious he relished the ostentation and deferential treatment that accompanied his position. For instance, he went everywhere by black limousine with flags flying on the fenders. Also, even though he was an outgoing friendly man, and well liked by the officers assigned to him, Kirk had definite ideas on how the peons should dress and conduct themselves.

On the night of the ball, Quentin decked himself out in his best trooper uniform. His trousers were creased to a knife-edge, his shoes were spit-shined to a mirror finish, and his blond crew cut was standing upright at rigid attention. He took his position by the front door, and since his duties demanded that he go in and out of the front door at times, he left off his hat. That's because he had been taught at Mother's knee that a gentleman never wore his hat indoors.

The crowd attending the inaugural affair was made up primarily of prominent Republicans from around the state, members of the legislature, wealthy local residents, and of course, their bejeweled spouses. A few of the crowd were from Perry and greeted Quentin by name.

He was beginning to enjoy himself and figured he was doing a good job of whatever he was supposed to be doing. Sometime later, when there was a lull in the arrivals, Kirk left the receiving line and came over to speak to him.

"Where's your hat, "he asked bluntly, "Or didn't the patrol give you one?"

That comment went over like a lead balloon with Quentin. He thought Kirk's manner was condescending, and his tone of voice sarcastic, and it flew all over him like stink on a hot turd.

Yep, he was definitely his father's son—-not only was he hardheaded, he also had Daddy's fierce pride. To him, there were some things that just could not be compromised.

"I knew right then that there would be more of that sort of crap I would have to swallow in the future. To me, there wadn't no job good enough, or salary big enough to give up my self-respect for. I guess I just wadn't cut out to be a boot-licker. Besides that, the job itself wadn't much of a challenge. The duties sure wadn't somethin' a man could take pride in."

I suspect there was another reason for Quentin's discontent. He had gotten used to the daily dangers he faced in the patrol. He liked living on the edge, and the adrenalin rushes associated with it. And he was proud of the work he did, the vigilant guardian of the public safety, so to speak. He was good at it, and he knew it.

Two or three nights after the ball, Quentin went to the airport and picked up the governor who had been gone for the day, and returned him to the mansion. After any trip, and after he had changed clothes to something more comfortable, Kirk would come downstairs for a drink. He had a closet in the basement where he kept his personal cache of booze—-some special brand of liquor—-and a bar for preparing his drinks.

"He came over and sat down and we started talkin'," Quentin said. "I got around to tellin' him in a nice sort of way that I didn't want the opportunity that had been offered to me. He said he understood and appreciated me comin' up from Perry. I loaded up what personal effects I had and went back home. I settled back down to my job and didn't try for a promotion again. By that time, I had been on the patrol ten years and was still a trooper."

Ironically, sometime later, Quentin was offered the opportunity to leave Perry and go to any county in the state with a promotion to corporal. Again, it was offered for the wrong reasons. Not because they felt Quentin had earned it, but to pacify a Taylor County man and get him off the back of the head HP honchos in Tallahassee.

Wesley Williams was the owner of a wrecker business in Perry, and he was also a big Taylor County Republican and supporter of Kirk's. As such, he enjoyed a certain amount of influence and was thought highly of, locally. At one time, anyway. That was before he began drinking heavily, divorced his longtime wife for his secretary, and became obsessed with having Quentin transferred. It all began with his wrecker business. He became greedy.

"We had a lot of wrecks in Taylor County because of the convergence of so many highways here. " Quentin explained. "The wrecker business was quite lucrative, but it wadn't lucrative enough for Wesley. He wanted more than his fair share and set about gettin' it any way he could.

"I was senior trooper here and always abided by the rotation wrecker list. We kept a log at the patrol station. Once a wrecker was used, that company was rotated to the bottom of the list. That seemed like a fair way to do things to me, but Wesley wanted me to ignore the list and throw extra business his way. I refused so he began a campaign of harassment against me that lasted several years. He told me to my face that he was goin' to get rid of me because I wouldn't 'cooperate.' To accomplish that, he began to keep a file on my activities. Actually, he became really paranoid and even—-I found out about this later—-hired a county deputy to keep an eye out for somethin' to hang me with.

"In the meantime, he began to spread rumors about me around Taylor County and constantly hounded the HP office in Tallahassee with false accusations. They were not happy with the situation atall . . . especially since I was tryin' to get Wesley removed from the wrecker list for bein' a damn crook. He hadn't been successful with me, but I knew he had recruited others. It was easy for an officer to be crooked if he was so inclined. If there was an accident involvin' a semi, for instance, the tow bill could run into the thousands. The officer could throw that business to Wesley and get a kickback. A few were doing just that and it made me mad as hell that they were gettin' away with it!

"I tried to get Capt. Cosson to back me and start an internal investigation but he wouldn't. He didn't like anybody to make waves and I reckon I had a way of makin' some big ones. Years later, when they finally did investigate, they found the night dispatcher at the patrol station was involved up to his eyeballs. He was the one who kept the wrecker log. Also, several city policemen and at least one county deputy were on the take."

Eventually, Quentin decided he had enough of the situation; his job was hard enough without having to contend with Wesley's constant harassment. So, he decided to meet with Wesley and see if they couldn't resolve their differences and come to some sort of amicable agreement. With that in mind, he drove down to Wesley's business and they sat in the patrol car, talking, and friendly enough at first. Then Wesley began the same old spiel, trying to get Quentin to throw more business his way. And once again, Quentin calmly explained that what Wesley was suggesting was dishonest and he wanted no part of it.

Wesley immediately bristled, "Honest, hell! Honesty won't make the payments on those trucks out there." He pointed to three top-of-the-line diesel wreckers that cost sixty to eighty thousand dollars each. Apparently he was having trouble making payments.

So . . . all the meeting accomplished was to make Wesley even madder and more determined than ever to get rid of Quentin.

"He blamed me for the financial squeeze he was in," Quentin said. "And the harder he worked to have me ousted or transferred, the more determined I became to stayin'. Durin' all this shit, I got no help from the patrol. When Gilbert was promoted and transferred to Panama City, a man named Ammison was put in charge here. He was no help because he was a damn crook hisself. He was a four-year sergeant and a Mason, had made corporal in two years, and lo and behold, I had to work for the sonuvabitch. Everybody on the patrol hated his guts.

"The president of the Senate at that time was a man named Stratton. He was from Nassau County where Ammison was a two-year trooper. Ammison latched onto the Senator who eventually became the most powerful man in the state next to the governor and cabinet. Stratton ordered Ammison's promotion to corporal, and then to sergeant two years later. If his order wasn't obeyed, he was going to hold up a $50 a month pay raise for all the troopers in the state. The HP in Tallahassee capitulated, naturally, because the Senate controlled their budget, too. So we were stuck with Ammison, and he wadn't about to give me any help with Wesley because they were both members of the local Shrine club and thick as thieves, which they were, actually. Right or wrong, the members look out for one another. It must be part of their secret oath or something."

Things came to a head the night Quentin worked a bad wreck south of Perry involving a refrigerated semi-truck. The driver, who owned the rig and its cargo of seafood, apparently went to sleep at the wheel and lost control. The truck turned over, blocking traffic and spilling its contents all over the highway, shoulders, and ditches on each side. It took Quentin all night to clean up the mess. The deputy who was on Wesley's payroll showed up sometime during the night to assist, but Quentin was too busy to give him much thought.

The truck driver, a Cajun from Louisiana, was scratched, bruised, and shaken up but not seriously injured. He told Quentin that the cargo was uninsured, and since there was no way he could salvage it before it spoiled, he wanted Quentin and the relief trooper to take what they could for their personal use. There were gallons of oysters, crab claws, and all sorts of good seafood, the kind Quentin couldn't afford on his trooper's salary. He knew how much it would help on the grocery bill and he was very appreciative, but not so much so that he would ignore the traffic violation. He thanked the driver, apologized for having to give him a ticket, and cited him for failure to have his truck under control. The man didn't seem upset about it. Quentin took him to the hospital to be checked over, and then to the Howard Johnson motel where he intended to call his wife in Louisiana to come pick him up. After that, he planned to get some needed sleep.

It had been a long night and getting some rest was what Quentin had in mind when his shift ended. He was relieved by the trooper on day duty, went home, and fell into bed in a state of exhaustion. But he didn't get much sleep, as it turned out.

"I had been in bed about three hours when the phone rang. Captain Cook, the troop commander, called me from the patrol station and told me in a curt voice to get down there. He had driven from Tallahassee to see me. I put back on my uniform, which was required even though I was off duty, and drove down to the station, wonderin' what the almighty hell I had done this time.

"When I arrived, it was obvious that Cook was pretty hot. It seemed Wesley had called Cook and told him he had proof that I was stealin' cargo from the wreck I worked. When he said 'someone had seen me,' I knew immediately it was Wesley's paid toady, the deputy who showed up to help me with the wreck. The SOB was a friend to my face and then took money to knife me in the back. I was tired and I began to get a bit steamed myself. I told Capt. Cook we were goin' for a drive and we could take his car or mine. He preferred his since it was unmarked.

"The more I thought about it the madder I got. I knew Wesley was behind it because I hadn't called him to work the wreck even though it wadn't his turn. The tow bill would run into the thousands and Wesley wanted it. I also knew Cook didn't like my ass either and he had been delighted to get the info. By the time we reached the motel I was furious but kept a lid on it.

"I didn't know how the truck driver would react since I had given him a ticket. Here was this poor man, beat up from the accident, who had just sustained mega-damage to his rig, lost all his cargo, and who had just gone to bed to get a little sleep. I had no idea whether he would back me up or cook my ass.

"He didn't say a word while I explained the situation. I told it all, knowin' Cook was sitting there, full of disapproval, and it took me about ten minutes. I gave him a fast history of Wesley and our relationship.'

"When I finished, I waited, not knowin' what to expect. First, the man complimented me on the professional way I had covered the accident. Then he turned on Cook and chewed out Cook's ass for botherin' me. Being a sharp businessman and understandin' the necessity, he got a piece of motel stationery and wrote me an authorization to take any or all of the thawin' seafood I wanted. He documented everything, signed it, and gave it to me for my records.

"Cook couldn't argue with that, the shoe was now on the other foot. No doubt Wesley had been jumpin' up and down with glee, thinkin' he had finally gotten rid of the burr under his blanket. I reckon he must've been really upset when he heard how it turned out. He tore up to Tallahassee in a rage, after callin' ahead for an appointment with Col. Beach, the biggest HP hotshot in the state. Cosson and Cook had been keeping Beach in the dark about most of the ongoing to-do in Perry, so when Wesley showed up in his office raising hell, Beach wadn't at all impressed, and physically evicted him from the office. Some friends who saw the whole thing, later told me all about it. That turned out to be my salvation on the patrol.

"It was only two or three days later that Cosson called me to Tallahassee and offered me the promotion and transfer to any county of my choice. I knew he had authorization from Beach because they wanted Wesley off their backs. Here I had been tryin' to get a promotion for years because I knew I deserved one, and now they were finally offerin' me one, not because they felt I earned it, but to get relief from ole Wesley. How sweet it was! Cosson came on pretty strong. 'Whittle, you can go anyplace you want to as a corporal. Just name it. Take it. Don't put up with that SOB anymore!'

"My meeting with Cosson was almost comical, but I wadn't laughin' at the time. Instead, I told him I wadn't goin' anywhere, that Wesley Williams wadn't going to run me out of Taylor County. I'd see him in hell first!"

"Instead of givin' me help in gettin' Wesley off the wrecker list, they were tryin' to ship me out of the county. Looked like they were between a rock and a hard place, and it would simplify matters if I just left. As it turned out, Wesley, with all his political connections and Mason friends, wadn't powerful enough to get my ass removed. Why? Because of Judge Byron Butler. He supported my position and he was powerful himself within the state. Besides being the county judge, he was also attorney for Buckeye Cellulose, campaign manager for Dickerson when he ran for governor, and he also controlled the bank where Wesley financed his trucks. That's the way that sort of stuff works."

So things continued along in the same vein until Quentin decided to start his own investigation to see who was taking payoffs and rigging the wrecker log. He set up surveillance and found out the night dispatcher was guilty, but the one he caught that gave him the most pleasure was Ammison. He had been stealing money from the coke and candy machine for the entire two years he had been stationed in Perry, and he was finally caught red-handed. The Perry HP group didn't grieve when he left.

During this time, Wesley continued to drink heavily. Sometimes he spent the night in his office, brooding, monitoring the HP radio and drinking. One night he got dog drunk, fell on a broken bottle, and then couldn't get up.

At three A.M. the patrolling city policeman noticed the lights in Wesley's office and stopped to investigate, but he couldn't get Wesley to respond. That's because he was passed out on the floor. The patrolman walked around the side of the building, peered in the window, saw all the blood, and reported it to the sheriff's office as a robbery.

Quentin was working nights, heard the radio report, and arrived at Wesley's office before the deputy. He broke the glass and unlocked the door.

"Wesley was pretty bloody from all the cuts," Quentin said, "but I knew his injuries wadn't life-threatenin'. When he came around, though, and saw all the blood, *he* thought they were. He looked up at me real pitiful like and said in a meek little voice, 'did you call the ambulance, Quentin? ' I said, hell no, you sonuvabitch! I ain't callin' no ambulance until you bleed to death!

"The black deputy who showed up was a friend of mine He wouldn't come in the office 'cause he didn't like the sight of blood, so I told him I would handle it and he stayed outside. The policeman had already gone. I let Wesley lie there and sweat it out for about fifteen minutes while he rolled around on the floor and begged. When the policeman finally stopped back by, I told him there was no robbery, just a drunk who had cut hisself and asked him to call an ambulance.

"Wesley lost his business right after that and left Perry. I heard he had gone to Puerto Rica. So, what goes round, comes round, as the saying goes.

"Many years later, about 1983, after I had retired from the patrol, I saw Wesley again one day as I was going into the courthouse here in Perry. Somebody hollered, 'Hey, Whittle, wait a minute! ' I looked up and there was Wesley, runnin' across the street between red lights. He shook my hand, and surprised the hell out of me by huggin' my neck. He said, 'Whittle, I just want to apologize to you and to tell you that through all the years you and I had our problems, and I've thought about this many times, I think you were probably the best friend I ever had in my life.'

"He was dead serious, but I just couldn't bring myself to be overly friendly to 'im. There was too much bad history between us. I just let it pass. He eventually ended up in South Carolina, got cancer, and died a few years ago."

29 | CHAPTER

Quentin makes friends easily and seems to have a special rapport with older people. One of his more unusual friendships began with a kidnapping. Actually, there were two kidnappings, and they both involved the same victim, an elderly man by the name of Dutton.

He was a white farmer in his early seventies, a small, wiry man about five-feet-four inches tall, and weighing about one hundred and twenty pounds. His old farmhouse sat in the middle of a thousand acres in Madison County, miles from the nearest neighbor. Mr. Dutton liked it that way. The nearest town was Lamont, a small settlement north of Perry on Highway 27.

"It had been rumored around the area for years that Mr. Dutton was extremely wealthy and didn't trust banks. "Quentin said, "Things bein' the way they were, I guess it wasn't surprisin' that, eventually, some foolish person would get the notion that Mr. Dutton had large amounts of cash hidden on the place. And, greed would eventually prod them into doin' somethin' stupid."

Two men and a woman who lived in Madison County and knew Mr. Dutton personally instigated the first kidnapping. They went to his house and overpowered him, which wasn't hard to do considering his size and age. Then, they took him to an old abandoned house on his property that was isolated and could only be reached through a locked gate. There, they tied him to a straight-backed, wooden, kitchen chair. His arms were tied together behind the chair, and his ankles were tied to the front chair legs. He was kept like that for three days. They would leave him for hours at a time, knowing they were safe, confident that no one could possibly know what was going on. They had him write a note to the mailman saying he was going out of town for a few days, so the mailman wouldn't get suspicious if he didn't see Mr. Dutton around the place.

The kidnappers found out pretty quick that the rumors weren't accurate. There were no large sums of cash hidden on the property. Mr. Dutton *was*, indeed, a very wealthy man, but he *did* trust banks and had accounts in several. No wanting to leave empty-handed, they had Mr. Dutton write checks made out to them, then took the checks to different banks in the area for cashing. Once all his accounts were cleaned out, they planned to kill him.

On the third night, two of the kidnappers checked the knots to be sure Mr. Dutton was tightly secured to the chair. Then, they went up to his house to get some sleep, confident he would be there when they returned. After all, where could the old man go? Tied to a chair and three miles from the nearest highway? They didn't reckon with the courage and tenacity of the tough old bird they had kidnapped.

After working at it awhile, Mr. Dutton managed to loosen his feet but couldn't free his arms. He backed against the door to open it, then shuffled the three miles to the highway, with the chair still attached to his back.

"He was a tough, hardheaded ole-timer," Quentin said. "Not many people would have, or could have, done what he did."

Somebody stopped on the highway and picked him up, then notified the authorities. Since Mr. Dutton knew the culprits, lawmen went to the house of the ringleader to pick him up, but he escaped out a back door and ran. Bloodhounds were brought in and tracked him toward the highway south of Lamont. He was eventually caught, his accomplices rounded up, and they were all sent to prison.

"Since the crime didn't occur in Taylor County, I wadn't involved in the trial, but I think they all got life sentences," Quentin said. "As for Mr. Dutton, I was really impressed with that old man, especially his coolheaded, calm manner.

"After that incident, I began checkin' on him about once a week, and we became good friends. Often, we would sit out on his porch and have some long talks about 'most anything, how it was when he was younger, life in general. He had two or three lakes on his property, and sometimes we would go fishin' together. He wouldn't let me paddle, but did it himself while I casted."

About 1975, Mr. Dutton was kidnapped a second time. That time it wasn't preplanned but occurred spontaneously as part of the circumstances. Again there were three people involved— two men and a woman, all white. They held up a store at Lebanon Station south of Perry and were headed north on U.S. 27 toward Tallahassee. There wasn't a trooper on duty in Perry at that time.

Capt. Cook, troop commander, was enroute to Tallahassee from Perry when he heard the radio report of the robbery. And he was just south of Lamont when he met the wanted vehicle. Since he knew there wasn't a trooper on duty, he decided to apprehend the robbers himself. He pulled them over to the side of the highway. Their location, at that time, was near the entrance to the gravel road that led to Mr. Dutton's place. Before Capt. Cook could disarm and handcuff the robbers, they over-powered him and took his service revolver. He wasn't shot, but they did shoot out all his tires and his radio. Then, they jumped back in their car, made a quick U-turn and headed back south toward Perry. Later, no one could figure out their reason for doing that.

Since traffic was fairly heavy on Highway 27, it wasn't long before a motorist spotted Capt. Cook. Once they stopped to assist him, word got out quickly.

"I was called out even though it was my day off. All law officers were, that was standard procedure. We all converged on the area, sealed off the main roads, and put up the patrol plane. I was on the road within minutes of the call so I knew they hadn't come into Perry. None of the other officers had spotted them so we knew they had to be in the woods somewhere in that area. We began to ride dirt roads lookin' for the car.

"About one-half mile south of where they had left Capt. Cook, and around a curve, they had taken a dirt road. This was in the southern tip of Madison County that extends down between Taylor and Jefferson Counties.

"Sergeant Williams and I were each in our own patrol car and we began to track them through the woods. The dirt road eventually dead-ended at an old farmhouse. Turned out it was located just across the swamp and about two miles from Mr.

Dutton's place. When the road petered out, the robbers just continued on past the house, out through a plowed field, and stopped in the edge of the woods. There were black people livin' in the house, and they were all sittin' on the front porch at first, scared to death.

"We were probably thirty minutes behind the robbers by this time. When we got to the house, spotted the car, and checked it out, we saw it was abandoned, and there were footprints runnin' into the swamp. Since they were on foot, we knew it would be easier to track them with the dogs, so we radioed the position and sat back to wait for reinforcements."

In the meantime, Mr. Dutton, unaware of what was going on, was peacefully plowing his field on the other side of the swamp. He was quite a distance from his house when he saw three people coming across his field, heading in his direction. Being a friendly sort of man, he stopped the tractor and waved at them. They waved back. He wasn't suspicious. Lots of local folks liked to hunt arrowheads and other Indian artifacts around plowed fields, and he figured that was what brought them there.

As soon as they got close enough, however, they quit acting friendly, pulled a gun, and made him take them to his house. While the female made herself at home in Mr. Dutton's kitchen, cooking something to eat, they openly discussed their plans for a getaway. They didn't care that Mr. Dutton heard. As soon as it was dark, they were going to take his gun collection, kill him, steal his pickup truck and hightail it to Georgia, using the back roads. They were relaxed, felt safe, had no idea the word was out and lawmen were hot on their trail.

Other lawmen had arrived near the abandoned car and were parked around the area, waiting with Quentin and Williams for arrival of the dogs.

Semie Moore was the sheriff of Madison County. It was his turf and he knew it well, every pig trail and swamp bog. As soon as he notified his deputies to bring in the bloodhounds, he decided to drive down to Mr. Dutton's farm. He knew Mr. Dutton personally, knew he was situated in a vulnerable position, and decided to warn him about the possible danger. When Semie reached the Dutton farm, he saw Mr. Dutton's pickup in the yard but there was no sign of any activity. The place was deadly quiet. He called Mr. Dutton and there was no answer. He began to get the gut feeling something wasn't right, so he stayed behind the car door with his mike in his hand.

In the house, the robbers were watching Semie through the window and saw he didn't seem to be in any hurry to leave. They decided to let Mr. Dutton step out the front door and speak to Semie, to allay any suspicions he might have by assuring him everything was all right.

One of the men jammed a pistol into Mr. Dutton's back and shoved him up to the door. "Step out there nice and easy and let that pig know you're fine. Say one word to make him suspicious and you're dead, both of you. You savvy, old man?"

Mr. Dutton calmly nodded and stepped out on the porch. He knew the robber was behind the door with the gun trained on his back, but he showed no nervousness.

"Howdy, Sheriff," he said.

"Mr. Dutton," Semie nodded in greeting and was beginning to relax a bit. "I just stopped by to let you know we have some people in the area who are armed and dangerous. Keep your truck locked and the keys inside and keep a sharp eye out. These are pretty desperate characters, and we don't want anybody to kidnap you again. Ha! Ha!"

As Semie spoke, he relaxed and began to move out from behind the car door. What happened then surprised him as much as it surely surprised the people inside.

Mr. Dutton suddenly yelled, "They're inside the house, Sheriff!" He was in motion even before the words left his mouth. He took one flying leap off the porch and rolled underneath the house, which sat up about eighteen inches off the ground. Semie immediately jumped back into the patrol car and backed it up until he could see both sides of the house. There were huge pecan trees on each side and cleared fields behind.

One of the men began cursing Mr. Dutton at the top of his lungs, while the other broke out a windowpane and began shooting at Semie. He hunched down behind the wheel of his car, keyed in the mike and began calling for help. "They're in Mr. Dutton's house! Need help! Shots fired!"

Meanwhile, back at the swamp, the bloodhounds had arrived and the posse was preparing to start the chase. Quentin and Sgt. Williams were talking quietly near the Sgt.'s patrol car, which was blocked by the other patrol cars, when the message from Semie came over the radio. They dived into Captain Cook's car—-the tires had been changed by then—-and took off, leaving Quentin's car and the Sgt.'s car behind.

"When a fellow lawman called for help, you got there as fast as you could, anyway you could," Quentin explained. "What Sgt. Williams did then was considered proper under the circumstances. Actually, it was kinda funny afterwards. He revved his engine, spun around, took off, and spread two patrol cars apart. He knocked 'em to the sides and kept going. Musta looked like some of that stuff you see in the movies. Needless to say, we were the first officers on the scene."

When they arrived, Quentin hid behind one of the pecan trees at the side of the house. From his location, he had a clear view of the back yard and the rear of the house. They had no way to escape, and it was almost dark. The plane was already circling overhead when Semie Moore called over his speaker, "You're surrounded. You have no place to go. Throw your guns out and surrender."

When they came out on the porch with their hands over their heads, Quentin was the closest and the first one to reach them.

"I recall that one of them had a dirty mouth and was lettin' it run freely, callin' Cook a dirty SOB, among other things, and said he should have shot him. I didn't care much for his sentiments, and when I handcuffed him, I gave him a nice smile and cinched those cuffs as tight as I could get 'em. He gave me a surprised look and changed his tune real fast. Before we got out of the yard, he was whinin' and beggin' me to loosen the cuffs. They know you aren't goin' to shoot 'em once they give up, and they want to act bad then. They tend to do a lot of cussin'.

"Once we had 'em cuffed, Mr. Dutton came crawlin' out from under the house, as calm as he could be. He never seemed upset or rattled in any way. Most of the officers present remembered him from the last incident and joshed him a little, about how he liked his solitude but always ended up in the middle of the action, and how they were going to send someone out to babysit and keep him out of trouble.

"Mr. Dutton certainly wadn't a talkative man. He never revealed much about his early life in all the years I knew him. He always dressed the same, in khaki pants and shirt. If a pocket fell off, he sewed it back on himself with a needle and thread. But he was always clean. And he didn't believe in doctors or hospitals. Said he hadn't been to a doctor in all his life.

Not long before he died, he told me that he had driven himself to Thomasville, Georgia and checked into the hospital there. Had some sort of problem with his prostate. He couldn't get over what they did to him there. I guess some of those tests really shocked him.

"I had retired from the patrol and was on a trip out west when Mr. Dutton died. I felt bad that I couldn't go to his funeral, and I wondered if any of his family showed up. He never talked about them, and I had too much respect for him to ask, but I always felt like they were missin' a lot. He was a fine old man and I really enjoyed his company."

CHAPTER 30

There's no doubt about it...listening to all Quentin's highway patrol experiences has given me a whole new perspective. About people, in general, I mean. Oh, I knew they could be irrational and unpredictable at times, but I had no idea to what extremes they would take their foolishness. Their reactions to the situations in which they found themselves was sometimes comical, sometimes downright stupid, and often very dangerous. For instance:

"I was on the midnight shift, patrollin' north of town again," Quentin said, "when I saw this one headlight comin' toward me. I thought it was a motorcycle at first, and then radar picked it up at 127 MPH. I thought . . . there's no way! So I cancelled it and immediately recalibrated it. In a half second it registered 126 MPH.

"About then he came flyin' by me and I saw it wadn't a motorcycle but a car. That was the fastest I ever clocked an automobile. I turned around and started tryin' to overtake him. I didn't turn on my siren or light. There wadn't nobody on the road that time of night but me and him, and I knew I could run faster than he was goin'. I was gainin' on him when all of a sudden he pulled over and stopped.

"He hadn't even noticed that I was behind 'im. I pulled over onto the shoulder and turned on my top light. When he got out and started back toward me, I recognized 'im. He was a local boy. Had two brothers but they wadn't with him then. None of them boys seemed to be wound too tight. I had other dealings with 'em later and knew 'em well.

"Anyway, I sat him in the patrol car to write his ticket. He had two passengers in his car, two ole boys he was tryin' to sell the car to. It was all souped up and he had told 'em it would run 145 MPH, could outrun anything on the road. They knew he had been runnin' it wide open. Now, he wadn't a bit worried about gettin' that speedin' ticket. He just didn't want me to tell those ole boys that we were only runnin' 127 MPH!

"It wadn't too many weeks later that I was workin' the three to midnight shift, had just got off, and was gettin' ready to go to bed. Still had my shoes on but no shirt. Then I heard cars coming, way up there, leavin' the four-lane highway. Tires were squallin', engines roarin'. I thought . . . God, they're not gonna make the S curve on that road. We were livin' in our house off Highway 27 North by then. I could tell there were two cars and they were racin'.

"I started runnin' for the patrol car when, lo and behold, they squealed around the corner and was comin' down the road in front of our house. Had it wide open. One of their hubcaps flew off and came rollin' down past the house. That road winds around and dead-ends in a subdivision over behind us. I could hear them doin' donuts and runnin' in circles over there. The sound carried real good. I knew they would have to come back sooner or later so I just waited, sittin' in my driveway.

"Finally they hit the hard road, headin' back towards me. When they got a couple hundred yards away, I turned on my blue light and pulled out in the road. They split me, takin' the ditches on each side, and kept goin'. I followed 'em. At the intersection down from the house, one went straight and the other hung a right. Got a good look at the car then and saw it was that same old Ford. I finally got it stopped and sure enough there was that same ole boy I had stopped for speedin'. He admitted the other driver was his brother and they were playin' a game of catch. That time he was pretty mouthy and we almost got in a tussle.

"He reminded me of that ole boy on the Andy Griffith show, Ernest T, who used to throw rocks. Obviously he hadn't sold the old car and it still had only one headlight. Still had it souped up and just liked to try it out ever once in a while, I guess."

"That episode with those boys reminds me of the drag-racin' days back in the late fifties and early sixties," Quentin said. "Got to be a real fad. It was a big thing, people came from out-of-state and there was a lot of money bet. The cars could run pretty fast anyway, but faster when they were all souped up. And it got to be dangerous, one man killed and a couple people hurt bad, so Raker and I tried to put a stop to it. We showed up at their race sites, chased 'em down and gave out a few tickets. It got to be a cat and mouse game, which added to the excitement for them, I guess. Sometimes I kidded around with 'em a little, but Raker was all business. He wadn't hard though, just one of the best troopers on the patrol in my opinion. He told it like it was and when his little ole Adam's apple stuck out, it was best not to give him any back talk. Everyone knew that, so they knew when to shut up.

"One night I had a boy by the name of Westberry ridin' with me. He was thinkin' about goin' on the patrol and wanted to see what it was like. We were hot after a drag racer, Butch Hoover, a local boy, who tried to lose us by turnin' out his lights and takin' off down a road that wadn't nothin' but two deep ruts of sand. It led through sand hills, scrub oaks, and pines and got pretty bumpy. We didn't have seat belts then. I had the steerin' wheel to brace myself with but Westberry, sittin' in the passenger seat, didn't have anything

"Butch really gave us a wild ride. He cleared up some old oak trees before I finally caught 'im. Westberry hit the top of my car so many times he was plumb addled, totally out of it. It knocked him senseless is what it did. He became a trooper later so I guess he didn't get too discouraged.

"After that incident, I put seat belts in my patrol car, a 1956 Ford. I designed 'em myself and used a parachute harness. They made me take 'em out, said they were unauthorized equipment. Actually, when I first went on the patrol, all we had in the way of extra equipment was a heater. No air conditioner. In the summer we had to wear those old heavy gabardine uniforms and had to wear our hat. We'd sweat like the devil, too. Our patrol cars only had two doors instead of four. Didn't have cages. They finally got cars with automatic transmissions in 1956.

"I still hear things about the patrol days. Marshall Hicks, a friend of mine who was into drag racin' and later became a county commissioner, told me once that he was passenger in a car I had stopped for speedin'. He said, 'The fine for speedin' was $35 and I heard you tell the driver that he was allowed $35 worth of talk and he had just used it all up.' I guess I probably said things like that but it was when they were tryin' to give me a hard time," Quentin said, grinning. "Actually, I gave 'em a break when I could, if they acted right.

"About 1963 I was workin' the midnight shift south of Perry. Traffic wadn't too heavy when I come up behind this car headin' south and started clockin' him. Usually when I did this I would clock three times, about a mile apart the first two times, and right close the last time to cinch it down. He was drivin' a 1963 black Chrysler 300. They had just come out with 'em and that was one hot car, heavy, with a 440 Magnum engine. We were movin' about 80 MPH. My patrol car was a 1963 Dodge, a lighter car, but it could move.

"When I got up behind 'im, he poured the coal to it. I stayed with 'im but backed off about fifty yards. Had my lights on but no siren. He crossed the county line goin' toward Cross City. There's some really bad curves on that highway, one called Eight Mile Curve where there's been a lot of wrecks and fatalities. I stayed with 'im and by then he knew he couldn't outrun me so he pulled over and stopped.

"There were three people in the car. Turned out the driver was the police chief from Mobile, Alabama, and the other two were police chiefs from a couple towns near Mobile. They were all headed to the National Police Chief's Convention in Tampa.

"He came back and flashed his badge right off the bat, nice as he could be. I wadn't a bit impressed. We had run close to 130 MPH and almost lost it a couple times on the curves. He apologized and said, 'I thought I could outrun you, this is the hottest car made.' I wrote him a ticket anyhow. He asked me how much it would have been if he hadn't tried to outrun me. I told him $35. Then he wanted to know how much the ticket was for and I told him to add $100 to it.

"He paid me in travelers' checks, then wanted to look under the hood of my patrol car, wanted to know what kind of engine I had. After that, the other two got out and began kiddin' and jokin' around. I imagine he'd been braggin' about how fast his car would go. Then he came across a little, ole, state trooper out there in wide-open country in the middle of the night and he thought he would show them. Uh huh! I bet those guys gave him a fit after they drove off. That sort of thing was almost a daily occurrence."

Sometime during that time frame, an incident happened that left a lasting impression on Quentin. An attorney from California called the Perry Patrol Station to tell them that he had a client there, a truck driver, who had just informed him that his truck was near Perry with a body in it. He had left his truck there, went all the way back to California and contacted his lawyer, before telling anyone about it. They had been studying a map of the area, as the driver wasn't sure of the location. He thought it was at a wayside park in Taylor County.

"I was thinkin' of the one north of Perry," Quentin said, "but I checked that one and there wadn't no truck there. So, I tried another park and there it sat. I had to get the Sheriff's Dept. out there because the truck was locked and we had to break in. It was summertime, I remember, and when we broke that window to get to the door, I started gagging. God Almighty! She was lyin' in the sleeper part of the semi with the curtains pulled and had been decomposin' in that heat for several days.

"Turned out she was a prostitute he had picked up at a truck stop in Haines City. He brought her up here and murdered her. Cut her throat and opened her up all the way down to her twot. I guess he musta panicked, because he just abandoned the truck, which was a company truck, a big semi, and took off back to California.

"We called out the EM Techs. I told them it was goin' to be a bad one and didn't know if they'd be able to handle it. Sgt. Williams, some of the deputies, and I were standin' around gaggin' and those EM Techs put on gloves and hats, climbed up in that truck, and handled that thing without ever changin' the expressions on their faces. I couldn't believe they could do that. They didn't even frown or nothin'! I just sat back and admired 'em."

There is one other subject concerning Quentin's days on the Highway Patrol that we haven't covered yet . . . and that's the relaying the troopers had to do. Since it took up so much of their time and the taxpayer's money, we can't ignore it. It, too, was directly related to politics.

A recruit had to have a letter of recommendation from his senator or representative before he could be considered for the

HP Academy. That, in itself, may have encouraged the role politics played in the everyday operations of the HP. And it was probably the reason the legislators, and other high-placed government officials, seemed to think the HP existed for their own personal convenience. The more power they had, the more they used the patrol. Chauffeuring and relaying personal items were the most frequent demands.

"Before I went on the patrol I had no idea such things went on," Quentin said. "They weren't talked around; they were just done and kept quiet by everybody. After awhile it got to be frustratin', not to mention downright disgustin'. We were called on to work overtime to do the relayin', usually two or three times a week. And during the legislative session, it was almost daily.

"Sometimes there wasn't a trooper out at night in Taylor County, or he might be workin' a wreck in Jefferson or Madison County. He would receive a radio message that a 10-5 was coming up from Miami to Tallahassee. That was the code for a relay, and that was one way it was hushed up. The trooper would have to stop what he was doin' and go to the county line to pick it up from the trooper in that county. The relay could be an article or somebody. He didn't know until he got there, then he took the relay across his county and gave it, or them, to the trooper in the next county.

"Sometimes a trooper would have to go farther than his county line. That happened if one trooper was workin' a bad accident and couldn't relay. Then the trooper had to sometimes cross two or more county lines, leavin' his county without coverage. I had to drive all the way to Chiefland once, and many times had to relay all the way to Tallahassee. Sometimes I didn't get home till daylight.

"The items most often relayed were citrus fruits, and strawberries when they were in season. Then there were hampers of beans, seafood of all descriptions, or anything that could be had gratis. Besides all that, we had government officials who had gotten fogged in at the airport and needed a chauffeur. Everything and everybody was dropped at the HP headquarters. Some of the relays were really ridiculous. I was called out of bed at night on a 10-5 call, south to the county line, to pick up a small Styrofoam cooler. It was so light I got curious about the contents and when I looked inside the damn thing was empty. There was a 99-cent price tag on it. It had been relayed all the way from St. Petersburg and was goin' to Tallahassee.

"Then there was the time I had to relay Tom Adam's hat. He was the Secretary of State at the time. He left his hat in a hotel in Miami. Instead of havin' it sent by Greyhound bus, he had us relay it. We were used for the politician's convenience and at the taxpayer's expense."

The trooper who met Quentin at the Taylor County line to relay the hat was from Brooksville. He was supposed to get off at midnight, but there was no trooper available between Hernando County and Taylor County at that time.

"I met him at the Steinhatchee River," Quentin said. "We stood on the bridge talkin'. I can't remember his name, but he was a good boy and an excellent patrolman. He was so totally disgusted and physically exhausted that he picked up that hat and was gonna toss it in the damn river, but I stopped 'im. He quit the patrol right after that.

"We troopers were all gettin' a belly full of relayin' so we began to speak more plainly on the radio, hopin' somebody would get wind of it. Hopefully the news media.

"Sometimes it got a little funny. Durin' strawberry season, I'd meet a trooper to pick up a relay and say, 'whatcha got?' He'd say 'damn strawberries' and he would be red all around the mouth from samplin' them, so I would help myself, too. By the time they were delivered there was about half as many as to begin with.

"You know what the partrol started doin'? We had to start signin' from the relay to relay . . . a damn inventory! Can you believe that? They didn't like us eatin' their berries and stuff. It really happened.

"There were some things I didn't mind relayin'. I was called out many times to relay eyeballs suspended in saline solution, medicines, and rare blood. Something like that was necessary and I didn't mind helpin' move it along one bit.

"There was one relay I never completed, though," Quentin said. "One of the HP officers —-I think it was Capt.Cosson but can't remember for sure—- had a brother who was an alcoholic. He had been sent about everywhere for treatment, but nothin' had done any good. We were told to relay 'im to the de-tox center down below Sanford. I picked 'im up early one morning as instructed, and started out for the Suwannee River. There wadn't a trooper on duty in Dixie County to help relay, so the trooper from Levy County was to meet me there. I told 'im we would be a little late because the man had decided he wanted to stop for breakfast.

"I drove into Cross City and stopped at a restaurant there. The man sat down at one of the tables while I went on through to the rest room. When I returned he was standin' beside the table chug-a-luggin' a beer and had another one in his other hand. All the local people who were sittin' there eatin' breakfast had seen us come in together. I was in uniform. I just kept walkin' right out the door and left 'im there.

"I got on the radio and called the Cross City patrol and told 'em that the 10-5 was at the restaurant. I also told 'em they could call the trooper down at Suwanee County to come get 'im if he wanted to because I wadn't takin' 'im any farther in my patrol car, and they could handle it anyway they wanted to.

"I came on back to Perry and nothing was ever said to me about it. Didn't know what happened and didn't care. We shouldn't a been relayin' him in the first place. When Burkett became top dog, he cut out most of the relayin'. About time, too.

"The troopers today don't know how lucky they are. I wonder if they have as many 'details' as we had back then . . . like the National Governors Convention in Miami, for example. I *always* had that one."

31 | CHAPTER

"Once a year governors from all over the United States met in Miami for several days, supposedly to conduct important business," Quentin said, "but they found time to do a lot of partyin', too. Each governor brought a large entourage with him, includin' wives and sometimes children. Back then the governors liked to have their meetin's in Miami or West Palm because of the weather and outside entertainment. Now they schedule 'em all over the U.S.

"Durin' the meetin's, troopers were pulled off the roads all over the state to cater to the visitin' governors' wishes and needs. Not just the governor's but everyone in his or her party, too. Usually three troopers were assigned to each governor, one to chauffeur and two to handle the baggage.

"The car dealers had a big promotional gimmick goin'. They made brand new cars available to the governors during their stay, and then sold them later as 'used,' but you can bet they didn't lose money. It was good advertisin', too."

Quentin was assigned to Gov. Rossilini, an Italian Catholic, from Washington State. He served as chairman of the convention, and Quentin served as his chauffeur. He was issued a new station wagon to drive the governor around in, and the two troopers who were detailed as baggage handlers were also given station wagons.

The troopers met the governors and their parties at the airport and transferred them to either the Fontainebleau or the Balmoral. The conventions were always held in the fanciest hotels and they sometimes took over the entire hotel. Usually the governors were booked into suites of rooms.

Most of the troopers didn't mind the assignment. It wasn't hard duty, as a rule. But according to Quentin that one week nearly did him in. That's because Governor Rossilini and his wife liked to party...almost all night...*every* night. They may have originated the term 'party animals' for it certainly described them. And, since it was Quentin's job to chauffeur, he had to accompany them wherever they decided to go.

The governors began their meetings at nine A.M. every morning and did whatever governors do at those things, while the troopers stayed at the "ready room" downstairs in the hotel. They had an elaborate setup with radios and telephones to insure they would be at the governors' disposal at all times. If the governors needed transportation, they drove them, and that applied to anyone in their party as well.

The wives spent their days touring and sightseeing, going to West Palm Beach shopping, or to Key West on boat tours. They were all constantly on the go with their troopers as chauffeurs. Most of the troopers were finished with their duties at night, however, but not Quentin or another trooper named John Polk. Polk's governor was a good friend of Rossilini's and he, too, liked to party. (Polk later became sheriff in Sanford.)

Every evening after dinner, Rossilini and his wife went juking with Quentin doing his chauffeuring duty. They toured most of the nightclubs in the area, but the Peppermint Lounge was one of their favorite hangouts. Quentin remembers it all.

"Rossilini had an uncanny memory," Quentin said. "He could get drunk as a coot and never forget anything. I've never met another human bein' like 'im in my life. He drank more than anybody I've ever seen, had an unbelievable capacity for booze, but even drunk he knew if the bartender shorted him one penny. I had to get him out of a couple fights.

"Everybody knew who the governors were, and us, too. Sometimes the bartenders, tryin' to take care of us poor little troopers, would hold out a dollar in change and try to slip it to us. They knew we couldn't afford the drinks. Rossilini caught that one time and created a scene. Hell, I didn't want his damn dollar, I was embarrassed by it all anyhow, but he seemed to like me. We would be on the go all night long. About one or two o'clock, the wife would give out and we would take her back to the hotel, and then keep right on partyin'. I kept hopin' he would quit when his wife did, just for one night, and let me get some rest. But no siree . . .

" 'Let's go, Whit,' he'd say and just the two of us would keep goin'. We saw the sun rise several mornings. His wife would go to bed about two and get a few hours sleep. About the time we got in, she was up and ready to go to early mass, bless 'er heart, and I had to take 'er.

"Meanwhile, the governor would catch a couple hours sleep and then he was good for all-day meetin's and more partyin' the next night. Damned if they didn't nearly kill me! I was really lookin' forward to the end of that week so I could get some rest. Finally, all the governors left...except Polk's and mine, that is, and they decided to stay another week. Rossilini even called the colonel and requested permission for me to accompany them to the Bahamas for a week. The Colonel refused, thank God, so Rossilini and his wife, with me in tow, resumed their partyin' in Miami for a second week. When they finally left, I had to drive my patrol car back home. Since Polk didn't have his car—-he had been relayed down—-I had to take 'im by Sanford on my way back. I'll never forget it. He throwed his junk in the back, crawled over into the back seat and went to sleep, dead to the world. I woke 'im up when we got to Sanford."

Getting sent on details was the rule rather than the exception, according to Quentin.

"The first few years I was on the patrol I was assigned almost every detail in Miami. I practically lived in Miami. Besides the Governors Conferences, the yearly AAA and VFW conventions, there were many more that I can't remember now. It was a political game the patrol played, an image-maker. Some of those details were borin', some exhaustin', and some I thoroughly enjoyed. Most, I thought, was a waste of taxpayers' money.

"One I remember real well was the time I was assigned to Governor George Wallace from Alabama. He had his wife with 'im. That time Nathan Sharon was chauffeur and was assigned a Cadillac. I took care of the baggage and drove a station wagon. It was durin' all the racial strife and Governor Wallace was gettin' a lot of press coverage and national attention, most of it bad.

"When we got to the hotel, all the media was out in force with their cameras. Besides that, there were about two thousand demonstrators across the street with their placards. They all knew he was comin' in, and they were all there waitin'.

"All the Cadillac's were pullin' into the reserved area in front of the hotel to unload the governors. We just pulled in behind the forward Cadillac. Governor Wallace climbed out of that damn car and looked straight out at all those people, and they didn't have any idea who he was. That was the funniest thing I've ever seen in my life. None of them recognized him. They didn't realize he was so short. That surprised me too. He only came up to my shoulder and I'm not all that tall.

"Me and Nathan got the luggage out with the help of the hotel porters, then walked on in with Governor and Mrs. Wallace to the elevators, then up to their rooms.

"One reporter, comin' through the lobby after goin' to the bathroom, happened to recognize Governor Wallace. He sailed in the elevator with us. He didn't have a camera or nothin' with him. We were all laughin' by that time, especially Governor Wallace. He said, 'Hell, none of them even knew me!' Then he made some remark about his shortness bein' the reason the demonstrators didn't spot 'im. He was actually disappointed, I think.

"Nathan said, 'Give 'em hell while you're down here, Governor!' and Wallace said 'I will, Son, I will.' He did too.

"There was one thing about that detail I really liked—-I got more rest than I did with Rossilini.

"I went to one detail in Miami where I did absolutely nothin'. I can't remember now why I was even sent down there. Me and Tidwell, a patrol pilot, went out to the airport and picked up a new slant-six, jet-black, Plymouth Valiant convertible that was made available for our use while we were there. We wore our civilian clothes and cruised around Miami day and night in that skeester, and every time we stopped at a red light, people on both sides would admire it and want to know where we got it. It was the first year Plymouth came out with that convertible, and it hadn't been put on the market at that time. Anyway, Tidwell, who was a real nut, would yell back that we stole it.

"One time we went out to the Everglades and rented a little two-seater trainin' plane. I scrooched up in the back seat, which had its own controls. We headed back to Miami with the intention of checkin' out the hotel roofs. It was rumored that women sunbathed in the nude on top of those hotels so we circled around them at sixty-five to seventy miles per hour. They did, sure 'nuff. There were cubicles up on those rooftops that were put up 'specially for sunbathin', and there was a woman in every one of 'em. Tidwell circled low, us lookin', and some of those women would sit up and flop their boobs at us. I ain't lyin'! They were as naked as jaybirds.

"We circled one hotel until we got a crick in our necks. When we decided it was time to head back to the airport, Tidwell found, to his horror, that he couldn't straighten the plane out. We were headed on a collision course with that hotel. Then Tidwell started yellin', 'Move your foot! Get your foot up!'

"There were pedals on the floor that controlled the flaps. They operated like gas pedals and clutches on a car. When you mashed those pedals the plane turned. I had been so engrossed in the scenery that I had my foot locked down on one of those pedals without realizin' it. It was a close call. We laughed about it later, but it was kinda scary at the time."

I remembered how motion sick Quentin got when he was in service and had to travel by ship or plane, so I asked him if he didn't get nauseated on that plane ride. He said, "No, not at all." Well, I reckon that's one quick and painless cure for motion sickness…nude women

(Tidwell, the patrol pilot, was stationed in Monticello, Florida. He retired after twenty years on the patrol and now runs the Ace Flying School in Tallahassee. He took Mark up for his first plane ride when he was five years old.)

Quentin met a lot of people during the years he was on the patrol and not all of them were felons. Some were just ordinary folks, down on their luck, and just passing through. After the big freeze wiped out the citrus crop in central Florida, many transient workers came through Perry heading west. Most of them were black, elderly, and penniless. All were hungry and dressed in rags. Often Quentin would take what money he had, go to the nearest store, and buy them a sack of Vienna sausage, sardines, and crackers. If there was any money left, he would toss in a can of Prince Albert tobacco and wrappers. They appreciated the food but were downright thrilled over the smokes, a real luxury.

One day, while he was patrolling, Quentin saw an old black man trudging along the highway. His clothing was in shreds and his shoes were so worn through they flapped when he walked. Quentin stopped, began talking to him, and discovered the man had walked all the way from central Florida. He was trying to get to Louisiana and hadn't eaten in two days. Quentin put him in the car and took him home for a hot meal, a bath, and a change of clothes.

Thais wasn't surprised when Quentin drove up with a strange man in the car. Similar incidents happened on a regular basis. Most wives who struggled daily just to make ends meet might have resented that compulsion of Quentin's to help any and all needy people he ran into, but Thais understood. Anytime he showed up with some ragged hobo, she just threw pots on the stove and started whipping up a meal with whatever she could find, or digging around in the closets for some clothes that weren't already worn out.

Behind his tough image there is a tender spot Quentin would just as soon people didn't know about. Giving a helping hand where it is needed isn't something he gives a lot of thought to. He just does it. It's the way he's put together and he doesn't feel comfortable talking about it, either. Actually, I had to pry it out of him. Pulling his eyeteeth with a pair of rusty pliers would have been easier. And there's one thing for sure...he never expects any sort of recognition for anything he does. A simple "thank you" is more than enough. Well, there were a couple times during his patrol days when he would have appreciated some sort of follow-up. Instead, he was left to wonder. One of those times was in 1981.

Quentin had a trooper friend, John Yawn, who had been diagnosed with a malignant brain tumor. One morning he took John to Tallahassee for his chemotherapy and they went in the patrol car. When they were returning to Perry on Highway 27, Quentin noticed a car with a Massachusetts license plate parked by the side of the road. The hood was up, and the car had a flat tire, but there was no one standing around outside the car, as he expected. Quentin slowed and pulled up behind the car and stopped. He could see through the back window that there was one occupant, a white male, sitting behind the wheel.

When he walked up to the driver's side and looked in, he saw a bearded man, who appeared to be in his thirties, slumped down in the seat against the door. Quentin thought at first that the man was asleep. Then he noticed that the man had a 370 Magnum pistol, cocked and pressed against his chin. His eyes were glazed, perspiration was running down his face, and he appeared to be in a state of shock.

"I saw what an agitated mental state he was in and knew he probably wouldn't recognize me," Quentin said, "so I started talkin' to him real slow and soft. I said, 'you don't really want to do this. I'm a state trooper and I'm here to help you. I was passin' by and noticed you had a flat tire'."

In the meantime, John Yawn got curious, left the patrol car, and was approaching on foot. Quentin heard him and discreetly waved him back. He knew if the man was suddenly startled he would most likely pull the trigger, leaving most of his head on the roof of the car.

Quentin continued to speak softly, then slowly reached up and gently pushed the gun to one side. As he did so, he put his finger between the gun and the hammer so that it wouldn't fire. The man released the gun and just sat there. It was then that Quentin saw a handwritten note lying on the dash. After he talked the man into getting out of the car, he slipped the note into his pocket.

He put John in the rear seat of the patrol car and the man in the front. After about fifteen minutes, the man seemed to become calmer and began to talk freely. His name was Steve, and as he talked Quentin began to see why he was so desperate and filled with despair. The note, which Quentin had put among his things and forgotten until recently, explained it all.

"Dear Mom and Dad, by the time you get this letter, I'll be gone. It makes no difference why or where. I can't take it anymore. Everything is going bad for me with no change in sight. I lost my job, my license, and my will to live. Please don't think too badly of me but I can't face anybody anymore. I'm a total failure and I don't want to live this way anymore. Please kiss the kids for me but don't tell them what happened to me. Love, Steve."

Quentin introduced Steve to John and explained John's problem. "I pointed out to Steve that John had no choice where his life was concerned, but he, Steve, did. That seemed to impress 'im, which is what I wanted, anything to get 'im past the notion of killin' himself.

"I kinda took him under my wing after that, felt kinda responsible for him, I reckon. Anyway, I took the spare tire off my pickup truck at home and changed his tire. Then I took him to the new shoppin' center that was under construction. The contractor, who was a friend of mine, hired Steve on as a carpenter. He had to work three days before payday, so I loaned him enough money to pay for three days in a nearby motel, and gave 'im enough food money to last.

"Three days later, Steve came by the patrol station and asked me if I would wait another week for the $83 he owed because the motel had to be paid in advance for the next week. He borrowed fifteen more dollars and told me he would see me the followin' Friday. He never showed up. When I asked at the motel and at the job, I found out that Steve quit the job after three days and left town. I never heard from 'im again. I always wondered where he went and what happened to 'im."

It wasn't long after that incident that Quentin found an out-of-state trooper and his family stranded on the highway south of Perry. He was broke and had run out of gas. Quentin bought him a tank of gas and gave him enough money to get back to his home in Alabama. He never heard from him again either.

Quentin probably felt let down from time to time, but he has never become hardened to the needs of others because of it. He continues doing his good deeds and keeping his mouth shut about it. Which, I suppose, makes him a contradiction of sorts. On one hand, he can give the word "frugality" new meaning; yet, at the same time, give anyone the shirt off his back if he figures the situation calls for it.

(Mother died suddenly on February 15, 1983 from chronic lung disease, which seems to run on the Carter side of the family. Losing our remaining parent left a big hole in our lives... but it also left us with some beautiful memories: her wit, love of nature, musical talent, creativeness, and devotion to family. She was a lady).

Quentin had so many tales to tell about his life as a highway patrol trooper I would be hard put to find a stopping place, but before I close out that period in his life, I must tell about the time he stopped a big crime boss for speeding. His name was Talifonta, he lived in Tampa, and he was on his way to New Orleans in a big, black, Cadillac limo. He was also under investigation by the FBI at the time, but Quentin didn't know that when he stopped him.

"I was on the midnight shift and they were doin' about 95 MPH when I pulled them over," Quentin said. "Talifonta was sitting in the back seat and his chauffeur was drivin'. They just quietly paid their fine and left. It was a long time later before I realized who he was and that they were fleein' to New Orleans, tryin' to outrun the federal indictments. They wouldn't have hurt me anyway. They like to keep a low profile where lawmen are concerned."

Quentin stopped anybody and everybody if they were speeding. It didn't matter how powerful they were, or how up on the political ladder they perched. To him the law applied to everyone equally. He would have given a ticket to Thais, too, if he'd caught her speeding. Well, maybe a warning ticket the first time. But he used to get called on the carpet regularly for stopping legislators. When they came through Perry driving over 80 MPH, he gave them a speeding ticket. The same as anyone else. Didn't matter to him who they were. The bigshots in the main office must have developed ulcers trying to appease those politicians. They would call Quentin up to Tallahassee and rake him over the coals. He never understood that. To his mind, they should have complimented him on doing his job. So, he just returned to Perry and continued doing his job, ticketing speeders, whoever they happened to be. To him, if they didn't want a speeding ticket they damn well shouldn't come through his county speeding.

Other decisions made by the patrol didn't make any sense to him either. For instance:

"I was to retire from the patrol the last day of December 1981," Quentin said. "That same month they sent me to school. Can you believe anything that stupid? It was a two-week school at the academy in Tallahassee. That wadn't all. After that school, they notified me that I was to attend a two-day seminar at the DOT building in Tallahassee to learn how to handle train wrecks or explosions. I drove over the first day and reported to Lt. Pfeiffer, the assistant troop commander under Cook.

"About midmorning we had a break and a few of us went outside for a smoke. I told Lt. Pfeiffer that I was goin' back to Perry. He said, 'you can't do that!' I said 'the hell I can't.' You get somebody up here in my place who's goin' to stay on the patrol. I'm leavin'. And I did. I got in my damn car and came on back to Perry. Pfeiffer was a company man from the word go, and he couldn't believe I would ignore my orders and just leave. Nothin' was said to me about that either. Not a word. The whole thing didn't make a bit of sense. I used to wonder who it was that made such asinine decisions."

So . . . after twenty-five years on the Florida Highway Patrol Quentin finally retired on December 31, 1981. He began as a trooper and almost retired as a trooper. From 1967 until his retirement, Quentin was a homicide investigator. In 1981 all homicide investigators were automatically promoted to corporal...with no increase in pay. Then, at retirement, he was automatically promoted to sergeant. That didn't help his retirement pay either, so Quentin still considered himself a trooper. As he said, the title meant nothing to him, just the amount of pay. He didn't see where adding a title to his name made him any better lawman. It was just the prestige of it and he didn't figure he needed to impress anybody.

His last day on the patrol included a big outdoor retirement party at the patrol station, with lots of people, lots of food, and lots of presents.

Now, there are a lot of people who don't know what to do with themselves when they retire. Not Quentin. For the next three years he enjoyed being a free man, doing all the things he had never had time to do. He bought a slide-in camper for his pickup and traveled. He hung out with friends at his hunting camp, playing poker and eating exotic Taylor-County-type food, like mullet and swamp cabbage. His pots of squirrel stew and beans became notorious. They sometimes simmered for days and were reported to be unbelievably potent...a sure-fire cure for constipation even if you weren't troubled with it. But his retirement wasn't destined to last...at least, not then anyway. That's because he took the notion to run for sheriff of Taylor County in the next election. He had his reasons.

32 | Chapter

Giving up his life of leisure and running for sheriff of Taylor County wasn't a decision he made lightly. When I questioned him about his reasons for doing so, Quentin said:

"There was a bunch of things that made me decide to do it, I guess. I'd been thinkin' about runnin' even before I got off the patrol. A lot of good local people had been talkin' to me and tryin' to get me to run. Then, after I retired from the patrol I found out my retirement pay didn't go very far. After a couple years trying to live on it, the sheriff's pay started to sound mighty good. In 1978, when Ronnie was about twelve, Thais went back to work in Tallahassee in one of the state offices. But even with her paycheck we still lived pretty tight.

"There was something else we had to consider as well. Ronnie was a straight A student, definitely college material. We were hopin' he'd get a scholarship when he graduated, like Mark did, but we couldn't depend on it. Donna had graduated and was working in Tallahassee but thinking about going into nurse's training. We knew she would need financial help as well.

"All those things influenced me, but I guess the main reason I decided to run for sheriff was because drugs were takin' over Taylor County. Made me sick. The year before I ran there was even an investigation into involvement by sheriff's department employees. A grand jury hearin' revealed that there were uniformed personnel suspected of dealin' in drugs, and a recommendation made that they be given a polygraph. It was never done. The sheriff didn't require it. He was a friend, we had worked together in the past, and I knew he was basically a good lawman. But...he did let things slip when he was in office. No doubt about it.

"After I retired from the patrol, I worked a lot with the DEA, Customs, and FDLE for free. I saw what went on . . . city and county officials, local residents, and even law enforcement officers . . . all in the drug business. I knew most of them personally, and I thought I could do something about it, if I could get elected

"Before I obligated myself to run, though, I decided I'd better do some checkin' around and see how much of a financial base I would need. Found out it would take between fifteen and twenty thousand dollars to back a campaign, but I figured I could do it for less. So, I opened a separate bank account and began savin' up. When I qualified to run I had five thousand dollars in my campaign fund. The man I defeated told me later that he spent nineteen thousand. But he did a lot of advertisin' and my campaignin' was mostly door-to-door. I don't reckon I missed many houses in Taylor County. Wore out a lot of shoe leather, too.

"The primary was held in September 1984 and I got 62% of the votes. Winnin' with that large a percentage made me feel real good. I didn't have Republican opposition so there wadn't a runoff in October. It's a good thing, too, 'cause all I had left in my campaign fund was $1.83. There's one thing I need to mention here . . . all my campaign money was saved up by Thais and me and wadn't from contributions. I refused all offers of financial help.

"The way I look at it, very few people donate to an election without expectin' a favor down the line . . . very few. I figured I could do a lot better job if I wadn't obligated to anybody. A lot of people didn't understand that. There were some who called me after I got in office and said, 'Sheriff, I voted for you and now I want you to do something about so-an-so.' I tried to handle those as tactfully as possible, but even then I guess I made a few people mad.

"There was a bunch of black preachers who offered to 'work' in my election but wanted me to 'pay their expenses.' They control their churches and the people vote the way their preacher tells them to vote. They don't think there's anything wrong with that. That's the way a lot of people get elected. Buyin' votes is what it was, though, and I didn't go for it.

"I really think one of the reasons my campaign was successful was because of Thais and the kids. Mark, Donna, and Ronnie were all born and raised here, and they were all thought a lot of. I'm convinced that was a big asset in the campaign. Besides that, I had worked in Taylor County for twenty-seven years, and I guess the people knew me pretty well and knew what kind of sheriff I'd make. Enough of them approved to get me elected, anyway.

"I took office on January 1, 1985, after defeatin' John Walker. There was another man runnin' on the Democratic ticket but I can't remember his name."

The job of sheriff turned out to be bigger than Quentin anticipated. All the patrol cars were worn out, most with over 100,000 miles on them. They had rusted-out holes in the floorboards, covered with car mats that flapped in the wind. Salaries were low and employee morale equally so. Investigative equipment was practically nonexistent. There was little money in the budget, and only $700 in the drug fund and that was all used for drug buys the first night.

One of the first things he did was restructure the employee insurance program, which he felt was unfair. As sheriff, all of his hospital insurance was paid, while the employees had to pay 50% of theirs. Under his plan, everyone...including himself... had to pay 25% and the sheriff's office paid the remaining 75%.

From his employees he demanded and received their respect. Anyone caught doing anything dishonest was fired. Some employees were promoted and salaries adjusted to better reflect their dedication. An ace investigator was hired from out of state.

Quentin set certain goals for his term as sheriff and one of the first was to update equipment, especially the patrol cars. Before he took office all new patrol cars were purchased in Perry from the local dealers at full retail price. He had no objection to buying the cars locally, as long as the prices were competitive, but he found out that hadn't been the case up until then. Since money was so short, Quentin felt he owed it to the taxpayers to make the best deal he could, and he set about doing so.

All patrol cars had to be police-equipped for safety. He found out he could buy those under state contract and save from

$2800 to $3000 per car. For his own use, and for his investigator and chief deputy, he bought low-mileage used-cars, either locally or from Hertz. He shopped around like a penny-pinching housewife, but he ended up with good safe cars for his employees and saved a bundle doing it. The taxpayers should have been proud! He felt he had an obligation to the people of Taylor County to spend their tax dollars as frugally as possible. Being frugal was easy for him anyhow. You might say he had been training for that part of the job all his life.

Quentin had to hire five additional correction officers almost immediately after taking office. The Dept. of Corrections required this and, at that time, the sheriff's office was under a lawsuit because of failure to do so. He also hired one new clerk and three resident deputies. His total number of employees was thirty-five. This included correctional officers, dispatchers, people manning the jail, investigators, support personnel, and a chief deputy.

(According to Quentin, five years after he left office, the sheriff's department had more than twice that many employees, and a budget three times greater. It's interesting to note that the number of arrests annually was about the same. However, they had a relatively new five-million-dollar jail to keep them in and forty-four correctional officers. Quentin operated with ten correctional officers and one supervisor. Their average daily jail count was sixty-eight, in a jail that will hold 183 people. Quentin's daily jail count was in the upper forties, but many times he had as many as sixty plus. Of course, if there had been more beds he could have made more arrests, but as it was, he could only sleep forty-seven. More than that got a mattress on the floor. So, to summarize, it costs the taxpayers three times as much money to incarcerate the same number of prisoners.)

Once Quentin settled in and had things running smoothly, he began concentrating on cleaning up the drug business in Taylor County. He had acquired an excellent supportive staff with Steve Spradley as investigator, Jack Underwood as lieutenant, and Carl Williams as chief deputy. (Williams had been a sergeant on the road patrol before his retirement.)

"Marijuana was the big moneymaker then," Quentin said, "and many of our local residents were involved. Taylor County has fifty-two miles of rural coastline. That's where the drugs were off-loaded from the mother ship and moved up the creeks and streams to where they were picked up by the dealers. To move in the shallow water they needed small draft boats, like mullet boats. So, they sucked in the old mullet fishermen by payin' 'em as much as $10,000 for one night's work. That was more than most of 'em made in a year fishin'. They weren't too smart, though, and began spendin' that money like crazy, buyin' new fancy automobiles and anything else their little heart's desired. Payin' cash for it, too. Naturally that sent up a red flag to me and I would start an investigation. When I sent that one off, seemed like there were two to take 'is place.

"One of the first things I did was contact the people I'd worked with in the different drug agencies. We had a good relationship. Up until then, they hadn't had much cooperation from the local law enforcement agencies, but they got plenty from me and my administration. We worked well together and that continued throughout the four years I was in office.

"It was in August of 1985 that crack cocaine began hittin' the street. Nobody knew what it was at first. It surfaced on the lower east coast, brought in from Jamaica by the Jamaicans and Haitians, and eventually turned up in Taylor County. Marijuana took up enough of my time but the crack cocaine turned out to be my biggest headache. That's because it's so highly addictive. I saw a lot of people's lives ruined because of it, good people I'd known for years. Some of 'em just tried crack as a lark, not realizin' that it only took a time or two to get hooked. So crime went up as the users began stealin' to support their habit. It wadn't unusual on our stakeouts to see a young white girl approach a black dealer and try to prostitute herself to get a supply.

"I decided I would stand a better chance of dealin' with it if I found out all I could about it. Something so powerful that it could cause a person to lose all pride, and sink down in the gutter just to get a fix, was damn scary. So I read everything I could find on it.

"It was through the Florida Sheriff's Association that I began to compare notes with some of the other law enforcement officers around the state and realized that crack cocaine wadn't just confined to Taylor County. It was spreadin' like wild fire all over the damn state. A few of us became concerned enough to contact Lawton Chiles for any federal assistance we could get.

He was still senator at that time, before he became governor of Florida.

"At his invitation we went to D.C. and briefed the heads of departments for the DEA, Immigration Service, and FBI. Besides myself, there were the sheriffs from Sumter and Citrus Counties, an investigator from the Tallahassee Police Department, and the chief of police from Hillsborough County. Chiles set up that meetin' in front of the National Press for television to give us as much coverage as possible. He was concerned and cooperated as much as he could, I guess.

"The reason the immigration officials were involved was because the cocaine was being brought into the country by aliens from overseas. I later worked with the FBI on a couple things but then they weren't all that involved with the drug problem. Turned out that the FDEA was the agency to help me most.

"To be honest, there was another reason why I went to D.C. I mean...besides wantin' to make people on the federal level aware of the destructiveness of crack cocaine, and of the problems we were confrontin' in tryin' to cope with it. I had found out that they were makin' a lot of seizures in South Florida on importation of marijuana. The U.S. Customs officials were seizin' boats and planes, which they were permitted to do under the law, and storin' them at taxpayer expense for hundreds of thousands of dollars. I figured they could donate them to law enforcement agencies that couldn't afford to buy them, like me. Then we would have a boat to patrol that fifty-two miles of rural coastline. Made a lot of common sense to me, especially since many of those boats were rottin' and sinkin' in the canals down there. Well, if there's one thing I discovered it's that the people on the federal level are not blessed with common sense. They're not a bit impressed when confronted with it, either. We needed federal assistance but we didn't get it, not then anyway.

"Chiles did stay in touch with me, though, and it was one of his aides who advised me to go to Camp Blanding. Seems they had some boats over there we might get. But, as we found out later, they were boats we couldn't use because our coastline is so shallow. The best things would have been airboats 'cause they have speed *and* shallow draft.

"Since that didn't materialize, I went to the FDEA (Federal Drug Enforcement Administration) for help and got the best reception of the trip. The man in charge was named Rabb, or something like that. He called me aside and was quite interested in workin' with me. Up until then, the FDEA had never worked street-level buys, and he wanted to start a pilot program aimed at reachin' the top dogs. They were too well insulated to get caught easily, but he figured it was time to make a stab at it. As it was, arrestin' the small fry wadn't makin' a dent in the drug traffickin'.

"So, the FDEA started a program and I worked with their office out of Gainesville. They financed everything at first, the drug buys, et cetera, and that suited me fine since my drug fund was practically nonexistent. Our plan was to start at the bottom and roll up. In other words, we began with the dealers not the users, and tried to get them to tell us where they got it—-which always turned out to be South Florida—-and then roll on up the line towards the top. We worked that system for four years. It was a good plan and proved successful, but in the process I made some of the state authorities mad.

"That's the problem in law enforcement and drug work. Each agency is jealous of the others. Consequently, it was rare that they freely cooperated with one another. None of 'em wanted to work with the others, and each of 'em wanted to work with me in Taylor County because it was such a lucrative spot to do drug work.

"I chose to work with the federal authorities rather than the state for several reasons, one being that I was already involved in a suit in federal court because I had the jail overfilled. A more important reason, at least to me, was because the federal people weren't hog-tied by guidelines like the state people were. In the state system you have to have three convictions before you actually have to serve time, and then you only have to serve about a fourth of that. That meant we were arrestin' the same people over and over, and it got real discouragin'.

"I only made a few cases with the state before goin' federal. We prosecuted a few locally; mostly individuals who went down to South Florida and hauled the drugs back themselves. But if I knew a drug ring was involved, I went federal. And the result of all that was . . . I made the state's attorney, Jerry Blair, mad as hell at me because we were in his circuit.

"All of our cases were good sound cases that almost guaranteed a 100% conviction rate. By goin' federal it made the federal prosecutors look good. I didn't care much; I got along good with the local prosecutors. We had few jury trials because we investigated, got all the material together, made the case, and turned it all over to the federal people. They took it from there. We made 232 drug arrests while I was sheriff, and we only lost one case. That one was by jury trial in Tallahassee. Only one. That's a pretty good record. And one reason for that was because I had such a fantastic investigator, Steve Spradley. He was jam up.

"Usually we would have several cases under investigation at once. Some of them were long-term, like four or five months. Durin' that time, the other agencies, mainly the FDLE, FDEA, or Customs, would bring in their investigators to assist in getting' together the evidence. We also had a joint local task force with the city. They had a good investigator, Clay Parker, who worked with us. He and Steve got along good and worked well together. In fact, we all had a good close workin' relationship.

"We would make as many buys and get as much documented evidence as we could. Then, I would get all the officers from the other departments in here and do a sting. We would have all the warrants made out, and within thirty minutes we would make all the arrests connected to that particular case. Then we would turn them over to the Feds for prosecution. I knew when they were sent up they wouldn't be back on the street for a long time. Then, too, I didn't have to hold them in my jail for long, which helped with the census. If it worked out that I did have to hold them for a while, the Feds paid me so much a day to house them. So, I made money off of 'em if they stayed in my jail. I liked that."

Quentin's first drug bust as sheriff was successful, but he almost got killed in the process. Not from a bullet either.

A man and woman in a florist van with a Madison County tag had been under surveillance for some time, as they sold cocaine and marijuana in Taylor County. Quentin notified the Madison County sheriff but no arrests were made. So, his men began to gather evidence. They made buys and recorded conversations.

The couple's drug transactions took place in a house east of Perry off Highway 27. Quentin's deputies had been watching the place up until the drug bust to make sure no one was there that night except the guilty parties. Quentin was running late and took off across a field as fast as he could go to get in position behind the house. Since he had never seen the place before, and it was pitch dark, he couldn't tell exactly where he was putting his feet. He couldn't use his flashlight without giving away his position. So, what happened was...he fell headlong into a deep hole. One minute he was running and the next minute he was flying through the air, ending up on his back with the wind knocked out of him. In the process, he dropped his flashlight and walkie-talkie.

After getting his breath back and making sure nothing was broken, he lit his cigarette lighter, looked around, and saw that his flashlight was smashed. From what he could see with his lighter, the hole appeared to be about three-yards-wide by ten-yards-long and about twelve-feet-deep. It was filled entirely with concrete blocks that had steel rods sticking up out of them every few inches to about three feet. Quentin fell in the only place in that hole he could have fallen without getting impaled on a steel rod.

The hole had straight sides and he kept trying to climb out without success. Finally he managed to pull himself up and over the top. By that time, the drug bust had taken place and the deputies were looking for him. He took them back in daylight and showed them the hole. They couldn't believe he fell in without ramming a steel rod through his body.

Didn't I tell you the boy had a way of tempting fate? His guardian angel must have been plumb worn out by that time.

33 | Chapter

Almost every night, if Quentin had no other pressing business to take care of, he would drive his unmarked car down to the black section of town. He knew a lot of drug dealing was going on under a big oak tree there, behind a juke, so he would sit on the hood of his car and observe the buying and selling. That this might be a dangerous thing to do never concerned him unduly, or if it did he just ignored it.

There didn't seem to be any racial barriers where drugs were concerned; both whites and blacks did business under that old oak tree. Physical handicaps didn't slow them down either. One of the most active dealers was a black man in a wheel chair. He had runners to deliver drugs and collect money for him, and he had quite a lucrative business going until he, too, was busted and sent to prison.

The dealers knew Quentin was there, watching. He knew most of them; some had even been his friends at one time. And even though all he did was watch and make mental notes, his presence there hurt business and made the dealers nervous. He liked that.

Eventually, Quentin set up surveillance with a video camera in a nearby house that was owned by an ex-drug dealer. When he was arrested, the dealer decided to cooperate with the authorities and maybe gain a few brownie points by letting them use his house as a base of operations. The investigators spent days and nights filmin' dealers doing transactions from that vantage point and, eventually, they made so many arrests the dealers moved their business to a different part of town...where it started all over again.

Some of the investigations were on-going and they could get stressful at times, but occasionally there were comic moments to relieve the tension.

"There were times," Quentin said, "when it seemed like everybody in Taylor County was either into drugs, was related to someone in drugs, or knew someone who was into drugs. Got right depressin'...but sometimes it did have a funny side if you could keep your sense of humor.

"We found out that a long-time post office employee was into drugs in a big way. He was importing cocaine and making crack in his kitchen. The dealer had a runner, called a mule, who worked for him and brought in the drugs from Miami, and we knew they were makin' hundreds of thousands of dollars annually. To get the evidence we needed to make a case, we brought in a DEA under-cover agent by the name of Mike. I won't use his last name. He was really good at his job. Looked the part too. Longhaired, unshaven, scroungey-lookin' clothes. He built up a relationship with the drug man by tryin' to get instructions on how to make crack. It was still pretty new and the instructions relatively simple.

"Eventually Mike made a deal to buy cocaine from the man so he could make a batch. The transaction was to take place in a local motel room. Before the meetin' was to take place, we set up the room with concealed cameras, one in the overhead light fixture and one in the base of the table lamp. We had the entire room covered for filmin' and for sound. Most of the equipment came from the DEA. They had all kinds of sophisticated gadgets I couldn't afford. "All the monitorin' equipment was in the adjoinin' room which had a common door. Me and a few investigators were next door, listenin' in and watchin' the proceedins'. There were times we got so tickled we thought we'd blow the whole set-up by burstin' out laughin'. I don't know how Mike did it with a straight face. But he was trained to it.

"He said, 'I went back to Gainesville and tried ta cook up a batch of that crack cocaine, but I musta done somethin' wrong 'cause when I mixed it up with that mayonnaise it just didn't come out right.'

"The drug dealer said, 'My-naise? I told ya to mix it in a my-naise JAR!'

"Here we were in the next room tryin' to be quiet and practically rollin' around on the floor laughin'.

"They agreed on a price and when the mule returned with the cocaine, Mike told the dealer that he wanted to check it for quality before he bought it. He pulled out his common drug test kit and put a pinch of cocaine in the test tube. Then he broke it into a little plastic bag. As he explained, a change in color would indicate the purity of the cocaine.

"The druggers were dumfounded. They'd never seen one of those kits before. After money had exchanged hands and the deal concluded, the big man decided he'd better do some testin' before buyin' from his source.

" 'He said, 'Where do ya get these here drug test kits?'

" 'Mike said, 'Oh, only law enforcement officers have 'em.'

He knew we already had enough evidence to make the case, so he just decided to have a little fun. What was really hilarious was the druggers didn't even pick up on that. The big man just said, 'Do tell' and then he asked Mike if he could have the used one. He stuck it in his cap, then put the cap on his head. It was almost impossible to stay quiet. We busted 'em right after that.

"I worked a lot with Mike, and also with another man who had been a helicopter pilot in Vietnam. He was just as nutty and crazy as Mike when it came to takin' chances. They did dangerous work You had to know the lingo, speak the slang, and look the part in order to fit into the drug scene, and it took somebody who was a perfect actor. If an undercover agent did it long enough, it became harder to revert back to his own personality and appearance. He developed this role he played and eventually he became that person, so much so that many times he was destroyed by it. Some even got into drug use. Mike stayed straight and eventually quit the under-cover work.

"We did a lot of sting operations with the FDEA and FDLE," Quentin said. "They brought in a lot of officers and equipment. One of the biggest stings we did was limited to marijuana and took months to set up. It started in California, was a multi-state/ multi-county affair, and was finalized at a motel here in Perry. Because it crossed state lines, Customs was also involved and they helped coordinate the sting. It was set up as an undercover operation with us as the sellers rather than buyers.

"A drug agent had been flipped down in South Florida. That meant he bad been busted and persuaded to come up to Perry and contact the drug brokers. Oh yeah, there were actual brokers who flew around the country checkin' out drugs. They operated a service like a CPA or an attorney. Deals were made and a day set for them to fly in for the buy. We had staggered appointments set up all day and couldn't afford to have any over-lappin'. Each buyer thought he was the only one we were dealin' with, so timin' was critical.

"They would fly into the Tallahassee airport and Mike or the helicopter pilot—-I can't remember his name—-took turns pickin' them up in a van. Hell, they had a regular shuttle service goin'! Others would take a cab from the airport to Perry. Some came in a motor home or would rent one to transport the drugs in. Tons of marijuana were sold durin' that sting, several hundred pounds to each person and the total money involved ran to about one-half million dollars. The exchange of money took place in the motel room, but they had to pick up the marijuana at a tobacco barn south of Perry, down in Levy County. That was under surveillance, too, and being video-taped as well. Those people were busted as soon as they drove off, before word could get back up here to Perry.

"The last dealer, one of the biggest, flew in from California and brought his three bodyguards. They were picked up by the pilot who drove like a scalded dog getting' back to Perry. It was getting' late and everybody was getting' anxious to finish up and close the sting down. It had been a long nerve-rackin' day, so I guess that's what made what happened later so damn funny to us.

"The three bodyguards checked into a motel across the street from where the drug deals were goin' down. We had been warned by informants in California that if they showed up to be aware that they were armed and dangerous. Their job was surveillance to see if any law officers showed, and they were good at it. They had all kinds of detection devices and stuff like that. What they didn't know was that while they were watchin' for us we had them under surveillance.

"When it come time to bust them, they were in Howard Johnson's eatin' supper. The place was full of people. We had no choice but to get them right then, because we were bustin' their boss in the motel next to Howard Johnson's. The arrests had to be timed within a few minutes of each other, and we knew we had to get them out of the restaurant to do it.

"They hadn't seen Mike, the undercover agent I liked so much, so he goes into the restaurant and slides into the booth with them while we're outside watchin' 'em from the parkin' lot. They look at him like he's nuts. He says, 'You'd better get out of here fast. The law's arrestin' everybody. Everything's goin' down. Y'all better get movin'. They jumped up and started gatherin' up their jackets from the back of the seats. Then, one of them turned to Mike and said, 'Well, who the hell are you?' and Mike said, without battin' an eye, 'Oh, I'm the one that drove the motor home down yonder.' Like that explained everything.

"They didn't even question it, which was funny. They paid their bill and hustled out. When they hit the parkin' lot, we busted 'em and started friskin' them. That's when we got the surprise of our lives...one of those bodyguards was a woman. I'm not kiddin'. Sure had us fooled. We had been watchin' them with binoculars and had them under surveillance all that time and never even suspected. Well, she sure looked the part. We had a real laugh over that.

"By that time it was good dark and we had to get a search warrant based on probable cause before we could check out their motel room. I wadn't involved in the room search, but the other agents found all kinds of automatic weapons and a sawed-off shotgun. Those dudes...and dudette...meant serious business. We were lucky.

"That sting was fun to me. It was good drug work, a coordinated effort by a lot of agencies in a lot of states. There wadn't much publicity afterwards, just a small article in the paper was all. When it was all over and we divvied up the money that was seized, I got about $54,000. I used most of it in drug investigations and bought some much-needed equipment for our surveillance work...like an airboat to patrol the coast. I shared some of the money with the city police because they helped with the sting and didn't have much in their drug fund. I found out later that some asshole in authority took the money out of the drug fund and put it in general revenue. Made me mad as hell, too, but wadn't nothing' I could do about it then."

Quentin was so determined to succeed at his goals as sheriff that he took little time off. His days were long and all-night stakeouts were common. He always accompanied his deputies if danger was involved and sometimes if it wasn't. Sitting behind the desk and shuffling papers wasn't his style; being in the thick of things was. He eventually gained the reputation of being fearless, but as with all things, there are exceptions. The only thing Quentin had a deathly fear of was snakes...any size, any type, any color. But he especially hated rattlesnakes.

Now, that snake-phobia could have started with the Howard Shell snakebite incident when he was eleven, or with the Billy Maxwell rattlesnake-trapping incident when he was on the patrol, but it increased over the years. He wasn't too keen on having people know about his one, teeny, little fear and spoiling his bold, daring reputation...but it came out anyway, eventually.

When an informant called to let him know a drug shipment was being flown in one night to an abandoned airstrip in the northern part of Taylor County, Quentin decided to check out the place beforehand. He drove out for a look-see that morning and saw that the area surrounding the airstrip was mostly sand, palmettos, and scrub oak. Lots of gopher holes, too. A good place or rattlesnakes. But he tried not to think about that. Instead, he concerned himself with locating the best places of concealment for his deputies and the other drug agents; places that would provide the best surveillance. It was to be a multiple agency affair with Quentin acting as the head honcho and doing the coordinating and directing of the operation.

About dusk dark he arrived back at the scene with his deputies and the other law enforcement officers. After deploying the men around the perimeter of the airstrip, he chose a place for himself among some bushes where he could be in close contact with the other men but couldn't be seen by the plane's occupants when they arrived.

He unrolled a sheet of plastic on the ground and lay down in a spot he had picked out earlier. From there he would have an unobstructed view of the field. Within reach he placed his flashlight, walkie-talkie, thermos of coffee, and his gun. It was a stifling, hot, summer night, not much breeze stirring. There was no moon and few stars to give light, so it wasn't long before the night turned so black he couldn't see his hand in front of his face. The time passed slowly. Quentin tried not to think of the night noises, the faint rustling sounds in the palmetto thickets. It had been a long day, full of the stress common to law enforcement work, and he was tired. Eventually, he dozed off.

He was awakened suddenly by a hard thump in the center of his back. Quentin froze, and he knew what it was right off the bat. There was no doubt in his mind. What he had always dreaded had just happened...he had been snake-bit by a big, diamond-back rattlesnake. His heart began to pound and he broke out in a cold sweat. Then it happened again. His next thought was...that sonofabitch wadn't just satisfied with bitin' me once; he had to go and do it again! That really made him mad. To hell with it, he thought, he's done bit me now...I'm gonna die anyhow, but before I do, by god, I'm gonna kill that sonofabitching snake!

He grabbed his pistol, jumped to his feet, turned on his flashlight, and got ready to blow the snake to smithereens. Only it wasn't a snake at all...just a good-sized toad trying to jump over him.

His deputies and the other lawmen started calling on their walkie-talkies, trying to find out what all the commotion was about. Quentin was too embarrassed to admit the truth, that he had just blown the cover on a carefully set-up drug operation because a toad frog had bumped him in the back. There are just some things a man can't admit without losing face, especially if he has the reputation of being fearless. Quentin finally told the men he had decided it was all a false alarm, that the plane wasn't coming in, and they might as well go on home and get some rest.

He was a little sheepish telling about the above incident but, being the honest fellow that he is, told it in its entirety while I laughed my head off.

34 | CHAPTER

Among the biggest headaches Quentin had as sheriff of Taylor County—besides the political games, which he hated—were the endless lawsuits. Inmates filed most of them. There were seven of those. Then there were the ones filed by the State Department of Corrections. One of those was waiting for him when he took office, and he was bound by it during the entire time he was in office. That one was for over-crowding and was mandated to the state by the federal courts.

Inmate suits were mostly trivial with no legal foundation, but they were filed for any reason that might make the inmate a few bucks. One of those suits hounded Quentin's heels even after he left office and was finally satisfied in Federal Court in Tallahassee in 1993. That case involved an A and M University student from a wealthy Gadsden County family. He was in Perry one night, pushing crack cocaine, and shot an eighteen-year-old girl through the window of her pick-up truck. The incident occurred in a black section of Perry as she was trying to make a buy. After driving on a couple blocks, she wrecked the truck and was slumped over the wheel, dead, when help arrived.

Quentin presented a strong case. The man was convicted and sent to state prison for twenty years. His lawsuit against Quentin was filed from prison and based on the conditions in the Taylor County jail while he was a prisoner there. Most of his allegations were totally false.

"One of his complaints was that at one meal his meat portion wasn't large enough," Quentin said, "and the inmate serving him didn't wear a hair net. The DOC guidelines said 'hairnets', but I didn't think they were efficient enough so I had all the waiters wearing full shower caps. The judge laughed about that one. Another of his grievances was that he had to sleep on the floor, and the commode ran over and exposed him to all kinds of diseases. There was plenty of room at that time, but for some reason or other many of the prisoners preferred sleepin' on the floor and would pull their mattresses off the bunks to do so. There were also recreational tables in the cells that he could have put his mattress on.

"Everything in the jail is documented, and our records showed that he spent one night on the floor. His complaint of a commode over-flowin' was true, but it happened on the second floor of the jail, and he was incarcerated on the first. That happened because the prisoners stuffed oranges and apples down the commode to stop it up. Most floodin' problems in a jail are intentional. He didn't get anything out of his suit, but it was time-consumin' and aggravatin' to me.

"Prisoner lawsuits are common nowadays. The inmates have a complete law library—another federal mandate—at their disposal and plenty of time to work up cases. Some of them get to be pretty good jailhouse lawyers. All their suits are accepted in federal court and are heard in federal court because of the civil rights fuss. The federal judges complain about being overbooked, but they will pass over cases that need to be heard in order to take care of the cases against sheriffs. It ridiculous, that's what it is.

"Those suits against me cost the tax-payers a bundle, not to mention lost man-hours. Some of the witnesses had left state employ and had to be subpoenaed. The time I had to spend tryin' to defend myself could have been better spent workin' up cases against criminals. Unfortunately, it seems that rights of the inmates take precedence over anything else. Since all the sheriffs are routinely faced with inmate suits, you can see what a problem it is state-wide."

There were other nuisances in the sheriff's job, small though they might seem. Some I got to witness first-hand. According to Quentin those usually popped up at night, when he was home, trying to get some rest. It seemed that way to me, too.

Every time we went down for the weekend, Quentin got calls at all hours. Most involved complaints that had nothing to do with a law violation. For example: the rooster next door was crowing and the disturbing one man, a dog was barking and keeping someone else awake, there was a cat under an old lady's trailer and she wanted it removed before it destroyed her insulation and she got killed by radon gas. And then there were all those property line disputes. These were all civil matters, according to Quentin, where law enforcement officials don't get involved except for serving papers. He handled all those piddling complaints with a lot of tact, to my way of thinking, considering how it cut down on his sleep and all. I imagine it's like that in all counties, especially the smaller ones.

But there were a lot of legitimate cases that he didn't mind staying up all night for. Like the following, which happened during his last year in office.

The young man's family lived in Perry but they were not natives of Taylor County. He had been in trouble with the law, had served time for assault and rape, and had just been paroled after serving only a portion of his sentence. He arrived in Perry in the late afternoon and began casing the downtown area, looking for a place to rob. After dark, as he slowly passed the few stores that were still open, he spotted a place he thought would do just fine. Besides the money in the register, the pretty, young, sales girl he could see through the window would be an added bonus.

She was a local girl, sixteen years old, from a good family, active in church, and thought highly of by everyone in the community. To earn some spending money, she had been working at a clothing store on the courthouse square. The owners, because they knew she was trustworthy and thought she would be safe, left her to close up the store at nine o'clock that evening.

When she didn't come home from work and no one answered the phone, her father became worried and went downtown to check on her. The store was still open, the lights were on, but the girl wasn't there and neither was her car—- a red hatchback Mustang.

The police were called. Blood was found on the storage room floor, and an APB was issued with a description of the car. Since a kidnapping had obviously taken place, the FBI was called in, as well as other law enforcement agencies.

As sheriff, Quentin was in charge of the investigation. He hoped that whoever had taken the girl would call in and demand a ransom. That way they could be pretty sure she was still somewhere in the area. The FBI put a monitor on the girl's home phone. Sure enough, a short time later, a call came in from a man demanding a large sum of money for her return. It was traced to the outside pay phone at Reams' store in Lamont.

By that time, in addition to the FBI, there were law enforcement officers from Jefferson County, game wardens, FDLE, and Quentin's people to help with the search. There was no question about the family paying the ransom. They were not wealthy people. The odds against getting the girl back safe seemed pretty high at that point.

Someone at Reams' store remembered seeing a red Mustang with a girl in it parked nearby. He also remembered seeing a man using the outside phone, and that they left the store heading south.

Quentin knew they had to be staying somewhere in the vicinity, so he divided that part of the county into grids, and the men began methodically searching each grid. About midnight, a game warden spotted the car in an isolated area near the Ecofina River. A command center was immediately set up at Cabbage Grove fire tower, about five miles west of where the car was located.

Quentin and Eddie Reynolds, a game warden, led the way in while the rest of the men stayed about fifty yards behind in case backup was needed. They figured two men could sneak up a lot easier and quieter than several could, and they hoped to catch the kidnapper by surprise.

The night was pitch black as they eased up to the car. Everything was deathly still so they figured the kidnapper was asleep. Their biggest concerns at that point were how the man was armed and whether the car doors were locked.

Quentin carried a big flashlight, and by holding the light down and covering the beam, he could see enough to note that the door was unlocked. The seats had been folded down to make a bed. The girl was lying on her back with her eyes open, frozen in terror. She looked up a Quentin and made eye contact. When he put his finger over his lips, she seemed to understand and didn't make a sound. The man was on the near side of the car, asleep.

Quentin quietly opened the door. Then, in one quick motion, he reached in, grabbed the man by his hair and shirt, and yanked him out on the ground. He was face down, and as Quentin explained later, "I kinda ground his face in the dirt a bit 'cause he woke up and was tryin' to resist a little. That wadn't nothin' compared to what I wanted to do to 'im. Found out he was carryin' a big knife and had raped the girl repeatedly, beginnin' on the storage room floor in the store. We found where he had cut off her blouse and bra with his knife. If we hadn't found them, he would have killed her and she knew it. She was really traumatized. I was afraid that what she had been through would ruin her life, and she was such a fine young girl."

Quentin has a temper. He doesn't show it often, but when provoked to the extreme, as he was at that time, he's not the kind of fellow you want to mess around with. When I asked him why he didn't just shoot the sorry son-of-a-gun and save the taxpayers a lot of money, he said with a grin, "Too many witnesses."

We both knew he had too much respect for the law he represented to give in to his impulses. But it sure didn't hurt to think about how satisfying it would be. I imagine all law enforcement officers can relate to that.

The girl was taken to the emergency room right afterwards for treatment. The kidnapper was brought to trial and sent back to prison, for how long Quentin couldn't remember. He was more concerned about the girl, and how much emotional damage she might have suffered from the incident. Years later, to his relief, he learned from a family friend who still lived in Perry, that she had married, had children, and seemed to be well adjusted.

Epilogue

August 2000

I began Quentin's biography about ten years ago and expected to complete the task within a few months, but Quentin seemed to be making history faster than I could write it down. At least that's what I have accused him of. Hardly a day passed during his law enforcement career that Quentin didn't experience some life-threatening, notable, or hilarious incident, and I have only touched on a few of them. It didn't stop with his retirement either. He bought a 29-foot, fifth-wheel trailer and a new Ford truck to pull it with, and he and Thais began their dream of traveling. The next few years they covered every state in the union, except Hawaii, some of them more than once, and spent several weeks in Alaska.

As was his usual habit, Quentin continued getting himself in all kinds of dilemmas...some funny and some really dangerous. Like the time he decided to go gold mining in Alaska, that time alone, and was forced off the Top of the World Highway by a distracted driver. His camper was torn up, he was knocked out, and only a small stand of saplings kept him from ending up at the bottom of a cliff. That was just a small example.

I haven't covered everything in his life by a long shot but decided there would have to be a cut-off point somewhere. So, basically, this book will end with his retirement as sheriff of Taylor County.

Quentin survived those four years a little the worse for wear but a whole lot wiser. During his time of public service, he didn't give a thought to his political image or waste any time trying to polish it, either. Instead, he devoted his time and energy to doing what he figured was his primary job...getting the bad guys off the streets and in jail. Since Quentin was never one to do things half-measure or side step issues, he stomped a few toes along the way and bruised a few egos. But he gained the respect of most of the people he came in touch with, even some of those he put in jail, and he made some lasting friendships. One thing seems to balance the other, or as the current saying goes, what goes round comes round.

He accomplished most of the goals he set for himself as sheriff, and that gave him a great deal of satisfaction. By the time his term ended, Quentin had one of the best-equipped and best-paid rural law enforcement agencies in Northern Florida. His deputies were paid even more than the deputies in Leon County, a much larger and more populous neighboring county, and employee morale was high.

Because he put so much of himself into his job as sheriff, however, Quentin's health suffered. He battled recurring infections, and had almost constant back pain. When he finally consulted Dr. Parker, his family physician, he was told the continuous physical and mental stress had left him with no resistance. It was for that reason, and on the advice of Dr. Parker, that Quentin decided not to seek a second term as sheriff, something he had originally planned to do. After retirement the symptoms gradually disappeared, and he became his old self again, which meant, of course, that he was back to flirting with danger every chance he got. Some things never change, but the years have left their mark.

Quentin's hair is white now, his face is lined and weathered, and he needs glasses to read. But he's just as sharp mentally and he still has that basic integrity that's so much a part of him. His sense of humor and zest for living remain intact, as does his deep devotion to family and friends.

He has my respect for being the kind of wonderful human being that he is, and my undying devotion for making my life so much fuller by being a part of it. I'm convinced the world is a better place because he exists, and I'm so very proud to call him my brother.

(As I mentioned at the beginning, Quentin tends to do everything in a dramatic way. Nothing simple. That hasn't changed. He continued to enjoy good health and a full life until about a year ago when he began having involuntary muscular twitching and cramping, and losing weight. At Shand's Hospital in Gainesville, Florida, on February 21, 1999, he was diagnosed with ALS...Amyotrophic Lateral Sclerosis...more commonly known as Lou Gehrig's disease. The cause is unknown and there is no cure at the present time although promising research is ongoing at many of the major medical centers across the country. It seems to be a race against time, but Quentin is facing this "dilemma" like he has all the others throughout his life...with unbelievable courage.)

I am reminded of a phone call I had from Quentin in June of 1993. He and Thais were spending some time on an island off Nova Scotia after touring Vermont and New Hampshire. When talking about a friend who had died suddenly, just after retiring, Quentin said, "Nobody knows when his time is up. Its just too bad he didn't get a chance to enjoy his retirement the way I have. I may die tomorrow but there's one thing for sure—-I've had one hell of a party!

I can't think of a better way to end his life's story.

Afterthoughts

Quentin and Thais' children:

Mark is a commander in the Navy and nearing retirement. He hopes to work for an airline so he can resume flying. He is stationed at the Pentagon, at present, and lives in Alexandria, Virginia, with his wife, Debi, and their four children...Chris, Amy, Ryan, and Zach.

Donna is a registered nurse, works for the Taylor County School System, and lives with her three children, Emily, Clare, and Mark...and her second husband, Pete Rooks, in Monticello, Florida.

Ronnie is a jet pilot and a major in the Air Force. He is stationed in Charleston, S.C. and lives in Summerford with his wife, Christy, and their two children, Allison and Andy.

Thais remains the "rock" of the family, trying to take care of everybody. Her serenity of spirit and non-complaining ways often remind me of Grandmother Whittle. To me there is no greater compliment than that.

About three years ago, Quentin re-established contact with his old Navy buddies, Frank Rosati, Emil Bazzoli, Joe Woods, and Bill Fischer and the foursome have visited, corresponded, and basically took up where they left off forty years ago.

Many of the people mentioned in this biography, people who had an impact on Quentin's life, whether in a positive or negative way, have since passed away...Cousin Jerry Collins, Captain Cosson, Commander Clifton, Lt.Gilbert, Ex-governor Lawton Chiles, Trooper Raker, and many others.

Billy Maxwell still works as a deputy sheriff in Live Oak, Florida, and goes fishing with Quentin occasionally. Ivey retired to the mountains in N.C. Jack Underwood and Jerry Wells still live in Perry and remain Quentin's good friends. Mike Latrell, the DEA agent, no longer works undercover and runs the agency in Sacramento, Calif. Joe Peavy is still sheriff, as of now. There are many I have missed, I'm sure, due to limited space, but it's my omission and not Quentin's, and I'm truly sorry I couldn't include everyone. And last, I would like to thank my brother-in-law, Carl Porter, who made it happen.

Edwina Hauversburk, a retired R.N., lives in the mountains of Western North Carolina with her husband Frank. (aka Harve)